PERENNIALS

PERENNIALS

CONSULTANT EDITOR
Judy Moore

WELDON OWEN

Conceived and produced by
Weldon Owen Pty Ltd
59-61 Victoria Street, McMahons Point,
Sydney NSW 2060, Australia
Copyright © 2003 Weldon Owen Pty Ltd
Revised edition copyright © 2010 Weldon Owen Pty Ltd

WELDON OWEN PTY LTD
CHIEF EXECUTIVE OFFICER Sheena Coupe
CREATIVE DIRECTOR Sue Burk
SENIOR VICE PRESIDENT, INTERNATIONAL SALES Stuart Laurence
VICE PRESIDENT, SALES: UNITED STATES AND CANADA Amy Kaneko
VICE PRESIDENT, SALES: ASIA AND LATIN AMERICA Dawn Low
ADMINISTRATION MANAGER, INTERNATIONAL SALES Kristine Ravn
PRODUCTION MANAGER Todd Rechner
PRODUCTION COORDINATORS Lisa Conway, Mike Crowton
PUBLISHING COORDINATOR Gina Belle

LIMELIGHT PRESS PTY LTD
PROJECT MANAGEMENT Helen Bateman/Jayne Denshire
PROJECT EDITOR Margaret Whiskin
PROJECT DESIGNER Avril Makula
CONSULTANT EDITOR Judy Moore

REVISED EDITION
PROJECT COORDINATOR Natalie Ryan
DESIGNER Christina McInerney
CONSULTANT EDITOR Anna Kruger

ISBN 978-1-921530-83-8

Printed by Toppan Leefung Printing Limited
Printed in China
A Weldon Owen Production

CONTENTS

HOW TO USE THIS BOOK

*T*he *Gardeners Handbooks: Perennials* is divided
into two parts. The first part is the general
section (sample page below) and the second part
is a plant directory (sample page opposite).
These combine to provide a comprehensive
guide to perennials.

Illustrations show various
perennials. There are many other
helpful illustrations in the book.

Colourful photographs
give you guidance
and inspiration in
planning and planting
your garden.

SOIL SOLUTIONS

Gardening would be easier if soil were
consistent, but it is a complex and
changing mixture of substances—there's
bound to be something (or lack of something) that makes gardening a challenge

ALKALINE ANEMONE
The delicate Japanese
anemone *Anemone x
hybrida* spreads by creeping
underground stems and
thrives in alkaline soil.

PLANTS FOR SOIL
pH 7.0 OR HIGHER
Baby's breath
*Gypsophila
paniculata*
Bergenias
Bergenia spp.
Coral bells
Heuchera spp.
Japanese anemone
Anemone x hybrida
Mulleins
Verbascum spp.
Peonies *Paeonia* spp.
Pinks *Dianthus* spp.

ADAPTABLE PHLOX
Phlox can adapt to alkaline
soil, as long as it has good
drainage and lots of organic
matter

ALKALINE SOIL
Most plants can live with a slightly
alkaline soil, but a soil with a pH above
8.0 starts to take its toll. Excessively
alkaline soils have chronic nutrient
deficiencies and resist attempts to acidify
them. In too-alkaline soils, phosphorus
and most micro-nutrients are insoluble
and unavailable to plants. On the other
hand, minerals such as sodium and
selenium may be abundant enough to be
toxic to plants. You may decide to grow
species that are adapted to high-pH soils.
The most effective material for
lowering the soil pH is sulphur. Apply
0.5 kg (1 pound) per 9.3 sq m (100 sq ft)
for each whole point you want to lower
the pH. Rake or dig the sulphur into the
soil and keep it moist.

Incorporating plenty of organic matter
can help lower the pH or keep it low if
you've added sulphur. Avoid fertilizers
that raise the soil pH, including wood
ash, bonemeal and phosphorus-based.

ACID SOIL
Excess acidity is among the easiest of soil
problems to fix. A slightly acid soil is a
great thing to have because most plants
thrive in it. But in too-acid soil, most
nutrients are bound up in unavailable
forms. A few minerals—aluminum, iron,
manganese—may become too soluble
and reach toxic concentrations. And soil
organisms are inhibited, so organic matter
breaks down more slowly.
Soil with a pH below 6.2 is too acid
for many plants, but there are some that
will thrive in those conditions. If your
soil is naturally quite acid, you may just
decide to grow adapted species, such as
chrysanthemums and lily-of-the-valley.
Observe what is growing well in your
neighbours' gardens and in your locality.

ACID FRIEND
Chrysanthemu
summer to aut
bloomers that v
well-drained soil
the acidic side an
to light shade.

RAISE THE pH
Add powdered lime to raise
the pH of acid soil, digging
or raking it into your soil.

64 PLANNING YOUR GARDEN

SOIL SOLUTIONS 65

Gardening tips and ideas,
and suggestions about
problems you may
encounter in your garden.

General information about
planting, propagating,
and caring for your plants
to get the optimum results.

Photograph of each individual plant, showing what it looks like when grown in the right conditions.

Quick-reference information on climate, height and spread, and flower season.

Botanical name

Family name

Common name

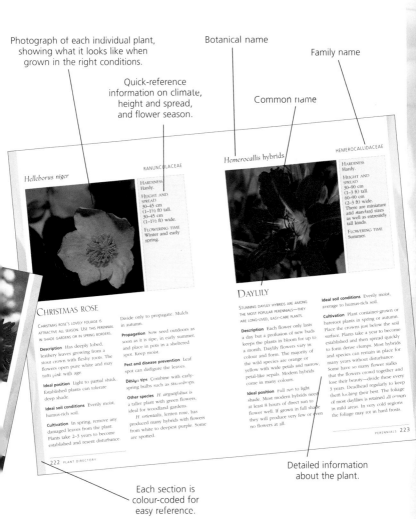

Helleborus niger

RANUNCULACEAE

HARDINESS
Hardy.

HEIGHT AND
SPREAD
30–45 cm
(1–1½ ft) tall.
30–45 cm
(1–1½ ft) wide.

FLOWERING TIME
Winter and early
spring.

Hemerocallis hybrids

HEMEROCALLIDACEAE

HARDINESS
Hardy.

HEIGHT AND
SPREAD
30–90 cm
(1–3 ft) tall.
60–90 cm
(2–3 ft) wide.
There are miniature
and standard sizes
as well as extremely
tall kinds.

FLOWERING TIME
Summer.

CHRISTMAS ROSE

CHRISTMAS ROSE'S LOVELY FOLIAGE IS
ATTRACTIVE ALL SEASON. USE THIS PERENNIAL
IN SHADE GARDENS OR IN SPRING BORDERS.

Description Has deeply lobed,
leathery leaves growing from a
stout crown with fleshy roots. The
flowers open pure white and may
turn pink with age.

Ideal position Light to partial shade.
Established plants can tolerate
deep shade.

Ideal soil conditions Evenly moist,
humus-rich soil.

Cultivation In spring, remove any
damaged leaves from the plant.
Plants take 2–3 years to become
established and resent disturbance.

Divide only to propagate. Mulch
in autumn.

Propagation Sow seed outdoors as
soon as it is ripe, in early summer,
and place in pots in a sheltered
spot. Keep moist.

Pest and disease prevention Leaf
spot can disfigure the leaves.

Design tips Combine with early-
spring bulbs such as snowdrops.

Other species *H. argutifolius* is
a taller plant with green flowers,
ideal for woodland gardens.
H. orientalis, lenten rose, has
produced many hybrids with flowers
from white to deepest purple. Some
are spotted.

DAYLILY

STUNNING DAYLILY HYBRIDS ARE AMONG
THE MOST POPULAR PERENNIALS—THEY
ARE LONG-LIVED, EASY-CARE PLANTS.

Description Each flower only lasts
a day but a profusion of new buds
keeps the plants in bloom for up to
a month. Daylily flowers vary in
colour and form. The majority of
the wild species are orange or
yellow with wide petals and narrow,
petal-like sepals. Modern hybrids
come in many colours.

Ideal position Full sun to light
shade. Most modern hybrids need
at least 8 hours of direct sun to
flower well. If grown in full shade
they will produce very few or even
no flowers at all.

Ideal soil conditions Evenly moist,
average to humus-rich soil.

Cultivation Plant container-grown or
bareroot plants in spring or autumn.
Place the crowns just below the soil
surface. Plants take a year to become
established and then spread quickly
to form dense clumps. Most hybrids
and species can remain in place for
many years without disturbance.
Some have so many flower stalks
that the flowers crowd together and
lose their beauty—divide these every
3 years. Deadhead regularly to keep
them looking their best. The foliage
of most daylilies is retained all season
in mild areas. In very cold regions
the foliage may rot in hard frosts.

Detailed information about the plant.

Each section is colour-coded for easy reference.

WINTER HARDINESS	
Hardy	Will survive winter
Frost-hardy	Survives outside in mild regions or in a sheltered site
Half-hardy	Needs protection from frost
Tender	Won't survive below 5°C (41°F)

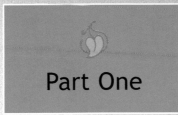

Part One

KNOW YOUR GARDEN

PERPETUAL PERENNIALS

Gardening with perennials is a joy. Whether your garden is large or small, sunny or shady, wet or dry, a wide variety of perennials will thrive there and provide beauty for years to come.

WHAT IS A PERENNIAL?

Perennial plants live and bloom for more than two growing seasons. Many survive a decade or longer if planted in the right location and hardy perennials come back year after year, so you don't have to buy and replant them each spring. But even the short-lived plants are worth growing. For instance, blanket flower *Gaillardia* x *grandiflora* blooms vigorously for a long

SHORT-LIVED BEAUTY
Some perennials, such as columbines *Aquilegia* spp. have short lifespans but set seed that replaces the parent plant.

CLOUDS OF COLOUR
The delicate Japanese anemone *Anemone* x *hybrida* is one perennial that can be propagated by taking root cuttings or by division.

period over the summer, although it seldom survives more than 2 years.

Occasionally a biennial plant such as foxglove *Digitalis purpurea*, which grows foliage the first year and flowers the second, will live for a third year. Despite their different lifespans, all these plants are called perennials.

Perennials are herbaceous, which means they lack woody stems—trees and shrubs are exempted from this definition because they develop woody stems and limbs.

Usually the foliage of perennials dies down to the underground roots each dormant season. A few, such as rock cress *Arabis* spp., have evergreen foliage.

Unlike annuals, most perennials flower for only a few weeks each season. They don't have to be replanted every year—these beauties come back on their own. They are cheaper than most trees and shrubs and they're relatively simple to move or dig up and replace if you want to change the look and layout of your garden. Perennials are dependable and easy choices for beginners, and they come in enough variety to satisfy even the most experienced gardener.

BEAUTIFUL BRACTS
Perennials come in all shapes and sizes. *Eryngium giganteum* is an unusually shaped, short-lived perennial with fascinating bracts surrounding the flowers.

SHOWY DAYLILY
Daylilies are dependable, hardy plants that produce brightly coloured blooms.

LONG-LASTING COLOUR

Centaurea dealbata 'Steenbergii' is a long-flowering knapweed cultivar, which is perfect for any full-sun position.

GRASSY COMPANION

Upright, arching, perennial grasses such as *Miscanthus sinensis* are ideal for planting with other perennials in a flower border.

NOT JUST FLOWERS

Shade-loving caladiums are grown for their showy leaves. Pinch off any of the small flowers that grow in summer.

A PERENNIAL FOR EVERY POSITION

Now that you know what a perennial is, you are able to start to explore the many possibilities for using them in your garden. With thousands of species and cultivars to choose from, there's a good chance that you'll find plenty of plant forms, leaf textures and flower colours and shapes to fit the garden you have in mind. Any plot can be accented with perennials. A few clusters of perennial flowers will bring colourful highlights to drab corners, and a garden full of perennials will become a landscape feature. You can use perennials as accents, focal points, masses of colour or scenes of change.

Choose perennials with colours, textures and forms that enhance your entire landscape. By combining perennials with annuals, biennials, shrubs and trees in one glorious garden, you will be able to enjoy the benefits of each kind of plant. For example, plant early-blooming perennials such as irises and peonies with annuals such as cleomes *Cleome* spp. and cosmos, which start blooming in early summer and carry on until early autumn. Put smaller clumps of dramatic perennials in strategic locations to highlight

the start of a path, the location of a door or the view from a window. Consider nesting three gold-centered, broad-leaved hostas (such as *Hosta* 'Gold Standard') at each side of the entrance of a woodland path. Or use a clump of red-hot pokers *Kniphofia* spp. to frame the top of a drive.

STANDING IRISES
A stand of irises is an impressive feature for any garden. They look really stunning planted in graduating colours.

Name That Perennial

One of the tricks to growing perennials successfully is to learn their names. Get to know their botanical names so you know exactly which plant you are talking about, planting or ordering.

What's in a Name?

Botanical names are usually given as two words. The first word, the name of the genus, refers to a group of closely related plants. The second word indicates the species, a particular kind of plant in that genus. You may grow several different species from the same genus. *Achillea millefolium* and *Achillea tomentosa*, for

AUTUMN FLOWERS

Helenium autumnale is great for moist soil. As its botanical name indicates, it is an autumn-flowering perennial.

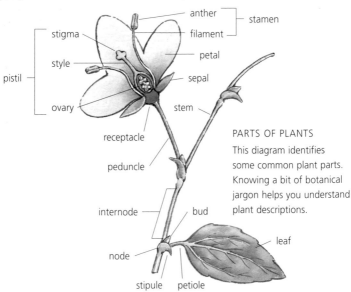

PARTS OF PLANTS

This diagram identifies some common plant parts. Knowing a bit of botanical jargon helps you understand plant descriptions.

example, both belong to the genus *Achillea*, known as yarrow. But *Achillea millefolium* refers to a species with finely cut leaves, while *Achillea tomentosa* refers to one with fuzzy leaves.

Horticulturists and botanists recognize two other classifications of plants: varieties and cultivars. Plants that develop a natural variation in the wild are called varieties and the varietal name is included as part of the botanical name after the abbreviation "var." Cultivars, whose names are set in single quotes after the botanical name, are plants that have been selected and propagated as part of a breeding programme or from a chance mutation in a garden.

You may also come across hybrids, which are blends of two species or, more rarely, two genera. One example is *Anemone* x *hybrida*—the "x" indicates that this plant is a hybrid.

In this book, you will find plants listed by their common name and their botanical name. When we use "spp." we are discussing related species in the same genus. For example, *Iris* spp. includes bearded, Siberian and Japanese irises.

CREEPING AJUGA

"Reptans" is Latin for "creeping." *Ajuga reptans* is a creeping perennial.

THE LOGIC OF NAMES

A botanical name tells us something about the plant it identifies, such as its flower colour or growth habit. Listed below are some words that appear in botanical names.

Albus: white
Argenteus: silver
Aureus: golden yellow
Caeruleus: blue
Luteus: yellow
Niger: black
Palustris: swampy
Perennis: perennial
Prostratus: trailing
Reptans: creeping
Roseus: rosy
Ruber: red
Spinosus: spiny
Variegatus: variegated
Vulgaris: common

CLIMATE

Climate—the seasonal cycles of rainfall, temperature, humidity and other factors—has a major influence on which perennials will thrive in different parts of your garden landscape.

THINK ABOUT TEMPERATURE

If you want to grow plants that will live for more than a year, you have to consider your area's average low and high temperatures. Plants that are naturally adapted to this temperature range will tend to thrive in your garden.

Try to limit your selections to plants that are reliably cold-hardy for your local area. Marginally hardy plants may survive for several years, but it's likely that they won't thrive and an unusually cold spell could even kill them off.

Unusually high summer temperatures will also affect your plants. Even if a plant can tolerate the heat, it may demand frequent watering in return, and it probably won't look great.

WATER WISE
Many delphiniums limp along in hot, dry sites and die out after 1 or 2 years, while the same plants grown in cooler, moister conditions can thrive for several years.

SHADE LOVERS
Moisture-loving plants such as astilbes, primulas and hostas thrive in cool, humid sites where the ground is reliably moist.

RAINFALL

Rainfall, like temperature, has a great impact on determining which plants will grow in your area. If you want to grow just a few moisture-loving plants, site them close to the house where you can give them special attention more easily. But if your goal is to save time, money and natural resources, you'll definitely want to include naturally adapted plants in your landscape. Small, fuzzy or silvery leaves are fairly reliable clues that a particular plant is adapted to dry conditions and will survive periods of drought.

MICROCLIMATES

Microclimates are small areas where the growing conditions differ from the norm. As an example, an L-shaped corner next to your house might be sheltered enough from cold winds and hold enough of the heat radiating from the house to allow you to grow a special, marginally hardy plant that would struggle along in the open. Similar microclimates can also exist for shade and water.

VARIABLE NEEDS

Some daylily cultivars are suited to heat, while others can't take it at all. Ask your local nursery for advice so you get the right plants for your garden.

SILVER-LEAVED YARROW

Plants with silvery leaves are often well adapted to hot, dry conditions.

TOPOGRAPHY

The topography of your plot will influence how you design your garden. Each kind of topography has its own advantages and disadvantages for perennial gardening.

GARDENING ON A HILLTOP

A garden on a hilltop will face different conditions than gardens just down the slope. The soil on a hilltop may be thin due to erosion, and is often very well drained. Hilltop sites can be windswept, and strong winds can topple tall plants, so you'll either need to stake your tall perennials or stick with shorter plants. Winds can also dry out plants quickly, so you may have to water more often. If excessive wind is a problem, you can decrease the force by setting a fence, hedge or vine-covered trellis between the prevailing wind and your garden.

GARDENING IN A VALLEY

At the base of a slope, perennial gardens are more prone to late-spring and early-autumn frosts. Frost and cold air inevitably concentrate in low-lying areas, known as frost pockets, slowing or damaging spring growth and autumn flowers. The same frost may miss plants growing in warmer areas slightly uphill. Gardeners in low-lying areas may want to wait a little later than those at higher levels to remove protective fleece or mulches.

Like frost, moisture will collect at the base of the slope. Valleys are rich in rainfall run-off and often natural water

OBEDIENT PLANT
Physostegia is ideal for those spots where water gathers in a valley garden. This moisture-loving plant likes full sun or light shade.

A SUNNY CORNER
A wall can act just like a stand of trees and create a warm, frost-free microclimate ideal for heat-loving plants.

Bugle *Ajuga* spp. and hosta
are two tough, dependable,
moisture-loving perennials
that are excellent for
shady gardens.

RAISED BEDS
Valley gardens often collect
water from surrounding
areas. If drainage is poor,
try planting in raised beds.

features, such as ponds and streams.
Topsoil eroded from surrounding slopes
tends to collect here, but if the soil is
clay, it may not drain well. A common
way to deal with this drainage problem
is to plant perennials in raised beds.
If poor drainage is really a problem,
you could install drainage pipes to
channel the excess water into another
area. In valleys and on flat terrain, the
best solution to poor drainage is often
to use the moisture around ponds and
water features to your advantage.
Let the reflective surface of a pond
become the focus around which you plant
water-loving perennials. Clothe the banks
with the flashiest of the moisture-lovers,
such as brightly coloured candelabra
primroses *Primula japonica*, red-spiked
lobelia *Lobelia cardinalis* or rodgersia
Rodgersia pinnata.

CASCADING COLOUR
Slopes tend to be well drained and are natural sites for rock gardens. Choose perennials such as *Arabis alpina* subsp. *caucasica*.

SLOPE STABILIZER
Ajuga reptans takes root and spreads rapidly to form dense ground cover—perfect for growing on shady slopes.

GARDENING ON A SLOPE

With a little imagination and work, you can transform a sloping site from a maintenance headache into a valuable landscape asset. Hillsides are awkward to mow and weed, so the best strategy is to cover them with plants that take care of themselves.

A hilly plot has great potential for interesting settings for your perennials. It also has more microclimates. In general, soils on slopes tend to be well drained but the topsoil may be thin because of erosion. Perennial gardens on slopes are less prone to late-spring and early-autumn frosts, as the cold air tends to settle down in the dip and the warm air rises up over the slope.

Slopes are ideal sites for rock gardens. If the slope isn't naturally rocky, you can add groupings of large boulders or layers of flat rock that resemble natural outcrops. Leave pockets of soil between the rocks to grow small perennials such as sweet violets *Viola odorata*, primroses *Primula* spp. and candytuft *Iberis*

SLOPING SOLUTIONS

Shallow basins or terraces trap moisture and minimize soil erosion (right). Another alternative is low-growing, spreading perennials such as mound-forming phlox for gently sloping sites (below).

ROBUST COLOUR

This clump-forming *Geranium* forms a glorious carpet of saucer-shaped, purple-blue flowers in early summer. It needs evenly moist soil to thrive.

sempervirens, along with small bulbs and dwarf conifers.

If you have a steep slope, think twice before stripping the existing vegetation to plant a perennial garden. The soil might wash away before most of the perennials can root and stabilize the slope. One way to handle slopes is by planting them with perennials that take root and spread aggressively, such as daylilies, bugle *Ajuga reptans* and cranesbills *Geranium* spp. Space the plants closely for more rapid bank stabilization, and plant through a weed-suppressing membrane to hold soil in place until the roots establish.

If you don't want to rely on plants alone to control erosion, you can terrace the hill or install a retaining wall to moderate the slope. A beautiful stone or timber retaining wall will give your landscape interesting structure and let you grow perennials that do not root strongly enough to survive on a slope.

ASPECT

Aspect refers to the amount of sun and shade your garden receives. It depends on where each garden is in relation to the house and to other shade-casting features such as trees and fences.

SOUTH-FACING SITES
Southern aspects have maximum light. Heat- and drought-tolerant perennials such as lavenders *Lavandula* spp. will thrive here.

EASTERN ASPECT
Eastern sites receive cool morning sun and up to a half day of direct light. They are sheltered from hot afternoon sun. Plants requiring afternoon shade do well here, such as lady's mantle *Alchemilla mollis* and cranesbills *Geranium* spp.

WEST-FACING SITES
West-facing sites are cool and shady in the morning but temperatures rise when strong afternoon sun hits. Try tough, drought-tolerant perennials that can take these conditions, such as daylilies.

NORTHERN ASPECT
North-facing gardens receive less light and remain cool. A bright, evenly cool spot is ideal for perennials that love shade and moist soil, such as hostas, ferns, primroses and some iris species.

MEETING THE CHALLENGE
Purple coneflowers (right) tolerate west-facing sites, which can be a challenge for plants.

Sun or Shade

How do you tell if a spot has full sun, partial shade or full shade? You'll have to consider not only the exposure, but also the shade cast by trees, shrubs, hedges, fences and other structures.

Understanding Sun and Shade

To understand a garden site, watch it over the course of a day (check on it every hour or so) and note each time whether the spot is sunny or shady. Any site with less than 6 hours of direct sunlight is shady. Perennials that prefer full sun need 6 hours or more of direct sunlight to grow well. A site that receives a few hours of morning or late afternoon sun but no direct midday sun is described as having partial shade. Many perennials that prefer full sun will also tolerate partial shade.

A generally bright site that receives little direct sun but lots of filtered or reflected light is said to have light or dappled shade. Typically, this kind of

SHADY COLOUR

Many interesting and colorful perennials, such as astilbes, thrive in the shade.

SECRET TO SUCCESS

The trick to successful perennial gardening is finding and combining plants that thrive in your particular conditions.

HAPPY HOSTAS

Hostas come in a variety of colours and shapes and are tough, dependable perennials that are excellent for shade gardens.

PURPLE ROCK CRESS

As its name suggests, rock cress (*Arabis*) is ideal for sunny rock gardens and rock walls.

shade occurs beneath high-branched deciduous trees that don't cast solid shadows. Full, dense or deep shade is darker and fewer plants grow well in it. The area under evergreens is in deep shade all year long. Plants growing under densely branched deciduous trees are in full shade most of the summer.

Shade changes during the year both because the angle of the sun changes and because deciduous trees grow and shed their leaves. A sunny summer site may be shaded by a tree in spring, when the sun is lower in the sky.

The deep shade of a deciduous tree disappears when it loses its leaves. Many spring wildflowers take advantage of this opportunity to bloom before overhead trees come into leaf. Even if your garden is deeply shaded the rest of the season, you can enjoy masses of colour in the spring and beautiful green and patterned foliage the rest of the year.

Soil Composition

Learning your soil's characteristics helps you choose the right techniques for dealing with it successfully. When your soil is in good shape your garden will naturally be healthier and more beautiful.

What Is Soil?

Just as the air you breathe is a mixture of different gases, your garden soil is a mixture of solids, spaces and living organisms. About 97 per cent of the solid part is old rock that's been broken down into tiny particles over millions of years. The remaining 3 per cent or so is organic matter, made up of decomposed plant and animal tissue. Intermingled with rock and organic matter is an almost equal volume of space, filled with air and water.

This mixture of minerals, organic matter, air and water can support a diverse population of living organisms, from algae and fungi to earthworms and small mammals. Most important to you, as a gardener, is that soil is a habitat for roots, providing the physical support, nutrients and water that your plants need to grow and thrive. Maintaining the right balance of these ingredients is the goal of good soil management.

WELL-DRAINED PEONIES
Peonies grow best in soil that has been enriched with organic matter. They like a nutrient-rich environment and need good drainage to avoid root rot.

SAND, CLAY AND SILT
Sandy soil (left) tends to be dry and low in nutrients; clay soil (centre) can be sticky when wet and hard when dry; and silty soil (right) is fine and powdery and compacts easily, like clay.

THRIVING PLANTS

Once you know the soil conditions of your site, you can choose perennials that will thrive—like these salvia and orange coneflowers.

SOIL MAKE-UP

Sand, clay and silt make up your soil and are categorized by size. Sand has the largest mineral particles. These leave loose pockets, called pore spaces, that allow water and nutrients to drain away. Sandy soils tend to be dry and infertile.

Clay particles are ultra-fine—about 1,000 times smaller than sand. They can pack together to make a tight, water- and nutrient-rich but poorly oxygenated soil. Between sand and clay are the medium-sized silt particles. Silt tends to have characteristics of both sand and clay.

STUDY YOUR SOIL

Soil structure refers to the way in which the sand, silt and clay particles join together to form clumps. A soil with high amounts of sand or clay will usually be too loose or too dense to support good plant growth. A well-balanced soil tends to form soft, crumbly, granular clumps. Soil with this loose, granular structure is also easy to dig.

Organic matter is a critical component of all soils. Healthy soils have 5 per cent organic matter or more (humus-rich soil). Soils high in organic matter tend to be dark, loose and crumbly and have a nice, earthy smell. Soil structure can be improved by adding organic matter.

Organic matter improves soil and encourages earthworms and other soil organisms, which in turn contribute nutrients and encourage root growth.

SOIL pH

Soil pH—the measurement of your soil's acidity or alkalinity—is another factor that can determine which plants will grow well because pH affects the availability of nutrients in your soil. Soils that have pH ratings below 7 are acidic and as the pH drops, the soil becomes increasingly more acidic. Soils with pH ratings above 7 become increasingly more alkaline. An acidic pH (5.5–6.5) is ideal for most flowering plants.

HUMUS-RICH SOIL

Humus, or partially decomposed organic matter, improves the quality of the soil. Ligularias thrive in a moist, humus-rich soil.

CARDINAL FLOWER

The shallow-rooted cardinal flower *Lobelia cardinalis* thrives in rich, evenly moist soil. It is frost-hardy.

SIMPLE TEXTURE TESTS

To see how much clay your soil has, rub a moistened ball of soil about the size of a grape between your palms. The goal is to make a "worm" or rope. If you succeed, your soil is more than 15 per cent clay. The longer the worm, the higher the percentage of clay.

To check for sand, place a chunk of soil in your palm and wet it enough to form a small puddle. Rub a finger in it: if it's gritty, your soil is sandy; if it's smooth, your soil is silty.

SOIL TUNNELLERS

Earthworms tunnel through the soil, consuming and breaking down organic matter and leaving behind nutrient-rich castings.

The depth of your soil has an impact on root growth and this in turn affects which plants—deep- or shallow-rooting—will thrive in your garden. Dig down into the soil with a spade. If you can go 60 cm (2 ft) without hitting rock or a band of dense, tightly compacted soil, you'll be able to grow a wide range of shallow-rooted perennials.

There is also abundant life in healthy soil. Beneficial bacteria can decompose organic and mineral elements, freeing nutrients for plants to use. Soil that is compacted, low in organic matter or excessively wet is low in soil organisms.

Fertility is the availability, not just the presence, of nutrients in the soil. In order to grow, plants draw upon large amounts of nutrients and trace elements. Many of these are released naturally through mineral-rich rocks breaking down. A soil test can tell you if you have the right balance for normal plant growth.

Part Two

PLANNING YOUR GARDEN

PLANNING

NOT JUST PLANTS

Don't restrict yourself to plants when planning your garden. Remember to include features such as bird baths.

NEVER TOO SMALL

Clouds of Japanese anemone *Anemone* x *hybrida* seem to drift in front of this window. They like moist, open shade.

D on't jump into perennial gardening without sufficient planning. By taking the few basic steps below, you'll create a beautiful, healthy garden that suits your landscape and requires the least upkeep.

LOOK AT YOUR LANDSCAPE

Before you start, walk around and look at your garden from all angles. Think about where a perennial planting would enhance your plot. The perennials could edge areas with shrubs, run along the perimeter of the patio or radiate out from the back door or French windows. In short, you want to give the garden a reason for being wherever it is.

PUT YOUR IDEAS ON PAPER

Once you've chosen a site and style for your garden, you can start putting your plans down on paper. Measure the length and width of the area you have targeted for your garden. Determine an appropriate outline and draw it to scale on a piece of graph paper. For example, if you decide to choose a perennial border that is 2 m (6 ft) wide and 4 m (12 ft) long, you could draw a replica plan with a scale of 2.5 cm (1 in) on paper to 60 cm (2 ft) in the garden. The resulting scale drawing would be 5 cm (2 in) wide and 15 cm (6 in) long. To fit a larger garden plan onto graph paper,

Once you decide on the plants and the effect you want, you're ready to take pencil and paper in hand and turn your list into a garden design.

> ### SET PRIORITY PROJECTS
>
> How you actually turn your ideas into reality depends on your time and budget. Don't try to convert the whole plot at once—a better route is to set priority areas based on the sections you feel most strongly about. Deal with the most time-consuming tasks first, which will free up more time to tackle the smaller challenges in the following years.

you could adjust the scale, with 2.5 cm (1 in) on paper equalling up to 1.5 m (5 ft) of garden. If you compress more than about 1.5 m (5 ft) of garden space to 2.5 cm (1 in) of graph paper your plan may be too small to include details you need.

Draw in the major features that surround your garden, such as buildings, trees, shrubs and existing paths. This is also a good place to jot down notes about the soil conditions in the area (is it frequently wet, often dry or evenly moist?), as well as the amount and type of sunshine available (does it get full sun, just a few hours of morning sun or no direct sun at all?). Now you are ready to choose perennials with colours, textures and forms that enhance your landscape.

A SPOT OF COLOUR

Even a small planting such as a patch of pinks *Dianthus* spp. and lamb's ears *Stachys byzantina* adds colour.

PLANT FOR ALL SEASONS
Pretty lamb's ears *Stachys byzantina* has lovely, velvety leaves that will provide year-long interest in a dry, sunny site.

A MASS OF COLOUR
You can depend on Michaelmas daisies to produce colourful blooms for your late-summer and autumn garden.

ALL-SEASON INTEREST

A good selection of spring-, summer-, and autumn-blooming perennials, plus a few plants with evergreen leaves for winter interest, will give you a landscape that is truly attractive all year long.

All-season interest starts with flower displays that spread beyond one season. Foliage and plant form are the other features you can use to keep your garden looking beautiful as flowers come and go. From spring through autumn, many perennials have leaves in attractive colours or interesting shapes, such as the starry leaves of blood-red cranesbill *Geranium sanguineum*.

Many wildflowers and shade-loving perennials bloom just as trees come into leaf, so spring is a good season to draw attention to areas that will be shady and green later on. Supplement early-blooming perennials with your favourite spring-flowering shrubs and trees.

As spring turns into summer, many cottage-garden perennials, including peonies, irises and columbines *Aquilegia* spp. reach their peak, making it easy to feature flowers.

As summer progresses, daisy-like perennials—including blanket flower *Gaillardia* x *grandiflora* and coreopsis *Coreopsis* spp.—take centre stage. Foliage keeps up appearances where early perennials have finished blooming. Silver leaves make dramatic partners for hot- or cool-hued flowers.

Michaelmas daisies, sedums and *Eupatorium* spp. keep blooming after autumn frosts nip most annuals. As flowers fade, foliage colour brightens—leaves of peonies and hardy geraniums

TIRELESS FLOWERERS
Foxgloves are easy-care,
summer-flowering perennials.
For a dramatic summer
display, use mass plantings
along a wall or fence.

YEAR-ROUND COLOUR

Put in a selection of
spring-, summer- and
autumn-flowering
perennials to ensure
all-season interest.
Plant spring-flowering
wildflowers and
cottage-garden peonies
and columbines for
summer colour.
For autumn, you can't
go wrong with asters.
For winter choose
perennials with
showy seedpods,
such as coneflowers
Echinacea and
Rudbeckia spp.

turn beautiful shades of red, the leaves
of amsonia (blue star) *Amsonia* spp.
turn bright yellow and many ornamental
grasses bleach to gold. False spikenard
Smilacina racemosa and Jack-in-the-
pulpit *Arisaema triphyllum* are perennials
with dramatic berries that may last
through autumn.

After the leaves drop, attention turns
to evergreen plants and those with
interesting seedpods, seedheads or fruits.
Perennials with attractive winter
seedheads include ornamental onions
Allium spp., coneflowers *Rudbeckia* and
Echinacea spp., sea hollies *Eryngium*
spp. and yarrow *Achillea* spp.

DRAMATIC EFFECT
The spiky leaves and flowers
of gay feather *Liatris spicata*
add summer drama.

RIGHT PLANT, RIGHT PLACE

Use the information you have gathered
about your site to decide which
perennials to grow where. You need to
decide whether to match the plant to
the site or the site to the plant.

Keep a wish list of all the plants that
you really love. Write down the flower
colour, shape, height, flowering season,
foliage appearance and cultural
requirements so you can compare them
all and group together the plants with
similar needs. Start matching up the
plants with your site conditions. Think
about how to organize the garden to get
the optimum result—consider factors
such as flower and foliage colours, size
and flowering season. It makes gardening
rewarding and simpler if you can match
the plants to the site.

If you have a fairly flat site with
moist, well-drained soil, you can plant
a wide variety of perennials almost
anywhere. But you still need to think
about other plant needs, such as sun
requirements, or exposure, and frost
hardiness. And the chances are that you'll
have at least one area in your garden

CONTRASTING STYLE

The colour and texture of the foliage of lamb's ears contrasts beautifully with the bold flowers of spiky speedwell—and they thrive in the same site conditions.

with more challenging conditions, such as slopes or boggy patches. If you have a difficult spot, you may decide to ignore it and limit your perennial plantings to the more hospitable areas. Or you may choose to take up the challenge and plan a garden of perennials that are naturally adapted to those tough conditions. You may be pleasantly surprised to see how well-chosen perennial plantings with similar needs can turn a problem site into a pleasing garden.

Quick-reference Guide to Some Favourite Perennials

The secret to having a thriving garden is choosing your plants well. When you have your list of favourites, check their hardiness and then group them together according to the position they like, flower colour and season of interest.

H = Hardy   H-H = Half-hardy   FH = Frost-hardy   T = Tender

BOTANICAL NAME	FLOWER SEASON	COLOUR	POSITION	HARDINESS
Achillea spp.	summer	yellow	sun/shade	H
Aconitum carmichaelii	late summer/autumn	blue	sun/shade	H
Agapanthus africanus	summer	blue	sun	H-H
Ajuga reptans	late spring/summer	blue	sun/shade	H
Alcea rosea	summer/autumn	various	sun/shade	H
Alchemilla mollis	summer	green/yellow	sun/shade	H
Alstroemeria aurea	summer	yellow, orange	sun/shade	H
Anemone x hybrida	late summer/autumn	white to rose	sun/shade	H
Aquilegia hybrids	spring/summer	various	sun/shade	H
Arabis alpinis	late spring	pink, white	sun	H
Armeria maritima	late spring/summer	pink	sun	H
Aruncus dioicus	late winter/spring	white	shade	H
Aster novae-angliae	late summer/autumn	various	sun/shade	H
Aster x frikartii	midsummer/autumn	blue-purple	sun/shade	H
Astrantia major	early to late summer	white, pink, red	sun/shade	H
Aubrieta deltoidea	spring	white, rose, purple	sun/shade	H
Begonia Tuberhybrida Group	summer/autumn	various	partial shade	T
Boltonia asteroides	late summer/autumn	white and yellow	sun/shade	H
Brunnera macrophylla	mid-spring	blue	shade	H
Caltha palustris	early to late spring	yellow	sun	H
Campanula glomerata	early summer	blue, purple	sun/shade	H
Campanula persicifolia	summer	blue	sun/shade	H
Centaurea dealbata	late spring/summer	pink	sun	H
Ceratostigma plumbaginoides	late summer	blue	sun	H
Coreopsis verticillata	summer	yellow	sun/shade	H
Cyclamen hederifolium	early autumn	pink, white	partial shade	H
Delphinium Elatum Group	early/midsummer	white, blue, purple	sun	H
Dendranthema x grandiflorum	late summer/autumn	various	sun/shade	H

BOTANICAL NAME	FLOWER SEASON	COLOUR	POSITION	HARDINESS
Dianthus spp.	early to midsummer	white, pink	sun	H
Dicentra spectabilis	early spring/summer	pink	partial shade	H
Echinacea purpurea	mid- to late summer	red, pink	sun	H
Gaillardia x grandiflora	summer	yellow and orange	sun	FH
Gaura lindheimeri	summer	white	sun	FH
Geranium endressii	early to late summer	pink	sun/shade	H
Helenium autumnale	late summer/autumn	yellow and orange	sun/shade	H
Heliopsis helianthoides	midsummer	yellow	sun	H
Helleborus niger	early winter/spring	white	light shade	H
Hemerocallis hybrids	summer	various	sun/shade	H
Heuchera hybrids	late spring/summer	white, pink, red	sun/shade	H
Impatiens New Guinea hybrids	summer	various	sun/shade	T
Iris sibirica	early summer	various	sun/shade	H
Kniphofia uvaria	summer	yellow, white, red	sun	H
Leucanthemum x superbum	summer	white	sun	H
Liatris spicata	midsummer	purple	sun	H
Lobelia cardinalis	mid- to late summer	red	sun/shade	FH
Lupinus hybrids	spring/summer	blue, yellow	sun/shade	H
Mertensia virginica	spring	blue	partial shade	H
Monarda didyma	summer	red	sun/shade	H
Nepeta spp.	summer	blue/purple	sun	H
Paeonia lactiflora hybrids	early summer	various	sun/shade	H
Papaver orientale	early summer	red	sun/shade	H
Phlox paniculata	mid- to late summer	various	sun/shade	H
Platycodon grandiflorus	summer	blue	sun/shade	H
Rudbeckia fulgida	late summer/autumn	yellow/orange	sun/shade	H
Salvia x superba	early to midsummer	blue-purple	sun	H
Scabiosa caucasica	summer	blue	sun	H
Sedum spectabile	mid- to late summer	pink	sun	H
Stokesia laevis	summer	blue	sun	H
Thalictrum aquilegiifolium	late spring/summer	lavender	sun/shade	H
Tiarella cordifolia	sping	white	shade	H
Viola odorata	spring	purple	sun/shade	H

DESIGNING

Great-looking gardens are basically sequences of many individual plant combinations that consider the quality, colour and texture of each plant's foliage as well as its flowers.

COLOUR COMBINATIONS

Different colours have different attributes. Warm colours—those related to red, orange or yellow—are bold. They are stimulating and appear closer to the viewer. Cool colours—those related to violet, blue or green—are more tranquil and appear to recede from view. Pure hues—like true yellow or blue—are more vibrant than lighter or darker versions of the same colour. Mixing warm and cool colours adds depth and interest.

Combining colour in your gardens is just as easy as combining colours in clothes. The green background of the foliage harmonizes with strong colours that you probably wouldn't think to combine in an outfit. While certain types and combinations of colours tend to create specific effects, only you can decide whether you like each particular effect.

Combining similar flower colours in the garden creates a harmonious effect. Try grouping reds with oranges and yellows, yellows with greens and blues, or blues with purples and reds. Colours sharing the same degree of lightness or darkness are also similar; for instance, several different pastels blend more harmoniously than several pure hues.

DRAMATIC EFFECT

It's hard to beat tall, spiky, bold-coloured flowers, such as these gay feathers (*Liatris*) for a dramatic touch.

POINT OF INTEREST

A bird bath of complementary colour adds interest to this bed of chrysanthemums.

FLOWERS AND FOLIAGE
The lacy leaves of this
Artemisia combine well with
different flower forms and
provide season-long interest.

If contrast and excitement are what
you're after, choose complementary hues,
such as yellow and violet or red and
green. Or place a light tint next to a very
bright or dark shade of the same hue.

White and grey play an important
role in the garden. White can be exciting
or soothing. Bright white is surprisingly
bold and stands out even in a group of
soft pastels. A dash of pure white in a
spread of harmonious colours has a
dramatic effect. Grey is the great unifier.
Silvery or grey foliage works even better
than green to soften the transition
between two complementary or bold
colours. Grey adds drama by contrasting
with neighbouring green foliage.

COLOURFUL SHADE

You can create colour and interest in shade gardens by using plants with variegated leaves and colourful flowers, such as this Jacob's ladder.

STRIKING COMBINATIONS

If contrast and excitement are what you're after, choose complementary hues, such as yellow and violet.

SPIDER CHRYSANTHEMUMS

These spidery flowers illustrate perfectly the use of contrast in colour, form and tone to give a great effect.

CONTRASTS AND COMPLEMENTS

Well-planned gardens balance contrast and similarity. Contrasting colours, sizes or other design elements are bold and stimulating. Use contrast to draw attention to a particular location and to add a lively feel. Overusing contrast, too many different textures or too many strong colours can give your garden a jumbled, chaotic look.

Similarity, or the absence of contrasts, increases the sense of harmony. Use variations of closely related colours and gradual height transitions to create soothing garden designs. Too much can be uninteresting, so add a touch of contrast for balance.

Repetition acts as a bridge between similarity and contrast. Repeating similar elements will unify designs. Exact, evenly spaced repetitions of particular plants or combinations create a formal look. Combine different plants with similar features to give an informal garden a cohesive but casual look.

TEXTURE AND FORM FACTORS

Two other plant characteristics, texture and form, are as important as colour in creating interesting combinations and landscapes with the desired effects. Masses of even-textured foliage can tone down bold colours. Dramatic leaf shapes can add extra zip to a pastel planting. Here are some other tips you can try to plan effective plantings:

• Balance rounded clump formers, such as shasta daisies *Leucanthemum* x *superbum* and coreopsis, with spiky plants, such as mulleins *Verbascum* spp., foxgloves *Digitalis* spp. and gay feather *Liatris spicata*.

• Contrast shiny leaves—like those of bear's breeches *Acanthus mollis* and hardy ginger *Asarum europaeum*—with velvety or fuzzy leaves, such as those of lamb's ears *Stachys byzantina* or lungworts *Pulmonaria* spp.

• Contrast fine foliage, such as lacy fern fronds, with the smooth, broad leaves of hostas and similar plants.

• Include spiky leaves, like those of irises and yucca *Yucca filamentosa*; they'll stand out from mat-forming or mounding plants long after their flowers fade.

• If you have a small garden that you'll see from a distance, use bold colours, bold textures or bold shapes to make it appear larger and closer to the viewer— the bolder it is, the closer it will appear.

STEELY COLOUR

This *Aconitum* sp. cultivar 'Stainless Steel' has beautifully coloured flowers. It looks great in borders with flowers of contrasting hues.

CREATING UNITY

Large masses of plants in a single colour can add unity to a garden design and avoid a "spotty" look—this adds a sense of serenity to a garden.

STYLES

There are traditional and non-traditional styles for flower gardens. These include formal gardens, cottage gardens, herbaceous borders, island beds, cutting gardens and other speciality gardens.

FORMAL GARDENS

Historically, formal gardens were found on large estates. But today, this style is spreading into smaller plots. They are usually laid out in squares or rectangles with low hedges of clipped box, hollies or other evergreens. Plant the beds symmetrically, using the same sequence of perennials and edging plants on either side of a central axis. Make your own patterns with lines, angles and curving rows. Choose carefully—limit your selection to plants that will stay in place and maintain uniform height. Try to keep the planting scheme simple with evergreens for year-round interest and splashes of colour in spring and summer.

CASUAL STRUCTURE
This delightful garden blends the casual feeling of a cottage garden with the structure of a double border.

A FLORAL EDGING
The floriferous, semi-woody candytuft *Iberis sempervirens* (above) is perfect for using as an edging in formal plantings (right), walks or walls.

Informal Gardens

Informal landscapes use curved lines to create a more natural feeling. These kinds of gardens generally include many different types of plants—trees, shrubs, annuals, herbs and climbers as well as perennials. Informal designs are relaxed and lively. Since the plants are free to spread, sprawl and lean on each other, they need less regular maintenance. You won't need to keep sharp edges on the beds and the few weeds that pop up won't immediately be obvious and ruin the look of the garden.

The classic informal garden is the cottage garden, where perennials, annuals, herbs and roses ramble and intertwine. Cottage gardens are traditionally enclosed within walls or fences, making them a natural choice for a house or garden flat with a large, enclosed outdoor space. Unify the scene with a focal point, such as a path through the garden's centre to a seating area.

COLOUR AND MOVEMENT

By using trees, paths, beds and borders in an informal way, this garden becomes full of interest and motion.

Cottage Collage

Create a pleasing jumble of colour and shape by keeping in mind the following "roles" plants can play:

"Feature" flowers have strong shapes—like spiky lupins and massive peonies—or bright colours.

"Filler" flowers are less obvious—baby's breath is a filler.

"Edgers" are low plants used in the fronts of beds or spilling over onto paths. Think of thymes and catmint.

CURVED BEDS

Island beds are suited to casual, or informal, plantings. Just make the beds curved.

BOLD BEDS AND BORDERS

The bold colours of Peruvian lily *Alstroemeria* cultivars are ideal for beds and borders.

PERENNIAL BORDERS

Most perennial borders are designed to be seen from the front, allowing you to set the shorter plants in the foreground and the taller plants in the back.

Borders typically are long, rectangular areas. Generally, the longer a border, the wider it should be—this will help to prevent awkward-looking squares. But there is no reason why you can't make a border any length and width you like. If you want a really wide border, put an access path through it so you can reach both sides from the middle without walking on your bed. If you only have room for a small border, place it close to the house and use small groupings of flowers. Look for plants with a long flowering season and attractive foliage.

ISLAND BEDS

Unlike borders, which are usually seen from only one side, island beds are designed for you to walk around and look at from all angles. Because they are located away from structures, they are exposed to maximum sun and air

SHADY BORDER

Monkshood (*Aconitum* spp.) is good for shade. The hooded flowers form dramatic spikes. Handle carefully: they are poisonous.

penetration—so the garden tends to be healthier and easier to maintain.

As with a border, tie an island in with existing structures. For the most natural effect, make island beds three times as long as they are wide. If you can view an island bed from all sides, put the tallest plants in the centre. If, on the other hand, you can view it primarily from only one angle, make the highest point at the back. Then you can add extra tiers of medium-sized plants.

FOOD AND WATER

Attract butterflies with a water source and a variety of different plants.

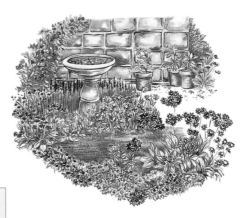

BEST FOR BUTTERFLIES

Astilbes
Bergamot
Blanket flower
  (*Gaillardia*)
Blue false indigo
  (*Baptisia australis*)
Butterfly weed
Fleabane (*Erigeron*)
Joe Pye weed
  (*Eupatarium*)
Lavender
Michaelmas daisies
Phlox
Pinks
Purple coneflower
  (*Echinacea*)
Red valerian
Rudbeckia
Scabious
Sedum
Shasta daisy
  (*Lencanthemum*)
White snakeroot
Yarrow (*Achillea*)

NOT ONLY COLOUR

Besides adding colourful blooms to your garden, rudbeckias offer nectar for butterflies.

ATTRACTING BUTTERFLIES

If you have a large plot, consider planting a meadow garden. If you don't have room, grow some of the many wildflowers that double as garden perennials, such as asters and coneflowers *Echinacea* and *Rudbeckia* spp. Scatter these plants throughout your landscape, or put several together in a butterfly garden. Large splashes of colour are easier for butterflies to find than a single plant, so group several plants of the same colour together.

You can take a number of steps to encourage butterflies to stay in your garden, including the following: set flat stones in a sheltered, sunny spot for butterflies to bask on; dig a small,

shallow basin and line it with plastic to form a butterfly-luring water source; allow a corner of your plot to go wild—woody shrubs provide protection from predators; and finally, create a safe, pesticide-free habitat by using safer techniques, such as hand-picking and water sprays, to remove pests.

Perennial Herb Garden

Plan your herb garden in the same way as a perennial bed or border. A basic garden could consist of raised beds separated by paths. For more formality, lay out the garden beds in geometric shapes, wheel spokes or intricate knots. If you don't have room for a separate herb garden, tuck your favourite herbs into other perennial beds and borders. Most herbs look good in formal designs and make a natural addition to informal gardens.

Sunny sites will suit the widest range of herbs. It is possible to grow some herbs in partial to full shade, but your choices will be limited. (Mints, lemon balm and sweet woodruff are your most likely subjects for success in shade.)

GROUPING OF HERBS
Herbs look wonderful however you use them—grouped into a special herb garden or mixed with perennials and other plants.

HERB FEATURE
Catmint (*Nepeta* spp.) is perfect for spilling over pathways in herb or other informal gardens.

MOISTURE LOVERS
A bog garden is a great site for many kinds of irises. The flowers are beautiful in early summer and the spiky leaves look good all season.

NOT ONLY FRAGRANT
Bergamot *Monarda* spp. leaves have a wonderful citrus aroma. This plant grows well in evenly moist soil.

BOUNTIFUL BOGS
Some perennials have an affinity for wet ground and will thrive at the edge of a pond or in boggy or marshy areas. Perennials suitable for low, moist places are plentiful, including Japanese flag iris *Iris ensata*, goat's beard *Aruncus dioicus*, turtleheads *Chelone* spp., marsh marigold *Caltha palustris* and cardinal flower *Lobelia cardinalis*.

If you already have a pond or wet spot, a bog garden is the solution. If you don't have a naturally wet area but enjoy bog plants, you can create your own bog. Dig a trench at least 30 cm (1 ft) deep and line it with a heavy plastic pond liner. Put an 8 cm (3 in) layer of stones on the base. Lay a seep hose on the top of the plastic and refill the trench with humus-rich soil. Turn on the seep hose to keep the soil evenly moist so your plants have the conditions they require.

THE FRAGRANT PERENNIAL GARDEN
When you mention fragrance in the garden, most people automatically think of flowers. Lavender and lilies are among

SHADE AND WATER

Rodgersias grow well in bog and water gardens and along streams. Plant them with hostas, irises, astilbes, ferns and ligularias *Ligularia* spp.

FRAGRANT PERENNIALS

Bearded iris

Catmint (leaves)

Daylilies (flowers of a few, especially yellow)

False spikenard (*Smilacina racemosa*)

Hosta 'Honeybells'

Lavender (leaves and flowers)

Lily-of-the-valley

Peonies (some *paeonia lactiflora* spp.)

Pinks (*Dianthus* spp.)

Phlox (*Phlox paniculata*)

HEADY SCENTS

Lavender is well-loved for its beautiful flowers and delightful fragrance.

the most well-known, but many others have pleasing scents. Grow scented flowers close to the house for their fragrance, or grow them near outdoor eating areas, patios and porches—any place where people linger.

A number of plants have fragrant foliage, but you need to touch these to smell them. Plant lavender and bergamot *Monarda* spp. where you'll brush against them as you walk by. Grow lemon balm *Melissa officinalis* near a garden seat so you can rub the leaves to release the delicious lemony odour.

The key to having a scented garden that you enjoy is smelling plants before you buy them. As you plan your garden, try to arrange it with just one or two scented plants in bloom at any one time. Then you can enjoy fragrances through the season without being overwhelmed by too many at once.

A Colourful Cutting Garden

Few people have enough space to put a cutting garden truly out of sight, but the more removed it is, the less you'll worry about making it look nice. Some gardeners allocate a corner of their vegetable garden to cut flowers; others create separate cutting beds along a garage, in a sunny side area, or wherever they can find a sheltered corner.

Wherever you put your cutting bed, you want it to be easy to reach and maintain and you want plants that will

STUNNING COLOUR
Peruvian lily *Alstroemeria aurea* 'Orange Glory' is a stunning flower to have in your garden or in a vase on your dining table.

MORNING HARVEST
Using sharp secateurs, harvest flowers in the morning before they fully open. Plunge the stems into a bucket of warm water.

> ### Keep It Simple
>
> You don't need a complicated design or a particular shape for a cutting garden. Just pick a suitable spot and line up your plants in rows, as you would for vegetables. Support the stems of floppy perennials, such as delphiniums, or stake them. Add annuals and bulbs to your cutting garden to extend your choice of materials for arrangements.

thrive in your growing conditions—if they don't grow well, they won't produce enough flowers for cutting.

Selecting plants for your cutting garden is much like choosing perennials for any planting. Here are some other things you'll want to consider when you're deciding what to include:

• If space is limited, concentrate on growing perennials in your favourite colours. If, on the other hand, you have lots of room, plant a variety of colours to give yourself lots of arranging options.

• Grow perennials of different shapes. Include spiky flowers and foliage for height, flat or round flowers and leaves for mass, and small, airy flowers and leaves for fillers.

• Look for perennials with long stems. Compact cultivars are great for ornamental plantings but their stems are usually too short for easy arranging.

• Don't forget to include foliage—it adds body and filler to arrangements. Use subtle greens and silvers—variegated leaves make striking accents.

To add extra excitement to your arrangements, include annuals, grasses and hardy bulbs in your cutting garden. Ornamental grasses are great with both flowers and foliage.

LONG LASTING
This pretty scabious can keep flowering from early summer until early autumn.

COLOUR THEMES
Gardens based on blue and purple flowers are peaceful and soothing. If you like these colours, grow them in a cutting garden so you can enjoy them indoors as well.

SOLVING PROBLEMS WITH PERENNIALS

Perennials are verstatile plants—you can find the right ones to suit any situation. Use them in permanent plantings, low-maintenance and container gardens and in different soil conditions.

PERMANENT PLANTING

More and more gardeners are discovering the advantages of using perennials and other colourful, adaptable plants to create a welcoming entrance that is both beautiful and low-maintenance.

Perennials, alone or in combination with hardy bulbs, trees, climbers and shrubs, offer attractive and colourful alternatives to a boring row of clipped evergreens.

Well-chosen perennials won't drastically outgrow their location, and they're usually dormant when winter arrives. Plus, perennials change continually through the season, which is more than can be said for the most commonly planted structural evergreens.

Planning a perennial area next to your house is pretty much the same as planning one in any other part of your plot. In the case of new building plots, growing conditions may be difficult and you'll need to bear this in mind when you choose your plants. Light levels and microclimates can vary dramatically on different sides of your house.

YEAR-LONG INTEREST

Mix perennials with evergreen leaves—such as heart-leaved bergenia *Bergenia cordifolia*—with hardy bulbs to create a planting with year-round appeal.

HAPPY HOSTAS

The ever-dependable hosta comes in a range of sizes and colours. Its tidy growth habit makes it ideal for shady permanent plantings.

HOUSE AND GARDEN
When you choose plants, look for flower colours that will complement the colours of your paintwork.

There are no special rules for designing permanent plantings—just choose the plants that can take the conditions and that look good to you.

Including some fragrant flowers, such as certain peonies and all pinks *Dianthus* spp., adds a welcoming touch. For a formal look, keep the lines straight with a path of bricks or square or rectangular flagstones and straight edges to plantings. For a less formal design, curve the edge of the bed to create a gentle, casual feel and to allow a few of the plants in front to sprawl over onto the path.

INTERESTING SHAPES
Include a mix of rounded and spiky blooms to add interest to your planting. Fragrant flowers are nice, too.

LOW-CARE COMPACTS
If you love bellflowers, go for a low-maintenance dwarf species, such as *Campanula portenschlagiana*.

LOW-MAINTENANCE
SUN LOVERS

The following are all easy-care and require full sun to thrive.

Coneflowers
 Rudbeckia spp.
Coreopsis
 Coreopsis spp.
Daylilies
 Hemerocallis spp.
Purple coneflower
 Echinacea purpurea
Sedum
 Sedum spectabile
Thrift
 Armeria maritima

STUNNINGLY EASY
Salvia x *sylvestris* has long-blooming showy spikes of purplish blue flowers, which are excellent as cut flowers.

LOW-MAINTENANCE PERENNIAL GARDENING

To some people, just the mention of low maintenance conjures up images of gravel-covered areas or expanses of boring, green ground-cover. But there's no reason why low care should mean no flowers. Planning for a low-maintenance perennial garden requires some thought. The trick is to choose perennials that don't need special attention such as staking, lifting for winter storage or frequent pruning. Look for plants that shrug off heat, scoff at drought and laugh in the face of pests. Although going the low-maintenance route eliminates some species, you'll still have more to choose from than you could ever hope to grow.

If you really want to avoid hard work, shun tall or floppy plants—such as delphiniums and baby's breath *Gypsophila paniculata*—that need staking. Steer clear of tender perennials, such as cannas and dahlias, that you have to dig up and store over the winter. Unless you want to cover a large area, avoid those that spread, like lamb's ears *Stachys byzantina* and lily-of-the-valley

Convallaria majalis. Avoid, too, those that die out after a few years, like many perennial asters *Aster* spp. And ignore those that seem prone to pests in your area, unless you can get a resistant strain.

What's left? A lot, starting with dependable spring bulbs such as irises, daylilies for summer (there are many to choose from), and hostas for shady areas. Try short cultivars of balloon flower *Platycodon grandiflorus* and bellflowers *Campanula* spp. Choose coreopsis *Coreopsis* spp. and wildflowers, especially in a natural garden. Don't forget old-time favourites such as bleeding heart *Dicentra* spp. Ornamental grasses such as fountain grass *Pennisetum alopecuroides* and blue fescue *Festuca glauca* are great for their foliage, and the interesting seed heads of *Pennisetum* may persist over winter.

For more ideas, look at gardens that seem to be in flower even though no one seems to garden in them regularly. Before you plant any perennial, research its growth needs to be sure it suits your conditions.

ROOM TO MOVE

Spiky speedwell *Veronica spicata* is a good choice for a larger, low-maintenance garden—cut them back each year if they get leggy.

EASY IRISES

Irises thrive for years without division and they look great with other easy-care perennials, such as hostas and astilbes.

CONTAINER SOLUTIONS

Containers can be the solution to any troublesome garden site—whether it be problems with soil, climate or topography. You can change all these things simply by using containers.

SOLVING PROBLEMS WITH CONTAINERS

With a little creativity, you'll find many different ways to use containers to solve problem spots. If you can't kneel or if you garden from a wheelchair, you can grow plants at a convenient height in raised planters. If your soil is too hard or rocky to dig, grow flowers in half-barrel tubs instead of in the ground.

If you've got a shady spot that's crying out for colour, try using potted annuals or perennials to create a rotating display. As flowers fade, move the shady pot to a sunnier spot and replace it with one that's been in the sun. Or tuck a few pots into a dull planting to add quick colour. If space is really limited, create your own garden paradise on a flat rooftop or in window boxes.

Don't limit your use of containers to just problem solving. Growing perennials in pots is a great way to experiment with different plant combinations before you commit to putting them in the ground. If you find that you don't like a particular combination, just

OVERFLOWING POT
Geranium (Cinereum Group) 'Ballerina' looks great spilling out of a container and its foliage is attractive all year round.

CONTAINER LIVING
Many lovely perennials, including Michaelmas daisies and bellflowers, adapt well to containers.

TOUCH OF INTEREST
Carefully chosen plants in well-placed containers can add another dimension to an otherwise uninteresting area of your garden.

separate the pots and group them with other possible perennials.

Containers can also make great garden accents. Choose bold, sculptural perennials such as *Yucca filamentosa* for formal designs—or mix lots of colours and cascading plants for a cottage-garden look. You can achieve any effect you wish with containers.

Choosing a Container

Possibilities are endless. You may buy plastic, ceramic or terracotta containers or make your own out of old barrels, sinks or even galvanised buckets. Large pots tend to provide the best conditions for growth, since they hold more soil, nutrients and water, but they are also quite heavy if you need to move them about.

Pots that are about 20 cm (8 in) deep are usually able to hold enough soil without getting too heavy. If you don't plan to move the planter, it can be as big as you want. Be creative, almost anything you can put drainage holes in—from catering-size food cans to old leather boots—can be pressed into service.

Solid-sided containers, such as plastic pots, hold water longer than porous terracotta. Plastics are great for hot, dry summers. Plastic pots are lighter and easier to move, but more prone to blowing over than terracotta pots. Empty these pots or bring them indoors before freezing weather because wet soil expands as it freezes and may crack the pot.

COLOUR IN A POT
You can combine different plants in one pot to create a particular colour combination.

CORAL BELLS
These popular plants with delicate flowers work well in containers.

FOCAL POINT
A special container can be a focal point in a garden. Terracotta pots are particularly attractive and natural looking.

OVERFLOWING FLOWERS

A "mass" container planting of baby's breath *Gypsophila muralis* 'Gypsy' not only looks great but gives you an ongoing supply of cut flowers to take indoors.

FOR CONTAINERS

Nearly any perennial will grow well in a pot. Plant several in one pot or group several in individual containers. Good choices include those with a long season of bloom, such as golden orange daylilies. Others that look great are those with attractive foliage, such as lady's mantle *Alchemilla mollis*, deadnettle *Lamium maculatum*, bergenias, heucheras, hostas and ornamental grasses. Foliage plants extend the period of interest.

CARING FOR CONTAINERS

Keeping the right water balance is a key part of successful container gardening. To help in this, you need to choose a growing medium that will hold some water but not too much. Improve garden soil by mixing 2 parts soil with 1 part potting compost and 1 part perlite. Or use sterilized, premixed "soil-less" potting mixes, which are peat-free. These mixes are free of soil-borne diseases and they weigh much less.

Regular watering is another way you'll balance each container's water supply. Some containers may need watering every day while others will only need water once a week. A good general rule is to wait until the top 2.5 cm (1 in) of soil is dry; then water until some comes out of the bottom.

Since their rooting space is limited, plants in pots need feeding more than plants in the ground. After they've been growing for a month or so, give plants diluted liquid feed every couple of weeks. Use liquid seaweed, granules or a balanced organic fertilizer. Follow the instructions on the pack to find out how often and how much fertilizer you should apply.

Soil Solutions

Gardening would be easier if soil were consistent, but it is a complex and changing mixture of substances—there's bound to be something (or lack of something) that makes gardening a challenge.

Alkaline Soil

Most plants can live with a slightly alkaline soil, but a soil with a pH above 8.0 starts to take its toll. Excessively alkaline soils have chronic nutrient deficiencies and resist attempts to acidify them. In too-alkaline soils, phosphorus and most micro-nutrients are insoluble and unavailable to plants. On the other hand, minerals such as sodium and selenium may be abundant enough to be toxic to plants. You may decide to grow species that are adapted to high-pH soils.

The most effective material for lowering the soil pH is sulphur. Apply 0.5 kg (1 pound) per 9.3 sq m (100 sq ft) for each whole point you want to lower the pH. Rake or dig the sulphur into the soil and keep it moist.

ALKALINE ANEMONE
The delicate Japanese anemone *Anemone* x *hybrida* spreads by creeping underground stems and thrives in alkaline soil.

Plants for Soil pH 7.0 or Higher

Baby's breath
  Gypsophila paniculata
Bergenias
  Bergenia spp.
Coral bells
  Heuchera spp.
Japanese anemone
  Anemone x *hybrida*
Mulleins
  Verbascum spp.
Peonies *Paeonia* spp.
Pinks *Dianthus* spp.

ADAPTABLE PHLOX
Phlox can adapt to alkaline soil, as long as it has good drainage and lots of organic matter.

Incorporating plenty of organic matter can help lower the pH—or keep it low if you've added sulphur. Avoid fertilizers that raise the soil pH, including wood ash and bonemeal.

Acid Soil

Excess acidity is among the easiest of soil problems to fix. A slightly acid soil is a great thing to have because most plants thrive in it. But in too-acid soil, most nutrients are bound up in unavailable forms. A few minerals—aluminum, iron, manganese—may become too soluble and reach toxic concentrations. And soil organisms are inhibited, so organic matter breaks down more slowly.

Soil with a pH below 6.2 is too acid for many plants, but there are some that will thrive in those conditions. If your soil is naturally quite acid, you may just decide to grow adapted species, such as chrysanthemums and lily-of-the-valley, or grow your favourite plants in containers. Observe what is growing well in your neighbours' gardens and in your locality.

ACID FRIENDLY

Chrysanthemums are late-summer to autumn bloomers that will tolerate well-drained soil that is on the acidic side and full sun to light shade.

RAISE THE pH

Add powdered lime to raise the pH of acid soil, digging or raking it into your soil.

Snow-in-summer is a low-mounding, spring-flowering perennial that can tolerate sandy or loamy soil.

PLANTS FOR SAND

Coreopsis
Coreopsis lanceolata
Cotton lavender
Santolina chamaecyparissus
Red-hot poker
Kniphofia uvaria
Sedums *Sedum* spp.
Snow-in-summer
Cerastium tomentosum
Statice
Limonium latifolium
White gaura
Gaura lindheimeri
Yarrows *Achillea* spp.
Yuccas *Yucca* spp.

TOLERANT THRIFT

Thrift *Armeria maritima* will tolerate poor, sandy soil that drains quickly.

MANAGING SANDY SOIL

Sandy soils are light to dig and don't get sticky when wet. They're well aerated. They warm up quickly in the spring. And it's easy to change their pH because they're not buffered by reserves of acidity or alkalinity. But sands have little clay or humus to hold water and minerals, which wash quickly away. Sand gets hot during the day and cools rapidly at night and there's little or no structure.

Compared to other soil quirks, excessive sandiness is easy to remedy—just add plenty of organic matter. With enough organic matter, sandy soils can hold water and nutrients while still being well drained and easy to work. Of course, with all that extra moisture to heat up, organically enriched sandy soils won't warm up as fast as they normally do in the spring. But they won't get as hot in the summer, either.

Because sandy soils are well aerated, micro-organisms burn through organic matter quickly. In one way, that's good, because humus forms faster; in another way, that's bad, because nutrient-rich organic matter doesn't last long. So add both fast- and slow-digesting organic matter. Manures, grass cuttings and

POOR SOIL DELIGHT

Sandy soil is generally infertile, and coreopsis grows best in soil that isn't very fertile—too much nitrogen can cause weak stems.

compost will break down quickly, building humus and improving the soil's ability to hold water and nutrients. Growing green manures over the winter is another good source of organic matter.

Sandy soils are so porous that if the top few inches have dried out, the next few inches below aren't far behind. It doesn't take as much water to soak the soil beyond the root zone, which encourages deep roots. But you will have to water more frequently.

Use any rocks you have dug up from your garden to make a raised rock garden. Mound topsoil over the top and plant in crevices and pockets between them.

PERENNIALS FOR ROCK GARDENS

Aubrieta
Aubrieta spp.
Blue cupidone
Catananche caerulea
Dalmatian bellflower
Campanula portenschlagiana
Gold dust
Aurinia saxatilis
Milkweed
Asclepias tuberosa
Thrift
Armeria maritima
Wormwood
Artemisia absinthium

Working with Rocky Soil

To gardeners facing a thin layer of soil over blocks of rock, the usual advice about deep watering and subsoils and double-digging seems pointless.

The obstacles these soils present are many. Plant roots have few places to go. Water and nutrients have little to cling to. Digging and planting can be very difficult. The usual remedy for building soil—adding ample amounts of organic matter—helps, but just isn't enough.

The best approach to gardening in rocky soil is to use native plants where possible or to use plants that are suited to rocky conditions—and to import soil for anywhere you can. Plants native to rocky regions have evolved to cope with short supplies of water and nutrients and little room to spread out. They generally

CASCADING COLOUR

Aubrieta 'Blue Cascade' is an excellent choice for sunny rock gardens.

ROCK JASMINE

Rock jasmine *Androsace* spp. is a low-growing, unassuming plant with light green or silvery grey foliage.

GRASSES

If you have a moist spot in your rock garden, try ornamental grasses to add depth and interest.

have shallow root systems that reach through whatever soil is available.

It's best to begin with the smallest plant possible. Seeds are ideal, although young potted specimens are more practical for difficult-to-germinate plants. Seeds and young plants can grow roots around obstacles in the soil rather than having to adapt an existing root system to new conditions.

Rocky soils dry out quickly, so water them frequently but for short periods. If you choose plants that are naturally adapted to rocky sites they may not need extra water at all once established.

Wildflower gardens normally feature durable, sun-loving flowers. Try turning an area with poor, rocky soil into a wildflower garden using plants that are naturally adapted to your rocky area. Look in wildflower gardening books and visit local nurseries to find out which plants will grow best in your area.

Once you've chosen the plants that will be in your wildflower garden, you'll need to prepare the ground well. Keep the soil moist and weed regularly for the first few years. Once the plants are established, strim in autumn and leave mowings to shed seed and dry before raking up and removing. Beyond that, you can let the perennials grow and mingle as they will.

Part Three

PLANTING YOUR GARDEN

Tools and Equipment

Caring for your garden is simpler if you've got good tools. Using the right tool makes any job easier, but when faced with a wall-long display of different tools, it can be hard to decide what you need.

SIMPLE NEEDS

If you garden only with containers or have a very small garden, the tools you need may be just a trowel and hand fork.

Basic Collection

Most gardeners can get by with a few basic tools. You'll need a spade to turn the soil, to dig large holes and for moving soil, compost and manures.

A garden fork is useful for turning the soil, working in organic matter and green manures, turning compost and dividing perennials. You'll also need a metal rake to smooth the soil, a hoe for weeding and a trowel for planting and transplanting. Secateurs are also useful for pruning perennials.

Caring for Tools

It's easy at the end of a long day in the garden to put tools away dirty.

EARTH MOVER

If you need to move any significant amount of soil, then a good wheelbarrow is essential to minimize injury and general aches and pains.

You may decide on a whole collection of garden tools, or you may buy only a few of the basics, especially if you are new to gardening. It depends on your needs and your budget.

But eventually the moist soil clinging to your tools will make them rust. Use a stick or an old wooden spoon to scrape off the soil residue. A good trick is to keep a bucket of sharp sand around and dip the tool up and down in it until the soil comes off.

Your spade and hoe will do a better job for you if you keep them sharpened. You'll get the best results if you sharpen them briefly and often rather than making it a big job you keep for the end of the gardening year. For most gardeners, a metal file is quite adequate. Use a file that matches the contour of the tool's surface. The aim is to keep the angle of the existing edge but to thin it a bit and remove any nicks. If you have many tools, a whetstone or grindstone will do the job more quickly. If you don't want to sharpen them yourself, you can take your tools to someone who does it professionally.

THE VERSATILE RAKE

A rake is a vital part of any garden tool collection. Use rakes for clearing stones, fallen leaves and twigs from paths, and from lawns and other grassy areas.

Selecting and Buying Plants

A basic step in ensuring a healthy garden is starting with healthy, disease-free plants. They'll become established quickly and you'll avoid importing pests and diseases that could spread to other plants.

Inspect the Root System

Strong, healthy roots are a vital part of plant health. If a plant is growing in a plastic container, gently remove the container and look at the roots. Roots should be uniformly white, moist and without breaks, bumps or brown spots. A few fine, exposed roots don't indicate stress, but avoid plants with lots of matted roots or plants tightly rooted to their neighbours. Separating closely rooted plants can severely damage individual root systems. This shocks the young plants and can set them back by several weeks as they grow new roots.

INSTANT COLOUR
Hellebores *Helleborus orientalis* are often sold when in flower and have an immediate impact.

A HEAD START
Starting with healthy, vigorous perennials, such as these lupins, is a key part of creating a beautiful garden filled with flowers.

SPOT THE DIFFERENCE

Learn to spot the difference between strong, healthy plants and weak, sickly ones that can be cheaper but won't be worth the money.

Check Plant Colour

Healthy young plant leaves are usually deep green, although you can expect colour to vary among plants and cultivars. An overall pale, washed-out appearance often indicates that a nutrient is lacking. If you're not sure what a particular plant is supposed to look like, compare it with a photograph from a book or catalogue. This will help you determine if those stripes, spots or colours are normal or if they indicate a problem.

Probe for Problems

Examine perennials carefully before you buy them and reject any that have clear signs of pests or diseases, or pest and disease damage. As you inspect the foliage of the perennials, make sure you turn the leaves over and carefully check their undersides as well as the tops—remember that the lower leaf surfaces are favourite hiding places for pests.

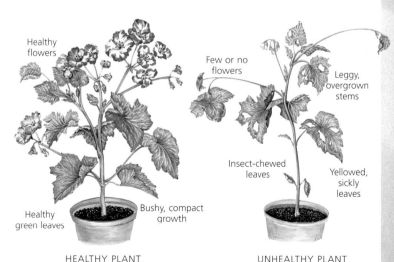

Healthy flowers

Few or no flowers

Leggy, overgrown stems

Insect-chewed leaves

Yellowed, sickly leaves

Healthy green leaves

Bushy, compact growth

HEALTHY PLANT

UNHEALTHY PLANT

CHECK BELOW

Gently slide a plant from its pot to check the roots before buying. Avoid plants with tightly packed, curled roots, below.

HEALTHY ROOT GROWTH

Good-quality perennials have healthy white roots that you can see are still growing through the soil ball, right.

CONTAINER-GROWN PERENNIALS

Perennials are most commonly sold in containers. Container-grown perennials are convenient and easy to handle. You can keep the pots in a well-lit location until you are ready to plant. Then you can slide the root ball out and plant it in the garden with minimal disturbance. However, there is a catch. Horticultural researchers are finding that roots tend to stay in the light, fluffy "soil" of synthetic mixes, rather than branching out into the surrounding garden soil. But you can avoid this problem by loosening roots on the outside of the ball and spreading them out into the soil as you plant.

Container-grown perennials come in different sizes, so their prices vary widely. Larger-sized pots, usually 4.5- and 9-litre containers, are generally more expensive. The cost may be worthwhile if you want immediate garden impact. On the other hand, you can buy younger plug plants inexpensively in trays or small pots. These sizes work fine if you don't mind waiting a season or more for them to fill out and flower with abandon. In fact, young plants tend to become established in the garden faster than older ones, catching up with the bigger plants in a short time.

Bare-root Perennials

You will come across many species of dormant bare-root plants for sale early in the growing season. In late summer or early autumn, you may also find bare-root perennials such as bleeding heart *Dicentra spectabilis* or even peonies. You may choose to buy bare-root plants to save money—they are usually less expensive than large container-grown plants. These plants look more dead than alive, but fortunately, in this case, looks are deceptive. If you keep the roots moist and cool and plant them quickly and properly, plants will recover.

Your plants' roots should be wrapped in a protective medium—keep this moist. Soak the roots in a bucket of lukewarm water for a few hours before planting. If you need to wait to plant, pot up the roots until you are ready.

WAYS TO BUY PERENNIALS
Container-grown perennials (left) may cost more, but they give your garden an instant effect. Bare-root plants (right) take a bit of care but are often less expensive.

FRAGILE HOLLYHOCK
If you start off with healthy young plants they will be less likely to attract pests and develop diseases such as rust.

Preparing the Bed

Preparing the planting bed is critical to the success of your perennial garden. If you do a thorough job here, you will be rewarded by quicker plant establishment and less weeding to do later.

Timing

If possible, start digging a season or a year before you plant. That way the soil will have a chance to settle. If spring typically is too wet to work the soil in your area, dig your bed in autumn instead. If you can't prepare the soil ahead of time, you can usually get the bed ready and start planting in the same season.

Making New Beds

When you're digging a garden bed in a lawn, strip off the turf with a flat spade by cutting long, spade-width strips across the width of your bed. Slide your spade under the strips to sever them from the soil and remove them. Or kill the grass

COLOURFUL RESULTS
With care, even poor soil can produce good results, such as these Michaelmas daisies.

TENDER LOVING CARE
These healthy late-summer flowers are the result of a good, granular soil structure. It's worth a little effort to prepare the soil well; your plants will thank you for it.

by covering it with black plastic, but this can take weeks, depending on the weather—the hotter it is the faster it works. Dig the turf back in once it decays.

Now break up the soil. If you're making a small bed you can usually loosen the soil to a depth of 15 cm (6 in) —or 30 cm (1 ft) if you double dig. Add well-rotted compost before planting and work it into the bed. For a heavy clay or light, sandy loam that is low in organic matter, spread a 10-cm (4-in) thick layer of compost over the entire area and work it well into the soil. Use less compost to grow perennials that like drier conditions. If your soil is on the acid side, add lime to make it more alkaline.

ALL IN THE PREPARATION
With good preparation, you will have a garden full of thriving plants, such as *Dicentra spectabilis* 'Alba' with healthy foliage and an abundance of flowers.

TO PREPARE A NEW BED

1. Outline the edge with rope or string.
2. Use a spade to strip off the turf and expose the soil.
3. If a soil test indicates the site is too acid, apply lime.
4. Spread a layer of compost over the surface and work it into the bed.

Double-Digging

Double-digging is hard work, but it can be worthwhile if you are gardening on heavy, clay soil or if you want to encourage perennials to root extra deeply in very dry areas. Remove the turf and weed roots first. Starting at one end of the bed, dig a trench that is 30 cm (1 ft) wide and as deep as your spade across the width of the bed. Put all of the topsoil you unearth into a wheelbarrow and move it to the far end of the bed. Now loosen up the exposed subsoil with a garden fork or your spade. Then back up to dig the next 30 cm (1 ft) wide strip. Shift that topsoil, with some extra compost or other organic matter, into the first trench and then loosen the new area of subsoil. Continue in this fashion until you reach the far end of the bed. Finish the last strip with the topsoil from your wheelbarrow and rake the bed smooth. Once you've prepared the bed, avoid stepping on it or you'll compact the soil and undo all your hard work. If you can't reach in from the sides to plant, lay a board across the soil and step on that. Remove it when you've finished.

SOIL IMPROVERS

Wood ash (above left) supplies potassium—it will raise the pH, so don't apply it to acid-loving plants. Gypsum (above right) supplies soil with calcium and sulphur.

POOR-SOIL SOLUTION

In poor soil, double-digging can help give your perennials the best possible conditions for root growth.

Dalmatian bellflower *Campanula portenschlagiana* likes average to rich, well-drained soil. Test the soil before you add any extra nutrients—you may not need to add anything.

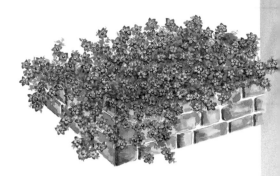

Use Compost

If you are preparing a new bed, work compost in as you dig. In an established garden, use compost as a mulch. As a general rule, cover the bed with 5 cm (2 in) a year for maintainance. Use more for moisture-loving perennials or if you want to control weeds. Use less around perennials that prefer drier, less fertile soils. Compost breaks down gradually over the growing season, so add more as needed.

LIKING IT LEAN

Some perennials, such as yellow chamomile *Anthemis tinctoria*, grow best if the soil isn't too rich.

Applying Organic Nutrients

How you actually apply organic nutrients to your garden depends on several quite different factors. If you are starting a new bed, for instance, you can spread compost, fertilizers and other soil improvers (such as lime or sulphur) over the surface and work the materials in before you plant. Once your perennial garden is established, you can supply your plants with nutrients by working slow-release fertilzers into the soil around the base of each plant and by mulching with organic materials, such as well-rotted garden compost. If they need a midsummer nutrient boost, you can spray the plants with a liquid feed, such as compost tea or seaweed extract.

CHRYSANTHEMUMS
These fibrous-rooted perennials are fast growing and need to be divided every 1–2 years to keep them vigorous.

QUICK FLOWERS
Blanket flower *Gaillardia* x *grandiflora* will flower in the first season after sowing.

PLANTING

Although you may have been anticipating the moment of planting for months, don't rush it. Planting takes time and a lot of bending. Work slowly to get each plant settled as well as possible.

WHEN TO PLANT

Once you've prepared your soil, it's time to get your carefully chosen plants in the ground so they can start growing. But planting your perennials at the right time is important to give them a good start.

Time your planting efforts so your new perennials will start growing in a period of abundant rainfall and moderate temperatures—usually spring or autumn. In areas with hard frosts, concentrate your planting efforts in spring. Spring planting, when the soil has warmed up sufficiently, allows the new plants time to establish strong root systems before winter. You can also plant in late summer for seasonally available perennials. In areas with mild winters, plant in autumn so perennials will be well established before the summer. In most areas you can plant perennials in autumn or spring.

UP, UP AND AWAY
Good soil preparation and careful planting will help get your chosen perennials off to a vigorous start for healthy future growth.

Container-grown Perennials

If you are planting perennials grown in pots from garden centres and nurseries, dig deeply enough so the surface of the container soil will be at the top of the hole.

Now, prepare the plant. Water it first so the plant will be easier to remove from the container and there is less likelihood that the roots will be damaged. Slide the plant out of the pot. Break up the edges of the root ball so the roots will have more contact with the surrounding soil. If the roots are wrapped around themselves, you may have to work them loose gently with your fingers.

After planting, firm the soil gently around the plant, water it well and mulch. Mulching your bed with organic materials, such as compost or fine bark chips, will conserve moisture and reduce weed competition. (New beds are especially weed-prone, since turning the soil exposes weed seeds.)

CONTAINER-GROWN

1. Dig a hole larger than the root ball.
2. Slide the plant out of its container and loosen the soil around the roots.
3. Set the plant in the hole, backfill with soil then firm lightly. Water well.

SPACING IS EVERYTHING

If you crowd plants, they will grow weakly and be more susceptible to disease. Before you plant, set them out in their pots to see how they look. Leave enough room for them to spread and mature to their full size.

ROOM TO MOVE

When planting, remember to space your plants evenly and give them the room they need to thrive.

BARE-ROOT PERENNIALS

1. Dig a hole large enough to hold the roots without bending them, leaving a mound in the centre.
2. Set the plant in the hole and spread the roots.
3. Backfill with soil, gently firm and water well.

BARE-ROOT PLANTING

Bare-root plants take more time to settle. Soak the roots in lukewarm water for a few hours. Identify how deeply the plants had been growing in the nursery. The parts above ground usually emerge from the root system above the former soil line. Plant so that these stay slightly above the soil in your garden.

Make a hole deep and wide enough to set the plant crown at the soil surface and stretch out the roots. Form a small mound of soil in the bottom of the hole. Set the root clump on it with the crown resting on top. Spread the roots in all directions and fill around them with soil. Firm the soil gently, water and mulch. Keep the soil moist for a few weeks to allow the plants to establish well.

Part Four

MAINTAINING PERENNIALS

MULCH

Mulching is important in almost any climate. It helps keep out weeds by preventing them from getting a foothold and it protects the soil. Organic mulches can add nutrients and organic matter.

USING MULCH

If you use mulch on frozen soil during the winter, it will keep the earth evenly frozen. This helps reduce the rapid freezing-and-thawing cycles that can damage plant roots and push plant crowns out of the soil. In hot summers, mulch will slow the rapid decay of organic matter in the soil so that each application will last longer. Whatever your local weather, if you choose carefully, mulch can also work as an attractive background to set off your perennials.

CONSERVING MOISTURE
Foxgloves like moist soil, so, in dry areas, apply a layer of mulch during summer to slow evaporation and keep the soil moist longer.

KEEPING IT CONSTANT
A generous layer of organic mulch will help moderate soil temperatures and conserve water.

> ### REMEMBER
> As useful as mulch is, there are situations when mulching can actually cause garden problems. If slugs and snails are your major pests, an organic mulch can provide them with the conditions they prefer. If you're gardening in heavy, wet clay, mulch can slow evaporation. In colder areas mulch in summer, when the soil has warmed, then remove and compost the mulch when you are clearing beds in autumn.

Mulching with compost is a good way to add nutrients to your garden. It may be all you need for light feeders, such as coreopsis *Coreopsis* spp., yarrow *Achillea* spp. and thrift *Armeria maritima*. Compost mulch will conserve moisture, but may not be very effective in eliminating weeds.

CHOOSING A MULCH

Many kinds of organic mulch are available for your perennial border. Leafmould makes a useful mulch and the leaves are free. Dark-coloured, fine-textured, well-rotted compost gives the soil a rich, healthy look as well as improving soil fertility. Grass clippings or straw may look too utilitarian for most flower gardens and bark or wood chips may be suitable for bold plants, but can dwarf small perennials.

Try to choose a mulch that won't pack down into dense layers. Dense layers of materials such as grass clippings tend to shed water—it runs off the bed instead of into the soil. If you use these kinds of mulches, mix in coarse, fluffy material such as shredded leaves and twigs.

WATERING

Fine-tune your watering depending on several factors, including the type of soil you have, the amount of natural rainfall you receive, the plants you grow and the stage of growth the plants are in.

FLOWERS FIRST TO GO

A garden that is actively growing and flowering will need a source of moisture at all times. If water is in short supply, flowers and flower buds are the first to suffer.

SMALL IRRIGATION

Hand watering with a watering can is often the most realistic option for irrigating small gardens.

How Moisture–retentive?

To answer this question, water a portion of the garden thoroughly. After 48 hours, dig a small hole 15 cm (6 in) deep. If the soil is reasonably water-retentive, the earth at the bottom of the hole will be moist. If it is not, you can improve it by working in lots of well-rotted compost. This acts like a sponge—if you add a lot of compost or other organic matter, you can water less frequently. But when you do irrigate, water extra thoroughly to saturate the organic matter.

Keeping Track of Rainfall

Monitor your rainfall and vary your watering accordingly. Overwatering can be as disastrous as underwatering, especially in heavy soils. You can tell how much rain has fallen if you leave out a rain gauge. If you don't want to

> ## HOW MUCH WATER?
> A good rule of thumb is that your perennials should get 25 mm (1 in) of water a week. This wets the soil deeply, encouraging roots to grow further underground. Of course, some perennials need more moisture and some need less, so you'll have to adjust your watering regime depending on the needs of all your plants.

buy a rain gauge, set a small, clean can in an open part of the garden and use a ruler to measure how much rainwater it collects. Check once a week.

DIFFERENT PLANTS, DIFFERENT NEEDS

Some perennials thrive in moist soils, others grow weakly or rot if water is abundant. Water more often if you grow perennials that need evenly moist soil. These include delphiniums, astilbes and moisture-loving bog plants such as candelabra primroses *Primula japonica*.

Let the soil dry out between waterings for drought-tolerant plants, such as lavender, candytuft *Iberis sempervirens* and red-hot pokers *Kniphofia* hybrids. These perennials may need no more than 12 mm (½ in) of water per week.

Expect to pamper newly planted perennials until their roots spread far enough to support the plants. If the weather is warm and dry, you may have to water daily until a heavy shower arrives. If the season is cool and rainy, let nature take care of the irrigation.

WATER OFTEN
Some hardy geraniums such as *Geranium endressii* thrive with evenly moist, humus-rich soil and need watering regularly.

Fertilizing

Supplying the nutrients that perennials need is critical to keeping them healthy. How much fertilizer to add to your garden will depend on how fertile the soil is and which plants you're growing.

Soil and Fertilizing

The texture and natural fertility of your soil will have a great impact on how much and how often you need to fertilize. A sandy soil will hold fewer nutrients than a clay soil or a soil that's high in organic matter, so you'll need to fertilize sandy soil more. If you prepared the soil thoroughly before planting you may not have to fertilize a new perennial garden for a year or more.

Varying Needs

Fertilizer requirements vary widely among different perennials. Some are light feeders, such as heleniums *Helenium autumnale*, heliopsis *Heliopsis helianthoides* and fleabane *Erigeron* spp. A light layer of compost applied once or twice a year should meet their nutrient needs. Other perennials are heavy feeders; these include delphiniums, astilbes and phlox *Phlox paniculata*. They need more frequent feeding to stay in top form.

You may want to give your plants a fertility boost to encourage new growth or rejuvenation. Feed in spring as they begin growing, after planting or dividing, and after deadheading or cutting back.

APPLYING FERTILIZER

Make holes in the soil and fill them with dry fertilizer (top). Or sprinkle slow-release fertilizer around the base of the plant (centre). Liquid feeds are easy to apply straight onto plant leaves (bottom).

ONCE A YEAR

A yearly application of a light fertilizer will supply all the nutrients many perennials need to thrive.

COMPOST TEA

If you want to turn your compost from a solid nutrient source into a quick-acting liquid fertilizer, make it into compost tea. Put one or two trowel loads of compost (or farm manure) into a big piece of sacking. Tie the bag securely at the top and submerge it into a large watering can or bucket of water. Let it steep for 1 week, then remove the bag. Dilute the remaining liquid until it is the colour of weak tea if you plan to spray or sprinkle it directly on your perennials, or use it full strength to drench the ground around the base of the plants.

APPLYING FERTILIZERS

When you feed plants, you can eliminate deficiencies by applying the feed in either liquid or dry form, or both. If you use a combination, make sure you don't apply more nutrients than your plants need. Remember, too much fertilizer can be as bad as not enough, leading to weak, sappy growth and disease.

Common liquid fertilizers include liquid seaweed and comfrey or compost tea. Use a single dose for a quick fix, or apply every 2 weeks for a plant boost. You can spray these directly on the plants, which absorb nutrients through their foliage.

Granular plant food is released to plants more slowly. Scratch them into the surface of moist soil in a circle around the perimeter of the plant's foliage, so the nutrients are released gradually. This encourages roots to extend outward.

MAKING COMPOST

1. Build your compost with high-carbon and high-nitrogen materials—add in layers or mix them up.

2. As you add new materials, water to moisten them if they seem dry.

3. Aerate the compost pile by turning it once every week or two using a garden fork. This hastens microbial activity.

MAKING AND USING COMPOST

Compost is the key to success in any kind of gardening. Compost is a balanced blend of recycled garden and household wastes that has broken down into dark, crumbly organic matter.

COMPOSTING

Why throw away kitchen scraps and plant waste when you can recycle them and turn them into food for your garden? Composting can take a while but provides high-quality organic material in a matter of months. There are different systems but they tend to have elements in common. Most require building up a heap in layers to ensure the right mix for good decomposition. For the best mix, use 3 parts of high-nitrogen material to 1 part of high-carbon material. Grass clippings, green plant material and vegetable waste from the kitchen are all high in nitrogen. Cardboard, paper, straw and shredded woody waste from pruning are all high in carbon. So, when you add grass clippings, for example, to your heap, always mix in plenty of cardboard or scrunched-up used kitchen towels or newspaper, so the grass doesn't coagulate into a wet mass that won't decompose effectively.

COMPOST BINS

A compost bin isn't strictly necessary, but it will help to keep all the garden and kitchen waste together in a neat pile.

Your local authority may provide plastic compost bins, or you can make your own from wood or chicken wire, supported by corner posts.

How long your compost will take before you can use it depends on many factors, particularly the size of the heap and how much heat it generates. Big heaps heat up more quickly than smaller ones and hot weather also accelerates the decomposition process. So, if your compost heap is in a sunny site, the material will decompose more quickly than if you locate it in a shady part of the garden. Turning your heap with a fork every month or two can also speed up the process. The good news is that all compost heaps will produce good compost eventually, even if it takes a year. And when most of the original material you put in is unrecognisable, your compost is ready to use.

HAPPY BELLFLOWERS
The time you spend making compost and applying it to your garden will be more than returned by improved soil and plant health.

COMPOST BIN
A homemade wire and timber frame keeps the compost heap neat and compact.

MAKE USE OF SCRAPS
Most kinds of kitchen scraps are suitable ingredients for your compost. Remember to avoid bones, meat and fat.

SUPPORTING AND TRAINING

Staking, deadheading, pinching out and cutting back are all techniques used to produce the most vigorous and beautiful perennials. These are tasks which good gardeners employ to help plants perform.

STAKING SECRETS

Support plants as they grow, don't wait until the stems are sagging—make a note on your calendar to set out your supports as plants emerge. If the foliage of your perennials is not full enough to hide the supports, you can plant low-growing annuals or perennials in front of them. They will fill in quickly and hide the stakes.

DEADHEADING MADE EASY

Deadheading can be done by hand or with a pair of sharp secateurs. No matter which tools you use, cut back to a leaf,

DROOPY LUPINS

Stakes and string can be used to support tall lupins.

START EARLY

Put up stakes early in the season so your plants can grow up and through them. For bushy plants, use something the plants can grow through, which they'll then fill out and hide.

Pruning shears are handy for snipping off spent flowers that have thick or wiry stems.

COLUMBINE HAIRCUT
Columbines *Aquilegia* spp. are beautiful in bloom but decline after flowering. Cut them back to encourage new growth.

bud or another stem. The exceptions are perennials with fine, wiry stems topped with flowers—with these plants, use shears to take off the top layer when the flowers fade.

PINCHING OUT

By removing the growing tip of the stem, you cut off the source of hormones that make it grow and elongate. This frees buds lower on the stem to develop into side branches. Pinching out will make leggy perennials more bushy and compact, with better branching and more flowers. Perennials that would otherwise need staking may be able to stand on their own if you pinch them back.

CUTTING BACK AND THINNING

You can cut back long or straggly stems to make a plant tidier and produce new growth. Cutting back is like a more radical form of deadheading.

Thinning removes whole stems, improving air circulation around the plant. Remove one-third to one-half of the stem length.

WEEDS

Weeds pop up in well-maintained gardens. The trick is to take care of the problem early, before they get large enough to compete with your plants for space, light, water and nutrients.

WHAT IS A WEED?

What separates unwanted weeds from desirable plants is often the speed with which they spread. Removing the roots of perennial weeds as you prepare the soil for planting will help keep them at bay. Mulching and regular weeding help prevent new weeds starting. If aggressive perennial weeds get completely out of control, it's often easiest to start again. Dig up your perennials and set them aside until you can dig the bed and remove all the roots of the weeds. Annual weeds may not have the invasive roots of perennials, but they reproduce from seed, often growing fast and spreading far. Remove annual weeds from the garden before they set seed. Cut them off or scrape them out with a hoe or hand weeder.

Uprooting gets rid of annual weeds but digging is a slightly better choice for perennial weeds, assuming you get all of the buried portions of the plant. If you don't, they can produce new weeds. When the weeds are too numerous to pull up individually by hand, a sharp hoe is a good solution. In most cases, hoes are best for young or annual weeds, but they can also be used

START EARLY

Removing weeds when they're small or preventing them from sprouting in the first place will make the job of weed control much easier.

SPREADING WEEDS

Many perennial weeds such as bindweed have rhizomes that spread quickly, engulfing desirable plants.

HEAVE HOE

Use a cultivator or hoe early in the season to break up the soil in your flowerbeds and loosen any weeds.

DANDELION DANGER

You may need to burn off or spray weeds in difficult spots, such as these dandelions between paving.

> ### BE WEED WISE
>
> Start while you are preparing your new garden bed. Look for the long, white roots of weeds and remove them completely—if you leave even little pieces, they sprout into new plants. Once your perennials are well established, you can control most weeds if you mulch and weed for the first year or two. By about the third year, there should be little room for weed invasion.

for some established perennials by forcing them to use their food reserves to replace the decapitated top growth. Hoe every 7–14 days to cut off the top growth before it starts sending food back to the roots.

One of the most common weed problems in perennial gardens is grass, which will creep in along the edges of beds and borders. You can block the invasion of grass by cutting along the edge of the border frequently with a sharp spade or edger and removing the errant sprigs of grass. Or you can take some preventive action when you dig the bed: add a metal, wood, stone, brick or plastic edging to form a barrier around the perimeter of the bed. Sink the edging at least 10–15 cm (4–6 in) deep to block creeping grass stems in their underground movement.

Pest and Disease Prevention

Creating and maintaining a naturally healthy garden isn't a simple one- or two-step process. Every decision you make, or don't make, plays a part in the results you get throughout the season.

Steps to a Healthy Garden

Diversity provides habitats for a range of insects and animals, and predators and parasites help to keep pest populations at a relatively constant level.

Good growing conditions give perennials a head start. Before buying new plants, make sure you can supply the conditions they prefer. If you have a struggling plant, move it or replace it.

Healthy soil produces healthy plants. Adding organic matter improves soil and encourages beneficial micro-organisms.

TAKE CARE
Hostas are dependable shade perennials, but remember they are prone to slugs and snails, so take precautions before they strike.

Remember

Vigorous plants grown in fertile soil attract fewer pests and are less susceptible to infection by plant pathogens than plants grown in poor soil. Start with a variety of healthy plants, give them the growing conditions they require and keep an eye out for potential problems. These simple steps will go a long way towards producing a successful garden, free from pests and diseases.

BEAUTY IN DIVERSITY
Including a diversity of flowering plants helps attract beneficial insects and makes your garden interesting.

ONLY THE BEST
Monitoring soil fertility will help ensure strong, healthy stems and leaves, vigorous roots and beautiful flowers, such as these *Aster* spp.

Checking your plants at least once a week can help you spot potential problems before they get out of hand.

Become familiar with diseases, pests and beneficial insects so you'll know which to control and which to leave alone.

Become familiar with available controls before you need to use them.

Keep track of when and where problems occurred and what you did to control them. Write down what worked and what didn't.

Pests

Pests are easiest to control if you catch them before they get out of hand. Inspecting your garden regularly helps you spot problems early. Identify the pest before you decide how to treat it.

Some Common Pests

Aphids are tiny, soft-bodied insects that can cause the plants to twist, pucker or droop. They breed at an alarming rate and leave a trail of sugary excrement (honeydew). Leafminers are the larvae of small flies. Mites are tiny, spider-like pests that attack, especially when it is hot and dry. Vine weevils eat notches from leaves and their larvae eat roots. Several bugs leave irregular holes or sunken brown spots in the middle of leaves. Slugs and snails can be a problem anywhere the soil stays damp. Thrips leave pale, silvery damaged areas.

Controlling Pests

If you find only a few pests, pick them off the plants by hand and crush them.

Catch pests in traps or deter them with barricades. Yellow sticky traps attract aphids in greenhouses and enclosed spaces. Trap slugs with a shallow container of beer or "slug pub" set in the soil so the top rim is at ground level.

You can use biological weapons such as nematodes that you water into the soil. They eliminate pests without harming people, animals or beneficial insects, and are effective against vine weevils and slugs.

BENEFICIAL LACEWINGS
Adult lacewings feed mostly on nectar and honeydew, but their larvae are voracious predators of insect pests.

APHID INFESTATION
If aphids are out of control and pruning is not an option, try a soap spray.

LOOK BEFORE YOU SPRAY
Before spraying, look for beneficial insects such as ladybirds. They may control the problem for you.

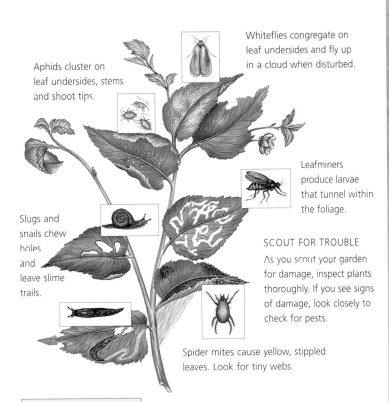

Whiteflies congregate on leaf undersides and fly up in a cloud when disturbed.

Aphids cluster on leaf undersides, stems and shoot tips.

Leafminers produce larvae that tunnel within the foliage.

Slugs and snails chew holes and leave slime trails.

SCOUT FOR TROUBLE
As you scout your garden for damage, inspect plants thoroughly. If you see signs of damage, look closely to check for pests.

Spider mites cause yellow, stippled leaves. Look for tiny webs.

"ORGANIC" CONTROLS

Some insecticides are derived from plants. Pyrethrins are effective on greenfly and blackfly. Derris can be used against aphids, caterpillars and flea beetle but may harm lacewings and ladybirds.

These controls have broad-spectrum activity, meaning that they will harm beneficial as well as pest insects. Pyrethrum, however, does not persist for long.

In a healthy garden, populations of beneficial insects will go a long way towards keeping pests under control.

If all else fails, try some of the less toxic insecticides. Apply these products according to package directions and apply them at the right time in the pest's life cycle, so they are effective.

Insecticidal soaps will kill soft-bodied insects such as aphids. And you can spray with highly refined horticultural oils to coat plant leaves and to smother insects such as aphids, leafminers, leafhoppers and mites. Read the label carefully and apply only when the weather is cool.

Diseases

Garden hygiene and proper plant selection go a long way to preventing and controlling diseases. Removing faded foliage and cutting back flowers after they bloom will remove sites of disease.

Some Common Diseases

Many different fungi attack perennials, causing a variety of symptoms. Rot can affect roots, crowns, stems and flowers, turning them soft and mushy. You will see rot most commonly on roots growing in wet, heavy soil or on crowns planted too deeply in the garden. Botrytis, or grey mould, attacks foliage and flowers, covering them in a fuzzy grey or grey-brown mould. Powdery mildew can strike many perennials, resulting in a fine powdery coating on the leaf surfaces. Remove foliage promptly and avoid overwatering. Fungal leaf spots disfigure and can cause defoliation.

Rust diseases turn foliage a rusty colour, often stunting growth and distorting leaf development.

Viruses can cause leaves or flowers to turn yellow or mottled. They cause stunted growth and poor flowering or sudden wilting and death.

Controlling Diseases

If soil-borne disease is a particular problem in your area, grow perennials in well-drained soil to reduce root diseases. Also, try not to damage the plant roots when you work the soil or weed.

VIRAL ALERT
Viral mosaic can attack pinks *Dianthus* spp. (above), chrysanthemums, delphiniums, peonies and poppies.

POWDERY PROBLEM
Powdery mildew is a fungal disease that forms a furry, white coating on leaves and can cause them to drop.

A BREATH OF FRESH AIR

Thin out the stems of bushy perennials such as *Helenium autumnale* to promote air circulation and good health.

PUZZLED?

Leaf spots can be caused by either fungi or bacteria. Removing infected foliage may stop the spread. If a plant's disease leaves you stumped, ask for help from your local garden centre.

Careful watering can help reduce disease outbreaks. Avoid wetting plant leaves; they stay wet overnight and fungal spores can germinate and attack. Overhead watering and even walking through wet foliage or cultivating wet soil can transfer disease from plant to plant. Use a ground-level irrigation system and don't work in the garden when plants are wet—and always keep your tools clean.

When a disease does strike, remove damaged parts promptly and either burn them or dispose of them. Don't put them on the compost heap. If you have any doubts, either throw the whole plant away, or plant it in an isolated spot. If it seems all right at the end of the season, move it back into the garden. If it's diseased, dispose of it permanently.

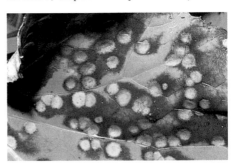

Seed Starting

Growing your own seedlings allows you to select unusual species and choose varieties that you can't buy at garden centres and nurseries. Use high-quality seed, and check the use-by date.

Sowing the Seed

Just as wild perennials self-seed naturally, you can sow seed directly outdoors in a well-prepared bed. Cover seed in loose soil to the depth indicated on the package and keep the soil moist until the seedlings emerge.

Although direct sowing is the easiest way, it is not the most dependable. When planted directly into your garden, your seed is very vulnerable. For a better survival rate, start seedlings indoors under lights or on a window ledge on the sunny side of the house.

Depending on the size of the seed and the speed of growth, you should start quick-germinating seed indoors in early spring. Some perennials can also be sown in autumn and then overwintered in a cold frame.

Other perennials will take much longer to germinate. You may need to expose the seed to a chilling period by placing the seed in the refrigerator for a certain number of weeks (known as stratification). If special treatment is needed, it will be indicated on the seed packet.

INDOORS OR OUTDOORS
Sea hollies *Eryngium* spp. can be started from fresh seed outdoors during autumn, or started indoors after stratification.

PROLIFIC SELF-SEEDERS
Rudbeckia spp. may self-seed if you don't cut off spent flowers in autumn. The seedheads look attractive in winter too.

PLANTING SEED

1. Sow seed evenly over a thoroughly moistened, sterile, seed compost.
2. Press the seed lightly into the surface—push larger seeds into the soil as deeply as they are wide.
3. Cover the seed according to packet directions and firm slightly.
4. Moisten with a fine mist of water.
5. Label the container.
6. Cover with clear plastic to keep soil evenly moist until the seed begins to germinate.

POTTING-UP SEEDLINGS

1. Gather your materials and tools together in a clean, shady spot.
2. Put some moist potting mix in the base of a new pot.
3. Gently squeeze the seedling container to loosen roots and to make it easy to remove the plant.
4. Carefully slide the plant from the container, taking care not to harm the roots.
5. Centre the plant in the pot and fill in with moist, but not wet, potting mix.

CARING FOR SEEDLINGS

When seedlings emerge, move them into bright light and remove the plastic. Set the container in a tray of water to soak up moisture, then keep moist.

Move seedlings to pots when they have two sets of true leaves and a bottom set of fleshy seed leaves. You can move most into 10-cm (4-in) pots if you intend to plant them outdoors soon. If not, move the plants up to larger pots to prevent root congestion. Feed lightly. If the weather is cold or hot, leave the young plants indoors under lights or near a sunny window. If it is relatively mild, move the plants out into a cold frame or another sheltered area.

DIVISION

Division is one of the easiest, fastest and most reliable ways to propagate clump-forming perennials. It is also a great way to revive older plants and to keep spreading perennials under control.

AVOID ROOT DAMAGE
Divide balloon flower *Platycodon grandiflorus* in spring or early autumn. Dig deeply to avoid root damage.

NOTHING TOO BIG
To divide a big clump, try prying it apart with two garden forks. If that doesn't work, try a saw or an axe.

REJUVENATED VIGOUR
A mature clump of iris will yield many new, vigorous plants once divided.

WHEN TO DIVIDE

How often you need to divide depends on why you are dividing. If you're using division to propagate, then it depends on how many new plants you want and how fast the plant you are dividing is growing. Divide annually to retard aggressive spreaders such as bergamot *Monarda didyma*, *Physostegia virginiana* and yarrows. If you want to rejuvenate perennials, you can divide them whenever flowering starts to decline. To keep performance high, you can divide Michaelmas daisies every year or two. Some perennials, such as peonies, daylilies, Siberian irises *Iris sibirica* and astilbes, can go for years without division.

How to Divide

Begin by digging up the root system. Shake off loose soil and remove dead leaves and stems. You may also want to wash most of the soil off the roots and crown to see the roots and buds clearly.

Perennials with fibrous roots, such as chrysanthemums and Michaelmas daisies, are the easiest to dig and divide. Pull them apart with your hands or with a spade. Others, such as daylilies and astilbes, can grow woody with age. You may have to pry these roots apart with two garden forks held back to back or cut them with a saw or axe. Discard the woody parts, which will not re-root well.

To renew an existing planting, slice the plant into halves, thirds or quarters. Discard old, woody growth from the centre of the clump and replant the vigorous outer portions.

When you want to build a larger stock of new plants, divide perennials into smaller pieces. Just make sure you keep several buds or growing shoots on the sections you will replant. Look for buds growing along the length of the roots or clustered in a central crown.

Work your compost, and any other soil improvers, back into the soil before replanting the division. Reset them at the same level at which the original clump was growing.

STEP-BY-STEP DIVISION
1. Divide the clump into several pieces.
2. Make sure each new piece has its own roots and some top growth.
3. Replant the pieces immediately, water well and apply a light layer of mulch.

Cuttings and Layering

Cuttings—small pieces of stem or root—are another way to propagate perennials. Cuttings take more effort than layering, which can be done with stems that root while attached to the plant.

Taking Cuttings

Take stem cuttings in spring or after flowering. When they shoot, remove the cover and move them into brighter light. To check if they have rooted, tug gently on the stem—if you meet resistance, they have. Transplant into larger containers.

Take root cuttings from autumn to early spring, while the plant is dormant. Lift the plant from the garden and wash the soil from the roots. Cut off pencil-thick roots close to the crown. Cut them into 5–10cm (2–4 in) pieces, making a straight cut at the top and a slanted cut at the bottom. Put into a pot filled with moist, sterile potting mix, so the top of each cutting is level or slightly below the surface. Put in a cold frame until they root then pot them into a larger pot—move them into the garden when ready.

ROOT CUTTINGS

Propagate Japanese anemone *Anemone* x *hybrida* by taking root cuttings after plants go dormant in autumn.

TAKING STEM CUTTINGS

1. Select a strong, young shoot and make a clean cut just below the node.
2. Snip the leaves off the bottom half of the cutting, exposing two to three leaf nodes, and insert the bottom half into a container of moist potting mix.
3. Cover with an upended jar to hold in moisture. Set in a bright place out of direct sun.

SIMPLE LAYERING

1. Select a flexible stem and bend it down to the soil.
2. Use a wire peg to firmly secure the stem, then cover the pegged stem with soil. Stake the leafy tip of the stem if it needs support.
3. Dig up the newly rooted layer and transplant it to another spot.

LAYERING WORKS

Good candidates for layering include pinks *Dianthus* spp. (above), and aubrieta.

LAYERING

Layering takes up space, you won't get many plants and it can take weeks or months—but it is easy and you get exact duplicates of the parent plant.

Leave the top three sets of leaves on the stem, but remove the leaves 5–17.5 cm (2–7 in) below the top greenery. Strip leaves from at least two nodes, leaving dormant buds undamaged. Loosen the soil where the stripped area will make contact and water it. Bury it 5–7.5 cm (2–3 in) deep with the leafy tip exposed and firm the soil.

Keep the area moist and mulched. The easiest way is to leave the plant in place until the following season. If you want faster results, check its progress by uncovering the stem and looking for roots or tugging lightly to see if it has become more secure. Once the roots reach about 2.5 cm (1 in) long, you can cut the shoot free from the mother plant. Wait several weeks for more rooting, then uproot and move the new plant.

Part Five

PLANT DIRECTORY

Acanthus mollis

HARDINESS
Hardy.

HEIGHT AND
SPREAD
75–120 cm
(2½–4 ft) tall.
90 cm (3 ft) wide.
Spreads to form
broad clumps.

FLOWERING TIME
Early to mid-
summer. Flowers
open sequentially
up the spike.

BEAR'S BREECHES

USE BEAR'S BREECHES AS STRUCTURAL
PLANTS OR AS ACCENTS IN FORMAL OR
INFORMAL GARDENS.

Description A robust plant with
lustrous, deep green leaves 30–60 cm
(1–2 ft) long and edged with
rounded or jagged teeth. It grows
from a stout crown with thick,
fleshy roots. It has unusual 2.5-cm
(1-in) flowers with three white
petals and overarching purple-pink
hoods carried on tall spikes.

Ideal position Full sun to partial shade.

Ideal soil conditions Evenly moist,
deep, well-drained, humus-rich soil.
Dry soil will reduce the size of
the leaves.

Cultivation Mulch the crowns of
newly planted bear's breeches in
the first winter, especially in areas
with cold winters.

Propagation Divide plants in spring
when they first emerge or take root
cuttings in spring or late autumn.
Roots left in the ground when
plants are divided will form new
shoots. Or propagate from seed.

Pest and disease prevention Slugs
and snails don't usually attack the
leaves, but if they do, put down
beer traps or use biological controls
such as nematodes. Powdery mildew
may be a problem; destroy affected
leaves and avoid overhead watering.

Acanthus spinosus

Design tips Good as a specimen plant in wide borders as it can cover large areas of ground when it matures. Good when combined with fine-textured plants such as yarrow for added contrast. A good plant for cutting and drying for flower arrangements. Bear's breeches release compounds that can stunt the growth of cucumbers, radishes and cabbage, so avoid planting near these vegetables.

Other species *A. spinosus* (pictured above) has large, deeply divided leaves, which are narrower than those of *A. mollis*. The flower spikes are similar to those of *A. mollis* and can grow up to 1.2 m (4 ft) tall.

Achillea filipendulina

HARDINESS
Hardy.

HEIGHT AND SPREAD
90–120 cm
(3–4 ft) tall.
90 cm (3 ft) wide.
Forms broad, tight clumps.

FLOWERING TIME
Summer. Flowers last for several weeks. Plants may re-bloom if deadheaded.

YARROW

YARROW IS A TRADITIONAL BORDER PLANT
AND IS PERFECT FOR COTTAGE-GARDEN AND
ISLAND-BED PLANTINGS.

Description This aromatic plant grows from fibrous roots and has deeply incised, ferny, olive-green leaves. It has many tightly packed, golden yellow flowers clustered in flat-topped heads 10–12.5 cm (4–5 in) across. Flowers bloom on several tall stems.

Ideal position Full sun to light shade.

Ideal soil conditions Dry to moist, well-drained soil. Overly rich soil creates growth but weakens stems.

Cultivation This strongly-growing yarrow is a tough, easy-care perennial. Plants spread rapidly and need frequent division. Lift and divide clumps to keep vigorous.

Propagation Take tip cuttings in spring or early summer. Divide in early spring or autumn. Replant healthy divisions into soil that has been enriched with organic matter.

Pest and disease prevention Plants can develop powdery mildew, especially in wet summers. Rot causes stems to blacken and collapse. Destroy all affected parts and dust with sulphur. Provide well-drained soil to avoid powdery mildew and rot.

Yarrow or milfoil *Achillea millefolium*

Design tips Plant at the front or middle of formal perennial borders or with grasses in informal gardens. Plant in naturalistic borders or wild-flower meadows and other informal settings. Use in cutting or herb gardens. Plants may re-bloom later in the season if the first flush of flowers is deadheaded.

Cultivars 'Gold Plate' has 15-cm (6-in) deep yellow flowerheads on 1.8 m (6 ft) stems.

'Cloth of Gold' grows 90–120 cm (3–4 ft) tall and has golden yellow flowers held on self-supporting stems.

Other species Yarrow *A. millefolium*, or milfoil, (pictured above) offers finely cut, deep green foliage. It has numerous tiny pink, white or red florets in dense, flat clusters 5–7.5 cm (2–3 in) across that are produced on stout stems. It flowers for several months in summer and grows 30–75 cm (1–2½ ft) tall and 90 cm (3 ft) wide. Plants may spread rapidly and become invasive.

Sow seed shallowly indoors in early spring or outdoors in late spring. Divide established plants in early spring or autumn. Choose a named selection such as 'Cerise Queen' or 'Terracotta'. 'Terracotta' (pictured on page 118) has beautiful flowers that begin as rich orange and fade to yellow. It grows to 90 cm (3 ft) and is reasonably drought-tolerant. It prefers a hot, full-sun position.

Yarrow continued

Yarrow *Achillea millefolium* 'Terracotta'

The closely related Galaxy series of new yarrows arose from hybrids with *A. aegyptiaca* (syn. *A. taygetea*). Plants resemble common yarrow with 5–7.5 cm (2–3 in) flowerheads on sturdy stems. Colours range from creamy yellow to salmon-rose and brick-red. Flowers fade with age, giving them a multicoloured appearance.

A. 'Moonshine' is a cultivar of hybrid origin. It grows 30–60 cm (1–2 ft) tall, with soft, blue-grey foliage and sulphur-yellow flowers.

A. 'Coronation Gold' is a cultivar of two species and grows 90 cm (3 ft) tall with stout self-supporting stems, grey-green leaves and 12.5-cm (5-in) wide clusters of mustard-yellow flowers.

Aconitum carmichaelii

HARDINESS
Hardy.

**HEIGHT AND
SPREAD**
60–90 cm
(2–3 ft) tall.
60 cm (2 ft) wide.
Open and
somewhat vase-
shaped, especially
in shade.

FLOWERING TIME
Late summer and
autumn.

MONKSHOOD

MONKSHOOD IS BEST PLANTED NEAR THE
MIDDLE OR REAR OF BORDERS WITH OTHER
AUTUMN-FLOWERING PERENNIALS.

Description A graceful plant with
lush, three-lobed, dissected leaves,
sturdy stems and deep-blue hooded
flowers in dense spikes. All parts
of the plant are highly poisonous.

Ideal position Full sun to light shade.
Afternoon shade in hot summers.

Ideal soil conditions Fertile, humus-
rich, moist but well-drained soil.

Cultivation Monkshood dislikes
disturbance once it is established.
Space plants 60–90 cm (2–3 ft)
apart with the crowns just below
the surface. Divide if plants become

overcrowded and always wear gloves.

Propagation Divide crowns in
autumn or early spring. Replant
strong, healthy divisions into soil
enriched with organic matter.

Pest and disease prevention Crowns
will rot if the soil is too wet and if
temperatures are hot. Give plants
the right situation to avoid problems.

Design tips Plant with ornamental
grasses or in groups with berrying
shrubs such as *Viburnum* spp.

Actaea alba syn. *A.pachypoda* RANUNCULACEAE

HARDINESS
Hardy.

HEIGHT AND
SPREAD
60–120 cm
(2–4 ft) tall.
50 cm (20 in)
across.

FLOWERING TIME
Summer flowers.
Autumn berries.

WHITE BANEBERRY

FOR A DRAMATIC TOUCH, PLANT THIS NORTH AMERICAN NATIVE AT THE EDGE OF A PATH IN A WOODLAND GARDEN.

Description Mature clumps of white baneberry in full fruit provide a stunning highlight in the autumn garden. The red-stalked berries are poisonous to people but savoured by birds. It has white flowers composed of a fuzzy cluster of broad stamens. The showy, oval white fruits, for which this plant is noted, are 6 mm (¼ in) long and borne on long stalks.

Ideal position Partial to full shade.

Ideal soil conditions Moist, humus-rich soil.

Cultivation Top-dress clumps with compost or leafmould in spring or autumn. Plants seldom need division.

Propagation Sow fresh seed outdoors in early to mid-autumn, after removing the pulp from the ripe berries. Wear gloves.

Pest and disease prevention No serious pests or diseases.

Design tips Mass plantings of white baneberry are breathtaking among ferns. Combine with bleeding heart *Dicentra spectabilis* and violets.

Agapanthus africanus

HARDINESS
Half-hardy.

HEIGHT AND SPREAD
45–90 cm
(1½–3 ft) tall.
30 cm (1 ft) across.

FLOWERING TIME
Mid- to late summer.

OTHER COMMON NAMES
African lily.

AGAPANTHUS

THESE DRAMATIC PLANTS MAKE A STUNNING FEATURE IN BORDERS OR IN CONTAINERS.

Description Agapanthus bear flowers on tall, upright stems. The many-flowered umbels—each separate flower head displays 20–50 individual blossoms—are borne on 90-cm (3-ft) stems and are known to attract bees. Attractive, arching, evergreen, dark green, straplike leaves arise from short rhizomes and fleshy roots. The pretty flowers are pale to deep blue and there are also white cultivars available.

Ideal position Full sun. Plants need protection in cold winters, so bring indoors or mulch the crowns well.

Ideal soil conditions Dry to moist, well-drained soil. These plants, with their strong, fleshy root system, are effective for use in binding less than ideal soil on steep banks if you live in an area with very mild winters.

Cultivation Remove spent flower stems before seeds mature if not wanted for propagating purposes. To ensure the plants remain neat and tidy at all times, trim dead leaves from the base of the plant when they become evident. To avoid overcrowding, and consequent poor flowering, divide the plants every 4–5 years and prune back overhanging shrubs

Agapanthus continued

Agapanthus campanulatus

to prevent excess shade, which can also inhibit flowering.

Propagation Divide in spring but only after the plant has become rootbound—usually in 4–5 years. Large clumps of roots form a tight network that can be very difficult to cut through. Fresh, ripe seed sown in autumn will give good germination results. If grown from seed, they may not flower for 3 years.

Pest and disease prevention No serious pests or diseases. Snails and slugs can use these fleshy-leaved plants as camouflage, although they don't seem to eat the leaves themselves. Place beer traps around the plants to lure these pests.

Design tips Agapanthus are perfect for rocky slopes and do well in coastal areas. They are also stunning in large tubs or containers. The flowers can last up to a week when cut.

Cultivars 'Blue Giant' is a mid- to late-flowering agapanthus that grows to 1.2 m (4 ft) and has large, rich blue flowers.

Headbourne hybrids are vigorous and hardy, growing to 90 cm (3 ft) with flowers in a wide range of colours.

In keeping with the trend toward smaller gardens, a range of miniature African lilies has been developed. These include 'Blue Baby', which grows to 45–60 cm (1½–2 ft)

Agapanthus praecox subsp. *orientalis* 'Albus'

tall and has dainty, straplike, evergreen leaves and pale blue flowers. There are other mid-blue flowering dwarf varieties of a similar size. White forms are also available.

Other species *A. campanulatus* (pictured opposite) is another frost-hardy agapanthus. *A. campanulatus* var. *patens* is smaller in both growth and flowering habit.

A. inapertus is a more unusual species with distinctive, elongated, bell-shaped flowers, which hang rather than form an open-ball shape.

A. praecox has starbursts of trumpet-shaped, rich lavender-blue flowers on large, spherical heads.

This species is not frost hardy and must be overwintered indoors.

A. praecox subsp. *orientalis* 'Albus' (pictured above) has white flowers.

Ajuga reptans

LAMIACEAE

HARDINESS
Hardy.

HEIGHT AND SPREAD
10–25 cm (4–10 in) tall. 20–25 cm (8–10 in) wide. Clumps may spread freely from a single plant.

FLOWERING TIME
Late spring to early summer.

OTHER COMMON NAMES
Ajuga.

BUGLE

BUGLE IS A TROUBLE-FREE GROUND-COVER PLANT THAT IS PERFECT UNDER TREES AND SHRUBS.

Description A low, rosette-forming ground-cover plant that spreads over the soil surface to form broad, dense mats. The spoon-shaped leaves are evergreen in mild regions. It has tiered whorls of small, intense blue flowers.

Ideal position Full sun to light shade.

Ideal soil conditions Average to humus-rich, moist, but well-drained soil. Will not tolerate extended drought or excessive moisture.

Cultivation Plant in spring or autumn. Spreads rapidly to form dense weed-proof ground cover and may become invasive.

Propagation Propagate by division in spring.

Pest and disease prevention Provide good drainage and air circulation to prevent crown rot and mildew.

Design tips Use as an edging or as ground cover.

Cultivars 'Catlin's Giant' (pictured above) has large, bronze leaves.
'Atropurpurea' has characteristic bronze-purple leaves.

Alcea rosea

HARDINESS
Hardy.

HEIGHT AND SPREAD
60–180 cm
(2–6 ft)tall.
60 cm (2 ft) wide.

FLOWERING TIME
Summer and early autumn. May bloom for 2 months.

HOLLYHOCK

PLANT HOLLYHOCK AT THE BACK OF BORDERS WHERE THE FOLIAGE IS OBSCURED BY BUSHY PERENNIALS.

Description A tall, short-lived perennial with rounded or lobed foliage. The flowers bloom along the upper half of the stem. Flowers range from white and pale yellow to pink, rose and red.

Ideal position Full sun to partial shade.

Ideal soil conditions Average, well-drained soil.

Cultivation Plant in spring or autumn. Hollyhocks are hardy but they need staking in areas that are prone to strong wind.

Propagation Sow seed indoors in early spring for summer flowering, or outdoors in late summer for flowers the following summer.

Pest and disease prevention If affected by rust, dust the infected foliage with sulphur. Deter spider mites by spraying infested plants with insecticidal soap.

Design tips Hollyhock is perfect when planted beside a garden shed, fence or garage wall.

Cultivars 'Chater's Double' has fully double flowers in a range of mixed hues or single colours.

Alchemilla mollis

HARDINESS
Hardy.

**HEIGHT AND
SPREAD**
30–45 cm
(1–1½ ft) tall.
60 cm (2 ft) wide.

FLOWERING TIME
Summer.

LADY'S MANTLE

THE GREENISH-YELLOW FLOWERS OF LADY'S
MANTLE ADD LIGHT AND INTEREST TO
SUMMER EVENINGS IN THE GARDEN.

Description Lady's mantle forms
mounded clumps of pleated foliage.
The 10–15-cm (4–6-in) pale green
leaves are covered in soft hair that
collects beads of water like jewels
on velvet. It has foamy clusters of
small, greenish-yellow flowers.

Ideal position Full sun to partial shade.
Heavy rain can damage foliage.

Ideal soil conditions Humus-rich,
evenly moist soil.

Cultivation Set the crowns at the
soil surface. Cut old foliage down
to the ground and new leaves

quickly appear. Mulch for evenly
moist soil.

Propagation Divide the crowns in
spring or autumn. Sow fresh seed
outdoors in spring. Lady's mantle
may self-seed.

Pest and disease prevention No
serious pests or diseases.

Design tips Plant at the front
of formal and informal beds and
borders or beside pathways.
Combine lady's mantle with other
plants that enjoy moist soil, such as
Siberian iris *Iris sibirica* and astilbe.

Cultivar 'Robusta' has firm, erect
flower stems.

Allium cristophii

HARDINESS
Hardy to half-
hardy.

HEIGHT AND
SPREAD
30–45 cm
(1–1½ ft) tall.
30 cm (1 ft) wide.

FLOWERING TIME
Early to
midsummer.

ALLIUM, ORNAMENTAL ONION

PLANT THESE STRIKING ALLIUMS AT THE FRONT OF BORDERS WHERE THEIR STALKS EXPLODE INTO BLOOM IN SUMMER.

Description Produces 45-cm (1½-ft) upright leaves arching out from the bulbs. Metallic, lilac-pink flowers in 20-cm (8-in) heads radiate from stalk tops.

Ideal position Full sun.

Ideal soil conditions Humus-rich, well-drained soil.

Cultivation New bulbs planted in autumn multiply slowly to form spectacular flowering clumps. Plants become dormant after flowering.

Propagation Divide mature clumps in spring. Sow ripe seed outdoors in summer or autumn. In areas with cold winters, provide a mulch.

Pest and disease prevention No serious pests or diseases. Mulch with organic matter to keep the soil evenly moist.

Design tips Alliums look good among mounding plants, such as cranesbills *Geranium* spp., as well as in containers.

Other species *A. giganteum*, giant onion, grows 90–150 cm (3–5 ft) tall, with 12.5-cm (5-in), rounded heads of deep-purple flowers.

Alstroemeria aurea

HARDINESS
Hardy.

HEIGHT AND SPREAD
60–90 cm
(2–3 ft) tall.
60 cm (2 ft) wide.

FLOWERING TIME
Summer.

PERUVIAN LILY

PERUVIAN LILY IS EXCELLENT FOR CUTTING GARDENS. PLANT IT IN BEDS AND BORDERS FOR A SUMMER SUPPLY OF CUT FLOWERS.

Description Peruvian lily has tall, leafy stems crowned by open clusters of orange or yellow flowers with brownish purple flares on the upper petals. The grey-green leaves are narrow and pointed. Plants grow from thick, fibrous roots.

Ideal position Full sun to partial shade. Needs protection from strong winds.

Ideal soil conditions Moist, humus-rich soil.

Cultivation Plant dormant roots in early spring or autumn. Growth begins early in the season and plants may be damaged by late frost. Mulch with organic matter in autumn to avoid frost damage. Achieves best performance after the third year.

Propagation Divide clumps in early spring. Sow fresh seed indoors after 3 weeks of pre-chilling.

Pest and disease prevention No serious pests or diseases.

Design tips Plant in partial shade with ferns or in containers.

Other species *A. psittacina*. This Brazilian native has narrow, red and green, bell-shaped blooms in early summer. It can spread easily from tuberous roots.

Alstroemeria Ligtu Hybrids

Cultivars Dr Salter's Hybrids. This group of hybrid cultivars comes in a wide variety of colours and the flower heads are slightly compact and heavily marked.

Dutch Hybrids. These hybrid cultivars (pictured opposite) are very popular in the flower trade. The flowers are broad petalled with compact umbels. They are heavily marked with stunning contrasting colours.

Ligtu Hybrids (pictured above). These popular hybrids were developed in the 1920s. The colours range from cream to yellow to orange and red. The plants die down after flowering.

Amsonia tabernaemontana

HARDINESS
Hardy.

HEIGHT AND
SPREAD
60 cm (2 ft) tall.
30 cm (12 in) wide.

FLOWERING TIME
Summer.

OTHER COMMON
NAMES
Willow amsonia.

BLUE STAR

USE THE SHRUBBY CLUMPS OF BLUE STAR TO ADD STRUCTURE AND INTEREST TO YOUR SUMMER GARDEN.

Description A tough, shrubby plant with lance-shaped leaves, stout stems and terminal clusters of tiny, steel-blue, 12-mm (½-in), starry flowers. Plants grow from a woody, fibrous-rooted crown.

Ideal position Full sun to partial shade.

Ideal soil conditions Average to humus-rich, moist, well-drained soil.

Cultivation May reach shrub-like proportions with age. Plants in shade may be floppy. If necessary, prune stems back to 15–20 cm (6–8 in) after flowering. New shoots will form an attractive, compact mound. Leaves turn bright orange to golden yellow in autumn.

Propagation Divide plants in early spring or autumn. Take 10–15-cm (4–6-in) stem cuttings in early summer. Sow ripe seed outdoors in autumn or indoors after soaking in hot water. Contact with the sap may irritate skin.

Pest and disease prevention No serious pests or diseases. Mulch with organic matter to keep soil evenly moist.

Design tips Grow either alone en masse or combined with other perennials.

Anaphalis triplinervis

HARDINESS
Hardy.

HEIGHT AND
SPREAD
30–45 cm
(1–1½ ft) tall.
30 cm (1 ft) wide.

FLOWERING TIME
A profusion of
flowers in mid-
to late summer.

PEARLY EVERLASTING

THE PAPERY WHITE FLOWERS AND SOFT
LEAVES OF PEARLY EVERLASTING ADD
BRIGHTNESS TO THE LATE-SUMMER GARDEN.

Description Unlike most silver-
leaved plants, pearly everlasting
grows well in moist soil. It has
white, double flowers with dark
centres borne in open, flattened
clusters. The flowers dry on the
plant and persist for weeks.

Ideal position Full sun to partial
shade.

Ideal soil conditions Moist, average
to humus-rich soil.

Cultivation Spreads to form large
clumps in moist soil. Divide

vigorous clumps every 2–4 years
to control their spread.

Propagation Cuttings root freely
during early summer.

Pest and disease prevention No
serious pests or diseases.

Design tips Grow pearly everlasting
in the front or middle of beds and
borders or in informal and meadow
gardens. Combine with Siberian iris
Iris sibirica. Ornamental grasses
also make excellent companion
plants, as do astilbes, daylilies and
phlox *Phlox paniculata*.

Anchusa azurea

HARDINESS
Hardy.

HEIGHT AND
SPREAD
60–120 cm
(2–4 ft) tall.
60 cm (2 ft) wide.

FLOWERING TIME
Late spring to early
summer.

ALKANET

FOR A STUNNING SPRING DISPLAY, PLANT
ALKANET AMONG SUCH FLOWERS AS SHASTA
DAISIES AND YARROWS.

Description Alkanet has lush,
oblong leaves covered in stiff hair.
Long branches bear terminal clusters
of brilliant blue, 18-mm (¾-in), five-
petalled flowers. It may reach 1.2 m
(4 ft) in height.

Ideal position Full sun to light shade.

Ideal soil conditions Humus-rich,
well-drained soil.

Cultivation Seed-grown plants may be
short-lived; choose a named cultivar
for better performance. Cut plants
back after flowering to encourage a
second flush. Plants may need staking.

Propagation Divide clumps in
autumn or winter. Replant into soil
enriched with organic matter. Take
root cuttings in early spring. Plants
freely self-seed, sometimes
excessively.

Pest and disease prevention No
serious pests or diseases.

Design tips Use en masse with
flowering shrubs.

Cultivars 'Dropmore' is a compact,
1.2-m (4-ft) selection with deep
blue flowers.
　　'Loddon Royalist' is 90 cm (3 ft)
tall with gentian-blue flowers.

Anemone blanda

HARDINESS
Hardy.

HEIGHT AND SPREAD
15 cm (6 in) tall.
10–15 cm
(4–6 in) wide.

FLOWERING TIME
Spring.

WINDFLOWER

THE DELICATE FLOWERS OF THE WINDFLOWER
LOOK STUNNING WHEN ALLOWED TO
NATURALIZE UNDER TREES.

Description The windflower blooms
in mid- to late spring. In regions
with mild winters, it may appear in
early spring. It has daisy-like blue,
pink or white flowers, which grow
to 5 cm (2 in) across.

Ideal position Full sun to partial
shade.

Ideal soil conditions Average to
moist, well-drained soil.

Cultivation Buy and plant tubers
in autumn. Soak them overnight
before planting, and set them in
individual holes or larger planting
areas dug about 2.5–5 cm (1–2 in)
deep. If you can see a shallow
depression on one side, plant with
that side up. Otherwise, plant the
tubers on their sides or simply drop
them into the hole. Space them
10–15 cm (4–6 in) apart. Windflowers
propagate themselves by spreading
and self-seeding.

Propagation Dig and divide the
tubers in spring, before replanting.

Pest and disease prevention No
serious pests or diseases.

Design tips Windflower combines
well with daffodils.

Anemone coronaria RANUNCULACEAE

HARDINESS
Half-hardy.

HEIGHT AND
SPREAD
45 cm (1½ ft) tall.
10–15 cm
(4–6 in) wide.

FLOWERING TIME
Mid-spring.

ANEMONE

COMBINE THIS ANEMONE WITH OTHER
ANEMONE SPECIES AND BULBS FOR A
SPECTACULAR SPRING FLOWER DISPLAY.

Description A tuberous-rooted
anemone that bears beautiful blue,
pink, red and white flowers in
spring. The flowers are solitary and
poppy-like, 2.5–3.5 cm (1–1½ in)
in diameter on stalks 22.5–45 cm
(9–18 in) long. Pick the flowers when
buds show plenty of colour and
are about to burst open. The black
stamens contrast with the colour of
the petals. They are long-lasting.

Ideal position Full sun. Tolerates
some summer drought, but keep
moist during autumn and spring.

Ideal soil conditions Average to
moist, well-drained soil.

Cultivation In autumn, plant tubers
7.5 cm (3 in) deep in a sunny spot.
Soak them overnight before planting.
In areas with cold winters, lift the
tubers and store them over the
winter in vermiculite.

Propagation Division of
tuberous rhizomes.

Pest and disease prevention No
serious pests or diseases.

Design tips Ideal for rock gardens,
beds, borders and woodland gardens.

HARDINESS
Hardy.

HEIGHT AND
SPREAD
15 cm (6 in) tall.
30 cm (12 in) wide.

FLOWERING TIME
Spring.

WOOD ANEMONE

WOOD ANEMONE, OFTEN FOUND WILD IN WOODLAND, IS A PRETTY AND EFFECTIVE GROUND-COVER PLANT.

Description Wood anemone is a very pretty, low-growing, spreading anemone with fine, creeping rhizomes. It has white (creamy) flowers with yellow stamens.

Ideal position Moist, shaded woodland conditions.

Ideal soil conditions Moist, humus-rich, well-drained soil. Will tolerate slightly drier conditions during summer when dormant.

Cultivation These plants form a mat about 10 cm (4 in) high and are best left alone in their humus-rich position where they will provide good ground cover dotted with flowers in spring.

Propagation Can be divided or sown with fresh seed.

Pest and disease prevention If the conditions are suitable, no serious pests or diseases.

Design tips Wood anemone is best planted en masse where it won't be overwhelmed by more vigorous plants.

Hybrids 'Rosea' has pink flowers in bud, ageing to deep pink.

Anemone x *hybrida*

HARDINESS
Hardy.

HEIGHT AND SPREAD
90–150 cm
(3–5 ft) tall.
60–90 cm
(2–3 ft) wide.

FLOWERING TIME
Late summer and autumn.

JAPANESE ANEMONE

JAPANESE ANEMONE LIGHTS UP THE AUTUMN
GARDEN WITH CLOUDS OF DELICATELY
COLOURED FLOWERS ON TALL STEMS.

Description Japanese anemone produces single or double flowers on slender stems. The deeply divided, hairy leaves are mostly basal. Plants grow from tuberous roots. Flower colour is from white to pink and rose.

Ideal position Full sun to light shade.

Ideal soil conditions Humus-rich, evenly moist soil.

Cultivation Spreads by creeping underground stems to form broad clumps once established. Thin overgrown clumps in spring if flowering is poor. Can spread vigorously.

Propagation Take root cuttings after plants go dormant in late autumn to winter. Sow fresh seed outdoors in summer or autumn. Divide in early spring.

Pest and disease prevention No serious pests or diseases.

Design tips Group with other late-season perennials and ornamental grasses. Combine with shrubs or ferns in dappled shade.

Cultivars 'Honorine Jobert' bears pure white single blooms on stems 90–120 cm (3–4 ft) tall.

Angelica archangelica

HARDINESS
Hardy.

HEIGHT AND SPREAD
1.5–1.8 m
(5–6 ft) tall.
90 cm (3 ft) wide.

FLOWERING TIME
Late summer.

ANGELICA

PLANT ANGELICA FOR ITS UNUSUAL HONEY-SCENTED FOLIAGE IN YOUR HERB OR SCENTED GARDEN.

Description This tall, sweet-scented herb resembles its close relatives, parsley and coriander. It has unusual, palm-like leaves and pale green flowers on tall stems. The young leaves can be infused as a tea and also used in salads.

Ideal position Partial shade.

Ideal soil conditions Moist, well-drained rich soil.

Cultivation Angelica can only be propagated from fresh seed, which germinates poorly if sown too deeply. Best sown *in situ* in early autumn. Seedlings do not transplant well, so ideally sow three to four seeds in a cluster at stations about 90 cm (3 ft) apart and thin to the strongest seedling.

Propagation Will self-seed or can be propagated from seed.

Pest and disease prevention No serious pests or diseases.

Design tips Angelica, a medicinal herb, is excellent in herb gardens and perfumed gardens. Plant it near a gate so you can enjoy the scent.

Antennaria dioica

HARDINESS
Hardy.

HEIGHT AND
SPREAD
5 cm (2 in) tall.
Spreads over a
wide area in time.

FLOWERING TIME
Late spring and
early summer.

CAT'S EARS

CAT'S EARS IS A CHARMING LITTLE GROUND
COVER FOR A DRY, SUNNY SITE. THE TINY
FLOWERS DRY WELL.

Description Cat's ears has rosettes
of hairy, silver-green, 2.5-cm (1-in)
wide leaves, which are topped with
off-white, pink-tipped flowers in
early summer.

Ideal position Full sun.

Ideal soil conditions Dry, sandy,
poor soil.

Cultivation Set plants 15 cm (6 in)
or more apart in light soil in spring
or autumn. Plants are generally
maintenance-free. The plant can
self-seed readily and provides good
ground cover in rock gardens.

Propagation Sow seed or divide
in spring.

Pest and disease prevention No
serious pests or diseases.

Design tips Cat's ears will spread
to form a good cover for hot, dry
spots in sunny rock gardens.

Cultivars 'Rosea' has rosy pink
flowerheads and grey-green,
woolly leaves.

Anthemis tinctoria

HARDINESS
Hardy.

HEIGHT AND SPREAD
Mounds to
60–90 cm (2–3 ft)
60–90 cm (2–3 ft)
wide.

FLOWERING TIME
Midsummer.

YELLOW CHAMOMILE

YELLOW CHAMOMILE PRODUCES A BRILLIANT DISPLAY OF GOLDEN FLOWERS, WHICH ARE LONG-LASTING WHEN CUT.

Description Yellow chamomile is a hardy, mounding plant with aromatic, fern-like foliage. It has tiny, golden, daisy-like flowers.

Ideal position Thrives in full sun.

Ideal soil conditions Average, well-drained soil and dry, poor soil.

Cultivation Cut back in autumn, after flowering, to ensure a tidy, well-shaped plant.

Propagation Can self-seed. Take cuttings during late summer or divide in autumn or spring.

Pest and disease prevention No serious pests or diseases.

Design tips Use in mixed borders or as edgings in island beds. Also ideal for rock gardens, sloping banks, cutting gardens and herb gardens.

Cultivars 'Alba' has cream-coloured petals and golden centres.

'E.C. Buxton' has soft yellow flowers, perfect for informal gardens among fine-leaved plants.

Other species *A. cretica* subsp. *cretica* has white flowers with yellow centres.

Aquilegia canadensis

HARDINESS
Hardy.

HEIGHT AND
SPREAD
30–75 cm
(1–2½ ft) tall.
30 cm (1 ft) wide.

FLOWERING TIME
Mid-spring to early
summer.

CANADIAN COLUMBINE

NATIVE TO THE EASTERN USA, THIS
COLUMBINE LOOKS PRETTY IN BORDERS
AND WOODLAND GARDENS.

Description This columbine may be
short-lived in the garden, but self-
sown seedlings are plentiful and
will replenish your plantings. The
red-and-yellow blooms hang down
from the top of delicate stalks with
divided, grey-green leaflets.

Ideal position Full sun to partial
shade. Fairly drought-tolerant.

Ideal soil conditions Plant in
average, well-drained soil.

Cultivation Set out young plants in
spring or autumn.

Propagation Divide or sow seed in
autumn or spring. Self-seeds readily.

Pest and disease prevention
Columbines can be attacked by
leafminers. Remove and destroy
affected foliage.

Design tips Use en masse with
flowering shrubs and small trees.
Combine with ferns and woodland
wildflowers such as hardy ginger
Asarum spp. and foamflower
Tiarella cordifolia. In naturalistic
schemes, plant them with hardy
geraniums and ornamental grasses.

Aquilegia hybrids

RANUNCULACEAE

HARDINESS
Hardy.

HEIGHT AND
SPREAD
60–90 cm
(2–3 ft) tall.
30–60 cm
(1–2 ft) wide.

FLOWERING TIME
Mid-spring and
early summer.

COLUMBINE

COLUMBINES ARE GRACEFUL PLANTS WITH
CURIOUS-LOOKING SPURRED FLOWERS. THEY
LOOK BEST IN GROUPS OR DRIFTS.

Description Plants grow in clumps.
They have single- or bi-coloured
variable flowers. Each flower has
five spurred petals surrounded by
five petal-like sepals. The spurs may
be 12–100 mm (½–4 in) long.
Yellow, red, blue, purple, pink and
white flowers are common.

Ideal position Full sun to partial shade.

Ideal soil conditions Light, average
to humus-rich, well-drained soil.

Cultivation Columbines may be
short- lived even under the best
garden conditions. They generally

live from 2–4 years, rewarding the
gardener with a month or more of
blooming. Plants self-seed prolifically
and new flower forms and colours
are always developing.

Propagation Sow seed outdoors in
spring or summer. Sow indoors in
winter after dry-storing seed in a
refrigerator for 4–6 weeks. Plants
develop quickly.

Pest and disease prevention The
leaves can be attacked by leafminers.
Destroy damaged foliage.

Design tips Plant with spring and
early-summer perennials and bulbs.
Combine with wildflowers, ferns
and hostas in light shade.

Columbine continued

Columbines often self-seed with variable results.

Try them in rock gardens.

Cultivars Biedermeier Hybrids come in mixed colours. Plants are only 30 cm (1 ft) tall.

'Crimson Star' grows to 75 cm (2½ ft) tall and has crimson-and-white flowers.

Dragonfly Hybrids are 25–30 cm (10–12 in) tall and come in mixed colours.

McKana Group is a strain of large-flowered hybrids in mixed colours.

'Nora Barlow', a popular variety, has double flowers in red, white and green combinations.

Other species *A. coerulea*, Rocky Mountain columbine, has graceful, upward-facing, blue-and-white flowers with long spurs.

A. chrysantha, golden columbine, has huge, 5–7.5-cm (2–3-in), yellow flowers with 10-cm (4-in) spurs.

A. flabellata, an alpine species, has showy, blue-green foliage and short-spurred, deep blue or white flowers.

Arabis alpinis subsp. *caucasica*　　CRUCIFERAE/BRASSICACEAE

HARDINESS
Hardy (except in
very cold winters).

HEIGHT AND
SPREAD
15–25 cm
(6–10 in) tall.
30–45 cm
(1–1½ ft) wide.

FLOWERING TIME
Late spring and
early summer.

ARABIS

THIS ATTRACTIVE ROCK PLANT LOOKS GREAT
TUMBLING OVER A STONE WALL OR CREEPING
THROUGH A ROCK GARDEN.

Description Arabis is an evergreen
ground-cover plant 10–15 cm (4–6 in)
high. The 2.5-cm (1-in) leaves are
clothed in soft hair and are often
obscured by the spring pink or
white flowers.

Ideal position Full sun. Usually hardy
but may not survive very cold winters.

Ideal soil conditions Average well-
drained soil.

Cultivation Spreads quickly to form
loose mats of foliage. Cut plants
back after flowering to encourage
new shoots and to keep them neat.

Divide every 2–4 years to keep
plants healthy.

Propagation Take cuttings in spring.
Layer by burying 15 cm (6 in) of a
low-growing stem and leaving the
leafy tip exposed. Divide in spring
or autumn.

Pest and disease prevention No
serious pests or diseases.

Design tips Interplant with spring
bulbs and small, early perennials
in rock gardens.

Cultivars 'Rosabella' has deep pink
flowers.
　　'Snow Cap' is a robust plant with
profuse white flowers.

Arenaria montana

HARDINESS
Hardy.

HEIGHT AND SPREAD
5 cm (2 in) tall.
13 cm (5 in) wide.
Larger with age.

FLOWERING TIME
Late spring and early summer.

MOUNTAIN SANDWORT

MOUNTAIN SANDWORT IS A VERY HANDY GROUND-COVER PLANT. YOU CAN EVEN USE IT IN CREVICES BETWEEN PAVING.

Description Mountain sandwort is dense and mat-forming with tiny, needle-like leaves and flat, white, five-petalled flowers. Plants grow from thin, fibrous roots.

Ideal position Full sun.

Ideal soil conditions Average to moist sandy or loamy, well-drained soil.

Cultivation Spreads slowly to form low, moss-like mats of foliage. It is very shallow-rooted, so keep moist during dry spells.

Propagation Divide in early summer. Sow seed outdoors in autumn or inside in early spring.

Pest and disease prevention No serious pests or diseases.

Design tips Plant among rocks in loosely constructed walls. Excellent in rock gardens and perfect between paving slabs.

Arisaema triphyllum

HARDINESS
Hardy.

HEIGHT AND SPREAD
40–50 cm (16–20 in) tall.
30–45 cm (1–1½ ft) wide.

FLOWERING TIME
Summer.

JACK-IN-THE-PULPIT

JACK-IN-THE-PULPIT IS A SUMMER-FLOWERING TUBER THAT IS PERFECT FOR PLANTING AMONG LOW-GROWING WILDFLOWERS.

Description The unusual green flowers, striped with yellow or purple, are hidden beneath single or paired leaves, each with three broad leaflets. Plants grow from a button-like tuber. Glossy, red berries ripen in late summer.

Ideal position Sun to partial shade.

Ideal soil conditions Evenly moist, humus-rich soil.

Cultivation Easy to grow and long-lived. Plant tubers 15 cm (6 in) deep in spring.

Propagation Remove the pulp from ripe berries and sow the seed outdoors in autumn. Seedlings develop slowly and may take several years to bloom. Propagate from natural offsets in spring.

Pest and disease prevention No serious pests or diseases.

Design tips Combine with bleeding heart *Dicentra spectabilis*, bloodroot *Sanguinaria canadensis*, hostas and ferns. Plant under shrubs or flowering trees.

Armeria maritima

HARDINESS
Hardy.

HEIGHT AND SPREAD
15 cm (6 in) tall.
15 cm (6 in) wide.

FLOWERING TIME
Late spring and summer.

OTHER COMMON NAMES
Sea pink.

THRIFT

THRIFT, WITH ITS PINK, BALL-SHAPED FLOWERS, LOOKS STUNNING AGAINST A WALL OR PLANTED IN ROCK GARDENS.

Description Forms dense tufts of grass-like, grey-green, evergreen leaves. The flower stalks arise from the centres of the rosettes. Small, pink flowers are crowded into rounded 2.5-cm (1-in) heads.

Ideal position Full sun. Good in coastal gardens.

Ideal soil conditions Average to humus-rich, moist, well-drained soil.

Cultivation Drought-tolerant once established, it will grow in rock crevices where water is scarce. It tolerates air- and soil-borne salt.

Propagation By semi-ripe cuttings in summer. Sow seed in autumn.

Pest and disease prevention No serious pests or diseases.

Design tips Combine with low plants such as snow-in-summer *Cerastium tomentosum*.

Cultivars 'Alba' has white flowers on 12.5-cm (5-in) stems.
'Dusseldorf Pride' has attractive wine-red flowers on 15–20-cm (6–8-in) stems.

Artemisia absinthium

HARDINESS	Hardy.
HEIGHT AND SPREAD	60–90 cm (2–3 ft) tall. 60 cm (2 ft) wide.
FLOWERING TIME	Summer.

WORMWOOD

THE SOFT GREY-GREEN FOLIAGE OF WORMWOOD IS LOVELY WITH ORNAMENTAL GRASSES OR IN FRONT OF CONIFERS.

Description Wormwood is a stout, shrubby perennial with stems that become woody with age. Soft hair on the deeply lobed, aromatic foliage gives the plant a muted grey-green tone. Inconspicuous yellow flowers are borne in terminal clusters.

Ideal position Full sun.

Ideal soil conditions Average sandy or gritty, well-drained soil. Does not tolerate winter wet.

Cultivation Thrives in all but the most exposed sites. Overly rich soils result in weak growth. Encourage compact growth by pruning back untidy plants by at least half.

Propagation Grow from stem cuttings taken in late summer. Dusting the cut surfaces with a rooting hormone can speed up production of new roots.

Pest and disease prevention No serious pests or diseases.

Design tips Use in sunny borders and rock gardens.

Cultivars 'Lambrook Silver' has deeply cut, silver-grey foliage.

Artemisia lactiflora

HARDINESS
Hardy.

HEIGHT AND
SPREAD
1.2–1.8 m
(4–6 ft) tall.
Up to 1.2 m (4 ft)
wide.

FLOWERING TIME
Late summer.

WHITE MUGWORT

WHITE MUGWORT HAS A SPECTACULAR SHOW OF WHITE FLOWERS THAT IS STUNNING AS A BACKDROP FOR A FLOWERBED.

Description Unlike its silver-leaved relatives, white mugwort can take light shade. It bears graceful, 60-cm (2-ft) long plumes of fragrant, white flowers in late summer.

Ideal position Does best in full sun but will tolerate light shade.

Ideal soil conditions Light, moist, fertile soil.

Cultivation Give plenty of space when planting seedlings. Feed lightly in spring and prune back minimally to stimulate growth. Water during dry spells. May need staking.

Propagation Propagate by cuttings in summer or by division in spring.

Pest and disease prevention No serious pests or diseases.

Design tips White mugwort makes a nice background plant in a flower border, especially when highlighted by late-summer flowers such as *Rudbeckia* spp., daylilies or Michaelmas daisies.

Aruncus dioicus

HARDINESS
Hardy.

HEIGHT AND
SPREAD
90–180 cm
(3–6 ft) tall.
90–150 cm
(3–5 ft) wide.

FLOWERING TIME
Early to mid-
summer.

GOAT'S BEARD

SHRUB-LIKE GOAT'S BEARD IS A GOOD
ACCENT PLANT WHEN COMBINED WITH
SUMMER-FLOWERING SHRUBS.

Description A showy perennial with large, three-lobed leaves and airy plumes of flowers. It has creamy white flowers with small petals. Male and female flowers are borne on separate plants.

Ideal position Best in partial shade.

Ideal soil conditions Moist, humus-rich soil.

Cultivation Plant 1.2–1.5 m (4–5 ft) apart to allow for the plants' impressive mature size. The tough rootstocks are difficult to move once established. Divide plants only if necessary to revitalize the clumps. Lift in early spring and replant strong, healthy divisions into soil enriched with organic matter.

Propagation Sow seed outdoors in autumn.

Pest and disease prevention No serious pests or diseases.

Design tips Use goat's beard with ferns, wildflowers and hostas in a lightly shaded woodland garden. It combines well with other perennials in beds and borders.

Asarum europaeum

HARDINESS
Hardy.

HEIGHT AND SPREAD
15 cm (6 in) tall.
30 cm (1 ft) wide.

FLOWERING TIME
Spring.

HARDY GINGER

THE GLOSSY, EVERGREEN LEAVES OF HARDY GINGER REFLECT LIGHT AND BRIGHTEN SHADED GARDENS.

Description A slow-creeping, evergreen ground-cover plant. The aromatic rhizomes creep at or just below the soil surface. The glossy, kidney-shaped leaves are mottled along the veins. Juglike, dull brown flowers are usually hidden under the foliage. The plant forms broad clumps with age.

Ideal position Partial to full shade. Best in regions with warm summers.

Ideal soil conditions Moist, humus-rich soil.

Cultivation Clumps spread steadily to form tight mats of weed-proof foliage. Divide crowded plants in early spring or autumn.

Propagation Divide in spring. Seed can take two years to germinate.

Pest and disease prevention No serious pests or diseases.

Design tips Hardy ginger is a good plant for ground cover. Plant along paths with ferns and wildflowers or in a shaded rock garden.

Aster novae-angliae

HARDINESS
Hardy.

HEIGHT AND SPREAD
90–180 cm
(3–6 ft) tall.
90 cm (3 ft) wide.
Matures into broad clumps.

FLOWERING TIME
Late summer and autumn.

OTHER COMMON NAMES
Michaelmas Daisy

NEW ENGLAND ASTER

THIS AMERICAN ASTER IS IDEAL FOR PLANTING AT THE BACK OF A BORDER IN INFORMAL AND FORMAL GARDENS.

Description A tall, stately plant with hairy stems and clasping, lance-shaped leaves. It has lavender to purple, 3.5–5-cm (1½–2-in) flowers with yellow centres. Flowers may vary in colour from white to purple, pink and rose.

Ideal position Full sun to light shade.

Ideal soil conditions Moist, humus-rich soil.

Cultivation Clumps will become quite large with age. Divide every 3–4 years in spring. Plants may need staking.

Propagation Take 10–15-cm (4–6-in) stem cuttings in late spring or early summer. Divide in early spring or autumn.

Pest and disease prevention Powdery mildew turns leaves dull grey. Thin stems to promote air circulation. Dust affected plants with sulphur.

Design tips Plant with autumn perennials such as sunflowers *Helianthus* spp., Japanese anemone *Anemone* x *hybrida* and ornamental grasses.

Aster novi-belgii

HARDINESS
Hardy.

HEIGHT AND
SPREAD
Depending on the
cultivar, 30–180 cm
(1–6 ft) tall.
30–90 cm (1–3 ft)
wide.

FLOWERING TIME
Late summer and
early autumn.

NEW YORK ASTER

LATE-FLOWERING NEW YORK ASTER IS A
COLOURFUL ADDITION TO THE AUTUMN
GARDEN, ESPECIALLY IN MASS PLANTINGS.

Description This plant is one of the
most useful for a perennial border.
It has pretty white, blue, purple
or pink single or double flowers,
3–6 cm (1¼–2½ in) wide, with
bright yellow centres.

Ideal position Full sun to light shade.

Ideal soil conditions Moist, well-
drained soil of moderate fertility.

Cultivation Pinch asters once or
twice before midsummer to make
them bushier and promote strong
stems so they are less likely to need
staking. Divide clumps every
1–2 years to renew the plant and
keep it vigorous.

Propagation Divide in early spring.

Pest and disease prevention Don't
overcrowd. This plant needs plenty
of fresh air to avoid mildew.

Design tips Use in clumps or en
masse in flower or mixed borders.
New York asters look good with
chrysanthemums *Dendranthema*
spp. and goldenrods *Solidago* spp.

Aster x *frikartii*

HARDINESS	Hardy.
HEIGHT AND SPREAD	60–90 cm (2–3 ft) tall. 60–90 cm (2–3 ft) wide.
FLOWERING TIME	Midsummer and autumn.

ASTER

THIS ASTER COMBINES WELL WITH LATE-SUMMER- AND AUTUMN-FLOWERING PERENNIALS AND ORNAMENTAL GRASSES.

Description Plant grows from short, slow-creeping rhizomes with fibrous roots. It produces open clusters of 6-cm (2½-in), lavender-blue flowers, with bright yellow centres, on loosely branched stems.

Ideal temperature Full sun to light shade.

Ideal soil conditions Moist but well-drained soil. Dislikes winter wet.

Cultivation This aster may be short-lived. Clumps spread slowly. Divide as necessary in spring.

Propagation Take stem cuttings in spring. Divide in early spring.

Pest and disease prevention This variety is said to be mildew-resistant.

Landscape use Combine aster with phlox *Phlox paniculata* and coneflowers *Rudbeckia* spp.

Cultivars 'Monch' has erect stems and deep lavender-blue flowers. Mulch after cutting back in autumn.
    'Wonder of Staffa' is more open in habit with paler flowers.

Astilbe x arendsii

ASTILBE

ASTILBE LOOKS SPECTACULAR BY PONDS WHERE THE PLUMES OF SHOWY FLOWERS ARE REFLECTED IN THE WATER.

Description Astilbe has ferny, dissected leaves with shiny, broad leaflets. The emerging spring shoots are often tinged with red. Upright, often-plumed flower clusters bear tightly packed, fuzzy blooms in shades of red, pink, rose, lilac, cream and white.

Ideal position Partial shade.

Ideal soil conditions Moist, slightly acid, humus-rich soil.

Cultivation Astilbes are heavy feeders and benefit from an annual application of balanced organic fertilizer. Top-dress with compost or lift and replant the clumps if crowns rise above the soil. Divide clumps every 3–4 years and replant into soil that has been enriched with organic matter. Keep plants well watered.

Propagation Propagate the true species by sowing fresh seed outdoors in early autumn. Propagate cultivars by division in spring or autumn.

Pest and disease prevention Vine weevils may be a problem. Treat with a biological control such as nematodes. Control root rot with good drainage and good air circulation.

Astilbe continued

HARDINESS
Hardy.

HEIGHT AND
SPREAD
60–120 cm
(2–4 ft) tall.
60–90 cm
(2–3 ft) wide.
Leafy clumps
spread steadily
outward. Each
clump maintains
a distinct crown.

FLOWERING TIME
Early to mid
summer.

Astilbe is perfect for planting in a moist shady garden or beside a pond.

Design tips In beds or borders, plant astilbes at the front or towards the centre, depending on their size. Combine with hostas and lungworts *Pulmonaria* spp.

Cultivars 'Amethyst' is an early bloomer with lilac-purple flowers on 45–60-cm (1½–2-ft) stems.

'Bridal Veil' has open, drooping clusters of creamy white flowers.

'Fanal' has deep red flowers on 30–45-cm (1–1½-ft) plants.

'Cattleya' is a mid-season bloomer with lilac-pink flowers on 90-cm (3-ft) tall stems.

'Glut' is a late-flowering red plant with long 45–60-cm (1½–2-ft) stems.

Other species *A. chinensis* is a shorter plant with rose-pink, late-summer flowers. 'Pumila' is low-growing and clump-forming. *A. chinensis* hybrids flower in late summer. 'Purple Lance' is 1.7 m (5½ ft) tall.

A. japonica hybrids are early-blooming with glossy leaves.

A. simplicifolia hybrids are mostly dwarf plants with glossy, deeply lobed leaves and open, drooping flower clusters.

Astrantia major

HARDINESS
Hardy.

HEIGHT AND SPREAD
60–90 cm
(2–3 ft) tall.
30–60 cm
(1–2 ft) wide.

FLOWERING TIME
Early to late summer.

MASTERWORT

MASTERWORT IS A TROUBLE-FREE PERENNIAL WITH BOLD FOLIAGE AND UNUSUAL FLOWERS THAT COMPLEMENT PERENNIALS AND SHRUBS.

Description Masterwort has deeply lobed, palmate leaves on a stout, fibrous-rooted crown. Leafy, branched flower stalks rise from the centre. It has creamy white, button-like flower heads surrounded by a whorl of starry, pointed bracts. The stiff bracts remain after the flowers fade, prolonging the display.

Ideal position Full sun to partial shade.

Ideal soil conditions Evenly moist, humus-rich soil.

Cultivation Clumps can become quite large with age. Divide to control their size and spread.

Propagation Divide plants in autumn or early spring. Sow fresh seed outdoors in autumn.

Pest and disease prevention No serious pests or diseases.

Design tips Plant in herbaceous borders or combine with *Thalictrum* spp., ornamental grasses and spiky mulleins *Verbascum* spp. in naturalistic planting schemes.

Cultivars 'Ruby Wedding' has deep red flowers and bracts.

Aubrieta deltoidea

HARDINESS
Hardy.

HEIGHT AND
SPREAD
5–15 cm
(2–6 in) tall.
15–20 cm
(6–8 in) wide.

FLOWERING TIME
Spring.

AUBRETIA

AUBRETIA IS AT HOME IN THE CRACKS AND CREVICES OF WALLS OR AMONG ROCKS IN SUNNY ROCK GARDENS.

Description A low, mounding, spring-flowering plant with weak stems clothed in sparsely toothed, evergreen leaves. It spreads by rhizomes to form broad clumps and has four-petalled, 18-mm (¾-in) flowers in white, rose or purple.

Ideal position Full sun to light shade.

Ideal soil conditions Well-drained, sandy or loamy soil.

Cultivation Plants tend to flop after flowering. Shear back clumps to promote compact growth and to encourage repeat flowering.

Propagation Divide in autumn. Take stem cuttings after flowering. Sow seed indoors in spring.

Pest and disease prevention Plant in well-drained soil to avoid root rot.

Design tips Plant at the edge of paths or at the front of beds and borders with spring bulbs, *Heuchera* spp., sedums and red valerian *Centranthus ruber*.

Aurinia saxatilis

HARDINESS
Hardy.

HEIGHT AND SPREAD
23 cm (9 in) tall.
30 cm (12 in) wide.

FLOWERING TIME
Spring.

GOLD DUST

GIVE GOLD DUST SUN AND GOOD DRAINAGE, AND IT WILL PRODUCE MASSES OF BRILLIANT YELLOW BLOOMS.

Description Produces mounds of 15-cm (6-in), oblong, grey-green leaves from a thick crown. Hairy leaves and deep roots help the plant endure dry soil and warm temperatures. It has brilliant yellow flowers, which have four rounded petals and are carried in upright, branched clusters.

Ideal position Full sun. Tolerates hot, dry conditions.

Ideal soil conditions Average, well-drained, loamy or sandy soil.

Cultivation Clumps spread by creeping stems and may flop after flowering. Cut stems back by two-thirds after flowering to encourage compact growth.

Propagation Take stem cuttings in early summer. Sow seed in autumn.

Pest and disease prevention Heavy moist soils will encourage root rot. Plant in well-drained soils only.

Design tips Gold dust lends colour to walls, rock gardens and paths.

Baptisia australis

HARDINESS
Hardy.

HEIGHT AND SPREAD
1–1.5 m
(4–5 ft) tall.
60 cm (24 in) wide.

FLOWERING TIME
Early summer.

OTHER COMMON NAMES
Baptisia.

BLUE FALSE INDIGO

SPECTACULAR BLUE FALSE INDIGO LOOKS EQUALLY ATTRACTIVE IN FORMAL BORDERS OR INFORMAL MEADOW PLANTINGS.

Description Mature plants form dense, rounded mounds of three-lobed, blue-green leaves. Deep blue 2.5-cm (1-in) flowers are carried in narrow, open clusters and resemble lupins. The dried grey pods are showy during autumn and winter.

Ideal position Full sun.

Ideal soil conditions Average to humus-rich, moist, well-drained soil.

Cultivation Grows slowly until its taproot establishes. Mature plants have massive, tough root systems that resent disturbance. Space young plants 90–120 cm (3–4 ft) apart. Division is seldom necessary.

Propagation Take cuttings after flowering or sow fresh seed outdoors in autumn. Treat stored seed by pouring near-boiling water over it and soaking for 12–24 hours before sowing. Divide clumps in autumn.

Pest and disease prevention No serious pests or diseases.

Design tips Plant towards the rear of the border with Siberian iris *Iris sibirica*, peonies and other bold-textured plants.

Begonia Tuberhybrida Group

HARDINESS
Tender. Grown as
annuals or lifted
and stored indoors
over winter.

HEIGHT AND
SPREAD
45 cm (1½ ft) tall.
30–45 cm
(1–1½ ft) wide.

FLOWERING TIME
Summer and
autumn.

HYBRID TUBEROUS BEGONIAS

HYBRID TUBEROUS BEGONIAS HAVE GORGEOUS
FLOWERS IN A WIDE RANGE OF COLOURS AND
ARE PERFECT FOR CONTAINERS.

Description These bushy plants
produce an abundance of single or
double flowers up to 10 cm (4 in)
wide in almost every colour except
blue, and many are edged with
other colours.

Ideal position Partial shade.

Ideal soil conditions Evenly moist
but well-drained soil that has been
enriched with added organic matter.

Cultivation Buy thick tubers 3.5–5 cm
(1½–2 in) across. Start growing
indoors in spring. Give developing
plants bright light and keep the soil
evenly moist. Set plants out when
night temperatures stay above 10°C
(50°F). Water and mulch to keep
the soil evenly moist. Feed several
times during the season. Pinch off
spent flowers to keep plants tidy.

Propagation Divide tubers in
spring, after bringing them out
of winter storage.

Pest and disease prevention Prevent
powdery mildew by giving plants a
site with good air circulation.

Design tips Plant in shaded beds,
borders and hanging baskets.

Other species This is a large genus
of plants with many hybrids of mixed
parentage, which have been placed

Begonia Rex-cultorum Group

into specific groups, including the bedding begonia *B.* semperflorens. These are often used as annual bedding plants. They combine glossy, colourful foliage with masses of pink, red or white flowers, which are held on the plants for months at a time.

Another group with hundreds of named cultivars of mixed parentage is the *B.* Rex-cultorum Group, (pictured above). Known as rex begonias, these plants are grown mainly for their colourful leaves, because the flowers are generally inconspicuous. They are half-hardy.

While there are many other begonias, a lot are considered to be shrubs rather than perennials.

Begonia grandis subsp. *evansiara* has large bronze-green leaves, reddish beneath. Leaves are 15 cm (6 in) long and emerge in late spring. It is best in light shade and may survive the winter if mulched.

Belamcanda chinensis

HARDINESS
Hardy.

HEIGHT AND SPREAD
60–120 cm
(2–4 ft) tall.
30–60 cm
(1–2 ft) wide.

FLOWERING TIME
Early to late summer.

BLACKBERRY LILY

THIS UNUSUAL BULB LOOKS GOOD WITH LARGE-FLOWERED PLANTS TO CONTRAST WITH ITS SMALL, STARRY FLOWERS.

Description This native Japanese plant produces showy, curved fans of foliage that resemble irises. Branched clumps grow from creeping rhizomes. Its six-petalled, 5-cm (2-in), orange flowers are speckled with red.

Ideal position Full sun to light shade in a sunny sheltered spot.

Ideal soil conditions Average to humus-rich, well-drained soil.

Cultivation Once established, plants spread by creeping rhizomes to form clumps. Divide as necessary to control spread. Self-sown seedlings often appear.

Propagation Divide in late summer or sow fresh seed in spring.

Pest and disease prevention No serious pests or diseases.

Design tips Combine blackberry lily with *Phlox paniculata* and daylilies for formal borders and informal gardens.

Bergenia cordifolia

HARDINESS
Hardy.

HEIGHT AND
SPREAD
30 cm (1 ft) tall.
30 cm (1 ft) wide.

FLOWERING TIME
Late winter and
early spring.

ELEPHANT'S EARS

USE ELEPHANT'S EARS AS ACCENT PLANTS IN
BEDS AND BORDERS, AT THE BASE OF WALLS
OR ALONG GARDEN PATHS.

Description Elephant's ears is a long-lived, handsome plant with broad, oval, leathery, evergreen foliage. The 25–30-cm (10–12-in) leaves emerge in a whorl from a stout, creeping rhizome. Nodding, pink or rose flowers are carried above the foliage on thick stems. Leaves may be tinted purple in winter.

Ideal position Full sun to partial shade.

Ideal soil conditions Moist, humus-rich soil.

Cultivation These plants creep slowly from rhizomes. As clumps age, they become bare in the centre. Lift in spring and remove old portions of the rhizome. Replant in humus-rich soil. Mulch regularly to aid healthy growth.

Propagation Divide in spring. Some cultivars can be grown from seed. Young plants will develop slowly.

Pest and disease prevention Exclude slugs with barrier strips of wood ash or sand.

Design tips Plant under shrubs for glossy, green ground cover. Or use them in borders or containers.

Boltonia asteroides

HARDINESS
Hardy.

HEIGHT AND SPREAD
1.2–1.8 m
(4–6 ft) tall.
1.2 m (4 ft) wide.

FLOWERING TIME
Late summer
through autumn.

BOLTONIA

CHOOSE BOLTONIA FOR THE REAR OF
FORMAL BEDS OR BORDERS OR INFORMAL
PLANTINGS AND COTTAGE GARDENS.

Description Boltonia is a tall, late-season perennial with lovely, grey-green, willow-like foliage. It has a profusion of 2.5-cm (1-in) white daisies with bright yellow centres carried in open clusters.

Ideal position Full sun to light shade.

Ideal soil conditions Moist, humus-rich soil. Dry soil will produce smaller plants.

Cultivation These easy-to-grow plants form dense, branching stems that sometimes need staking.

Propagation Divide oversized clumps in spring. Seed collected from cultivars will produce seedlings. Sow in spring.

Pest and disease prevention Powdery mildew may attack plants. Provide good air circulation.

Design tips Combine with autumn-flowering perennials such as asters, Japanese anemones *Anemone* x *hybrida*, goldenrod *Solidago* spp. and *Eupatorium* spp.

Brunnera macrophylla

HARDINESS
Hardy.

HEIGHT AND
SPREAD
30–45 cm
(1–1½ ft) tall.
60 cm (2 ft) wide.
Foliage reaches
mature size in
summer.

FLOWERING TIME
Mid- to late spring.
Flowering often
continues for
3–4 weeks.

BRUNNERA

BRUNNERA HAS BOLD SUMMER FOLIAGE,
A PERFECT FOIL FOR FINE-TEXTURED PLANTS
SUCH AS ASTILBES AND FERNS.

Description The 20-cm (8-in), heart-shaped leaves rise in a mound from a short, fibrous-rooted rhizome. The 6-mm (¼-in), pale blue flowers look like forget-me-nots and cover plants before leaves emerge, and whiten with age.

Ideal position Partial shade. Tolerates short, dry spells once established.

Ideal soil conditions Evenly moist, humus-rich soil.

Cultivation Plants are tough, increase slowly and seldom need division. Self-sown seedlings appear regularly. Keep moist.

Propagation Divide clumps in early spring or autumn. Take 7.5–10-cm (3–4-in) root cuttings in autumn or early winter. Transplant self-sown seedlings to desired position.

Pest and disease prevention No serious pests or diseases.

Design tips Use to provide ground cover under trees or shrubs with bulbs, wildflowers and ferns.

Cultivars 'Hadspen Cream' has leaves with creamy white borders.

Caladium bicolor

HARDINESS
Tender. Grown as annuals or lifted and stored indoors over winter.

HEIGHT AND SPREAD
30–60 cm
(1–2 ft) tall.
60 cm (2 ft) wide.

FLOWERING TIME
Late spring.

CALADIUM

CALADIUM IS A TENDER PLANT GROWN FOR ITS SHOWY LEAVES. PINCH OFF THE SMALL, HOODED FLOWERS.

Description This shade-loving plant likes a sheltered, warm site.
It produces bushy clumps of usually heart-shaped leaves that are shaded and veined with combinations of green, white, pink and red.

Ideal position Partial shade.

Ideal soil conditions Moist but well-drained soil.

Cultivation Start tubers indoors in early spring. Set them with the knobby side up in pots of moist potting mix and cover with 5 cm (2 in) of mix. Keep in a warm, bright spot with moist soil. Move to the garden only when night temperatures stay above 16°C (60°F). Keep soil moist until late summer. When leaves die down, dig up the tubers and store them.

Propagation Divide tubers in spring, after bringing them out of winter storage.

Pest and disease prevention No serious pests or diseases.

Design tips Caladiums provide colour in shady beds and borders, especially in warm summers.

Caltha palustris

HARDINESS
Hardy.

HEIGHT AND
SPREAD
15–45 cm
(6–18 in) tall.
Up to 60 cm
(2 ft) wide.

FLOWERING TIME
Early to late spring.

OTHER COMMON
NAMES
Kingcup.

MARSH MARIGOLD

MARSH MARIGOLD GROWS IN MOIST SOIL
AND SHALLOW WETLANDS. IT IS THE PERFECT
PLANT FOR WATER GARDENS.

Description Marsh marigold produces
yellow spring flowers over mounds
of rounded leaves from a thick crown
with fleshy, white roots. Butter-
yellow, 3.5-cm (1½-in) flowers have
five shiny petals in open clusters.

Ideal position An open, sunny site.
Grows, even when covered with
2.5–10 cm (1–4 in) of water. Once
flowering is complete, moisture is
less critical.

Ideal soil conditions Boggy, humus-
rich or loamy soil.

Cultivation Divide overgrown plants
1 month after flowering.

Propagation Divide after flowering
in early summer. Sow fresh seed
outdoors immediately upon
ripening. Plants will not germinate
until the following spring.

Pest and disease prevention No
serious pests or diseases.

Design tips Plant with primroses,
irises and ferns in bog gardens.

Cultivars 'Flore Pleno' has fully
double flowers that last for a week
or more.

Campanula carpatica

HARDINESS
Hardy.

HEIGHT AND SPREAD
22.5 cm (9 in) tall and a slightly wider spread.

FLOWERING TIME
Early to mid-summer.

OTHER COMMON NAMES
Carpathian bellflower.

BELLFLOWER

ADAPTABLE BELLFLOWER PRODUCES A LIVELY DISPLAY OF FLOWERS AND IS PERFECT FOR BORDER PLANTINGS.

Description Spreads to form tidy mounds of dark green leaves topped with cup-shaped, blue-purple or white flowers.

Ideal position Full sun or light shade.

Ideal soil conditions Well-drained, fertile soil.

Cultivation Mulch with compost during summer. Water in drought.

Propagation Short-lived unless you divide and renew plants every couple of years. Deadhead for an extended flowering period or leave a few flowers on so the plant can self-seed.

Pest and disease prevention Exclude snails and slugs with barrier strips of wood ash or sand. Alternatively, bait them with shallow containers of beer set flush with the soil surface.

Landscape use This bellflower looks pretty in clumps at the front of a shrub or flower border. Or use plants individually in a rock garden or beside a patio.

Cultivars 'Alba' displays a show of pure white flowers.

Campanula glomerata

HARDINESS
Hardy.

HEIGHT AND SPREAD
30–90 cm
(1–3 ft) tall.
60 cm (2 ft) wide.

FLOWERING TIME
Early summer.

CLUSTERED BELLFLOWER

ROBUST CLUSTERED BELLFLOWER IS A FAST-GROWING PERENNIAL, PERFECT FOR BORDERS.

Description Erect, leafy, flowering stems and hairy, 12.5-cm (5-in) oval leaves. It grows from slow-creeping rhizomes with fibrous roots and has purple to blue-violet flowers in tiered clusters.

Ideal position Full sun to partial shade.

Ideal soil conditions Moist, humus-rich soil. Tolerates alkaline soil.

Cultivation Cut back flowering stems after blossoms fade to encourage a second flush. Divide overgrown clumps.

Propagation Divide in autumn or early spring. Self-sown seedlings will appear. Take cuttings after flowering.

Pest and disease prevention Exclude slugs with barrier strips of wood ash or sand.

Design tips A good choice for cottage-garden schemes and with irises.

Cultivars 'Crown of Snow' has large clusters of white flowers.
'Joan Elliot' is a delicate, floriferous selection with deep blue-violet flowers.
'Superba' grows to 75 cm (2½ ft) with violet flowers.

Campanula persicifolia

HARDINESS
Hardy.

HEIGHT AND SPREAD
30–90 cm
(1–3 ft) tall.
30 cm (1 ft) wide.

FLOWERING TIME
Summer.

PEACH–LEAVED BELLFLOWER

THIS ELEGANT BELLFLOWER HAS SHOWY FLOWERS AND COMBINES WELL WITH YARROW.

Description Produces mounds of narrow, 10-cm (4-in), evergreen leaves from a fibrous-rooted crown. Has open, bell-shaped, lavender-blue flowers, which make long-lasting cut flowers.

Ideal position Full sun to partial shade.

Ideal soil conditions Moist but well-drained, humus-rich soil.

Cultivation This bellflower spreads slowly by sideshoots from the central crown. It may self-seed.

Propagation Take tip cuttings in early summer. Divide clumps in early spring.

Pest and disease prevention Weak plants may be susceptible to rust. Slugs can be lured into beer traps.

Design tips Plant in the middle or rear of borders. Or use them in drifts as accent plants.

Cultivars 'Alba' displays a show of pure white flowers.

'Blue Bloomers' has large violet-blue flowers.

'Telham Beauty' has large, pale blue flowers on 90-cm (3-ft) stems.

Canna spp.

HARDINESS
Half-hardy.

HEIGHT AND
SPREAD
60–180 cm
(2–6 ft) tall.
30–60 cm
(1–2 ft) wide.

FLOWERING TIME
Mid- to late
summer.

OTHER COMMON
NAMES
Indian shot.

CANNA

MASS PLANTINGS OF SHOWY, STURDY
CANNAS MAKE A DRAMATIC AND EYE-
CATCHING SUMMER BORDER DISPLAY.

Description Cannas grow from thick
rhizomes. They produce tall stems
with large, oval, green or reddish
purple leaves from spring until early
autumn. Clusters of broad-petalled
flowers up to 12.5 cm (5 in) across
bloom in shades of pink, red,
orange, yellow and bi-colours.

Ideal position Full sun to light shade.

Ideal soil conditions Average to
moist, well-drained, humus-rich soil.

Cultivation Start rhizomes indoors
in spring in a warm place. Set out
when all danger of frost is over.

Cannas are drought-tolerant, but
mulch and water during dry spells.
In cold areas, lift the rhizomes in
late autumn after the first frost and
store over winter.

Propagation Divide clumps in
spring. Divide rhizomes into pieces
about 15 cm (6 in) long.

Pest and disease prevention No
serious pests or diseases.

Design tips Use canna alone en
masse or as part of an "exotic"
scheme. Good in containers.

Catananche caerulea

HARDINESS
Hardy.

HEIGHT AND
SPREAD
45–60 cm
(1½–2 ft) tall.
25–30 cm
(10–12 in) wide.

FLOWERING TIME
Summer to early
autumn.

CUPID'S DART

THE STRAWLIKE FLOWERS OF CUPID'S DART
LOOK GREAT IN THE SUMMER GARDEN AND
DRY EASILY FOR FLOWER ARRANGEMENTS.

Description Cupid's dart produces
tufts of narrow, woolly leaves from
a fibrous rootstock. Its blue 5-cm
(2-in) flowers resemble asters and
are carried singly on wiry stems.

Ideal position Full sun.

Ideal soil conditions Any light, well-
drained soil. Good drainage for
healthy growth.

Cultivation Plants may be short-
lived, especially in heavy soil.
Divide each year for longevity.

Propagation Divide in autumn.
Take 5–7.5-cm (2–3-in) root cuttings
in autumn. Sow seed indoors in
early spring. Plants will bloom the
first year.

Pest and disease prevention No
serious pests or diseases.

Design tips Use en masse in rock
gardens or at the front of a dry,
sunny perennial garden. Combine
with yarrows.

Cultivars 'Alba' has white flowers.
'Major' has lavender-blue flowers
on 90-cm (3-ft) stems.

Centaurea dealbata

HARDINESS
Hardy.

HEIGHT AND SPREAD
75 cm–1 m
(2½–3 ft) tall.
45 cm (1½ ft)
wide.

FLOWERING TIME
Late spring and
early summer.

KNAPWEED

KNAPWEED IS A GREAT COTTAGE GARDEN
PLANT AND IS PERFECT FOR ANY INFORMAL
BEDS AND BORDERS.

Description Knapweed has lobed
leaves with 8 to 10 woolly divisions.
The leaves clothe thick, weakly
upright stems over fibrous-rooted
crowns. The fringed, mauve-pink
flowers have broad, white centres
and are borne one to a stem. Use
the blooms as fresh, cut flowers or
cut them for drying.

Ideal position Full sun.

Ideal soil conditions Any well-
drained soil. Will tolerate poor soils.

Cultivation Remove flower heads as
they fade to promote more flowers.

Cut plants back to remove floppy
stems when flower production
wanes. Divide clumps every 2–3
years to keep plants vigorous.

Propagation Divide in spring. Sow
seed outdoors in autumn.

Pest and disease prevention
Powdery mildew can be a problem
in damp conditions.

Design tips Combine knapweeds
with ornamental grasses and other
cottage-garden plants in informal
settings.

Cultivars 'Steenbergii' is a long-
flowering, compact selection with
magenta flowers.

Knapweed continued

Centaurea cineraria

Other species *C. cineraria* (pictured above). This shrubby plant has beautiful silvery grey, finely cut leaves. It is grown mainly for its foliage and has small, thistle-like, lilac-pink flower heads. It is fairly drought-tolerant and needs fertile, well-drained soil. To propagate, take cuttings, sow seed or divide in spring or autumn. Mix with flowers of contrasting colours and foliage textures.

C. macrocephala, globe cornflower. This yellow-flowering species has foliage similar to that of a large dandelion. It grows up to 90 cm (3 ft) tall and flowers from early to late summer.

C. montana, perennial cornflower. This plant grows to 75 cm (2½ ft) tall with beautiful violet, lacy flowers in early summer. It spreads slowly to make good-sized clumps, but is not invasive.

Centranthus ruber

HARDINESS
Hardy.

HEIGHT AND
SPREAD
30–90 cm
(1–3 ft) tall.
60 cm (2 ft) wide.

FLOWERING TIME
Spring and
summer.

RED VALERIAN

THE STRIKING, BRIGHT RED FLOWERS OF RED
VALERIAN ADD VIBRANT COLOUR TO THE
SPRING AND SUMMER BORDER.

Description Red valerian is an
upright perennial with opposite,
grey-green oval leaves. Plants grow
from a fibrous-rooted crown. Small
red flowers are carried in domed,
branched clusters. Rose, pink and
white selections are also available.

Ideal position Full sun. Grows
readily in walls and rock crevices
where soil is limited.

Ideal soil conditions Average, sandy
or loamy, neutral or alkaline soil.

Cultivation Plants may become
floppy after blooming. Cut them
back to promote compact growth
and further flowers.

Propagation Sow seed outdoors
in summer. Plants often self-seed
prolifically. To reproduce plants
of a specific colour, remove basal
shoots and treat them like cuttings.

Pest and disease prevention No
serious pests or diseases.

Design tips Perfect for wall and
rock gardens. The red flowers
combine well with the neutral
colours of stone.

Varieties *C. ruber* var. *albus* has
off-white flowers and var. *coccineus*
has deep red flowers.

Cerastium tomentosum

HARDINESS
Hardy.

HEIGHT AND
SPREAD
8–10 cm
(3–4 in) tall.
30–90 cm
(1–3 ft) wide.

FLOWERING TIME
Late spring and
early summer.

SNOW–IN–SUMMER

SNOW-IN-SUMMER IS AN UNUSUAL PLANT WITH A PROFUSION OF FLOWERS IN SPRING ROCK GARDENS.

Description A low-mounding plant with small, woolly leaves and clusters of white flowers on wiry stems. Snow-white 12–25-mm (½–1-in) flowers have 5 deeply notched petals that give the impression of a 10-petalled flower. Plants grow from a dense tangle of fibrous roots.

Ideal position Full sun.

Ideal soil conditions Average, sandy or loamy, very well-drained soil.

Cultivation Cut back after flowering to promote fresh, compact growth.

Clumps spread easily and may overgrow their position.

Propagation Divide in spring.

Pest and disease prevention No serious pests and diseases if planted in a sunny, dry site.

Design tips Use snow-in-summer for cascading over a wall, a bank, or for planting in a rock garden.

Ceratostigma plumbaginoides

HARDINESS
Hardy.

HEIGHT AND SPREAD
15–30 cm
(6–12 in) tall.
30–45 cm (1–1½ ft)
wide, wider with
age.

FLOWERING TIME
Late summer, often
into autumn.

LEADWORT

LEADWORT WORKS WELL AS GROUND COVER
UNDER FLOWERING SHRUBS OR AT THE FRONT
OF THE PERENNIAL GARDEN.

Description A creeping, semi-woody
perennial with russet stems and
sparse wedge-shaped leaves. Plants
die back to the ground each year.
Deep gentian-blue flowers are carried
in clusters at the tips of the stems.

Ideal position Full sun in a sheltered
site. Leadwort provides useful
ground cover and is a good plant
for rockeries.

Ideal soil conditions Light, moderately
fertile, moist well-drained soil.

Cultivation Prune stems back to
the ground in autumn or spring and
prune out any winter-damaged
stems by late spring, when new
growth emerges. Foliage often
turns orange in autumn.

Propagation Divide in early spring.
Take tip cuttings in early summer.

Pest and disease prevention No
serious pests or diseases.

Design tips Interplant the creeping
stems with spring- and autumn-
flowering bulbs such as crocuses,
miniature daffodils and autumn
crocuses *Colchicum* spp. The striking
flowers look pretty in rockeries.

Chelone lyonii

HARDINESS
Hardy.

HEIGHT AND
SPREAD
30–90 cm
(1–3 ft) tall.
30–60 cm
(1–2 ft) wide.

FLOWERING TIME
Late summer.

PINK TURTLEHEAD

PINK TURTLEHEAD, A NORTH AMERICAN
PLANT, MAKES A STRIKING DISPLAY IN MOIST
BEDS AND BORDERS.

Description A bushy perennial with
leafy stems from a stout, fibrous-
rooted crown. The 10–17.5-cm
(4–7-in) leaves are broadly ovate
with toothed margins. Pink, inflated,
tubular flowers resemble a turtle's
head with jaws open.

Ideal position Full sun to partial shade.

Ideal soil conditions Evenly moist,
humus-rich soil.

Cultivation Divide the crowns to
increase vigour and reduce size of
large clumps in more mature plants.

Propagation Divide in spring or
after flowering. Take stem cuttings
in early summer. Remove any
flower buds. Sow seed outdoors in
autumn or indoors in late winter
after stratification. To stratify, mix
seed with a moist potting mix in a
plastic bag. Close bag with a twist-
tie and refrigerate for 4–6 weeks.
Then sow mixture as you would
normal seed.

Pest and disease prevention No
serious pests or diseases.

Design tips Combine with asters,
phlox and goldenrod *Solidago* spp.
for late-summer colour.

Cimicifuga racemosa syn. *Actaea racemosa*   RANUNCULACEAE

HARDINESS
Hardy.

HEIGHT AND
SPREAD
1.2–2.1 m
(4–7 ft) tall.
90–120 cm
(3–4 ft) wide.

FLOWERING TIME
Midsummer.

OTHER COMMON
NAMES
Black snakeroot
and bugbane.

BLACK COHOSH

GROW THIS UNUSUAL-LOOKING PERENNIAL
IN A WOODLAND GARDEN WITH FERNS
AND WILDFLOWERS.

Description The wand-like spires of
black cohosh wave above an open
cluster of large compound leaves
with toothed leaflets. Plants grow
from a stout, fibrous-rooted crown.
The small, 12-mm (½-in), creamy
white flowers have a dense whorl
of fuzzy stamens (male reproductive
structures) and no petals. They are
carried on tall, sparsely branched
spikes.

Ideal position Dappled shade.

Ideal soil conditions Moist,
humus-rich soil.

Cultivation Black cohosh is an
extremely long-lived perennial.
Young plants take several years
to reach flowering size, but clumps
increase each year.

Propagation Divide clumps in
autumn or spring. Leave at least one
bud per division. Sow fresh seed
outdoors in autumn.

Pest and disease prevention No
serious pests or diseases.

Design tips Place at the rear of
borders with bold flowers such as
phlox and daylilies.

Coreopsis verticillata

COREOPSIS

USE COREOPSIS IN A MASS PLANTING WITH
SHRUBS OR COMBINE WITH ORNAMENTAL
GRASSES.

Description An airy, rounded plant
with threadlike, three-lobed leaves
and bright, summer, starry flowers
from butter to golden yellow. Plants
grow from a fibrous-rooted crown.

Ideal position Full sun or light shade.

Ideal soil conditions Average to rich,
moist but well-drained soil.

Cultivation This plant is easy-care,
demanding little attention once
established. Plants eventually die
out at the centre. Divide old clumps.
Replant in rich soil.

Propagation Divide in spring.

Pest and disease prevention No
serious pests or diseases.

Design tips Perfect for the front
of the border with cranesbills
Geranium spp., yarrows, daylilies
and coneflowers *Rudbeckia* and
Echinacea spp.

Cultivars 'Golden Gain' grows to
45 cm (18 in) tall with golden-
yellow flowers.

'Moonbeam' is a showy spreading
plant from 30–60 cm (1–2 ft) wide
with pale yellow flowers.

HARDINESS	Hardy.
HEIGHT AND SPREAD	30–90 cm (1–3 ft) tall. 60–90 cm (2–3 ft) wide.
FLOWERING TIME	Throughout summer.

Coreopsis 'Schnittgold'

Other species *C. 'Schnittgold'* (pictured above) is a relatively short-lived perennial with masses of single yellow flowers produced throughout summer. The species grows to around 45 cm (1½ ft); however, its compact cultivar 'Nana' grows to a height of only 15 cm (6 in) and makes a colourful addition to the front of the border.

C. grandiflora has clear, yellow, single flowers topping pale green foliage and is one of the easiest species to grow. It is native to the southern and eastern United States. There are some choices of cultivar available, including the semi-double 'Early Sunrise' and the tall-growing 'Mayfield Giant', which has flower

stems up to 90 cm (3 ft) tall carrying bright yellow single blooms.

C. lanceolata is the parent of many cultivars with additional colouring to the blooms, including 'Sternataler', with interesting brown rings.

Specialist nurseries offer a much wider range of coreopsis and other perennials than garden centres, if you want to try different species.

Corydalis flexuosa

FUMARIACEAE

HARDINESS
Hardy.

HEIGHT AND SPREAD
20–30 cm
(8–12 in) tall.
20 cm (8 in) wide.

FLOWERING TIME
Late spring to early summer.

CORYDALIS

CORYDALIS IS IDEAL FOR PROVIDING A SPLASH OF VIVID BLUE IN THE SHADE OF EMERGING SPRING GROWTH IN A WOODLAND GARDEN.

Description Corydalis has a mass of blue, long-spurred, tubular flowers that are about 2.5 cm (1 in) long. It is the amazing colour of these flowers, set over pale green fern foliage, that makes corydalis so popular with gardeners and a welcome choice as a perennial.

Ideal position Partially shaded, fairly moist position.

Ideal soil conditions Moist but well-drained soil.

Cultivation Grow corydalis in partial shade such as that provided in a woodland garden where deciduous trees provide a continuing supply of humus. They can be easily naturalized in moderate climates and they can self-seed.

Propagation Either by seed or by division.

Pest and disease prevention No serious pests or diseases.

Design tips Corydalis is perfect for mass plantings, especially in a woodland garden.

Cultivars 'Purple Leaf' forms a 20 cm (8 in) mound with purplish leaves and dark blue flowers.

Yellow corydalis *Corydalis lutea*

Other species *C. lutea,* yellow corydalis (pictured above). Yellow corydalis is the easiest corydalis to grow and has one of the longest blooming seasons. It is a mound-forming, rhizomatous plant with attractive, soft, bright green foliage. It grows to about 30 cm (1 ft) tall and 45 cm (1½ ft) wide. The lovely foliage is topped with bright yellow flowers from spring through to early autumn if growing conditions are to its liking. It will grow happily in walls, between paving stones and in rockeries, and it makes a colourful ground-cover plant. It grows best where drainage is good but will tolerate alkaline soils.

C. ochroleuca. This white-flowering corydalis prefers partial shade to full sun and dry soil.

C. solida. This corydalis has pink to dark purple flowers in spring. It requires full sun. 'George Baker' has rich red flowers. 'Beth Evans' has pretty, pale pink flowers.

C. wilsonii. This low-growing species has pale, blue-green foliage and yellow flowers in spring. It grows to 20 cm (8 in) tall and 20 cm (8 in) wide, and may not be widely available.

Cyclamen coum

HARDINESS
Hardy to half-
hardy.

HEIGHT AND
SPREAD
10 cm (4 in) tall.
10 cm (4 in) wide.

FLOWERING TIME
Winter to spring.

CYCLAMEN

CYCLAMEN MAKES A PERFECT GROUND-COVER PLANT WHERE ITS INTERESTING FOLIAGE CAN BE SEEN TO BEST ADVANTAGE.

Description A hardy, tuberous perennial with attractive silver-marked leaves and winter to spring flowers. Colours range from creamy white to deep pink.

Ideal position Best in partial shade.

Ideal soil conditions Provide good drainage in a moist position with grit. Prefers soil that dries out in summer.

Cultivation Plant the tuber at a depth of about 5 cm (2 in). Once the plants have become established, leave them alone. In cold regions, provide a dry mulch in winter.

Propagation Best results may be achieved by soaking seed for up to 24 hours to help germination, which can be erratic. Sow into a moist medium in summer or autumn and keep in a warm position.

Pest and disease prevention No serious pests or diseases.

Design tips An attractive ground-cover plant under deciduous trees or shrubs.

Cultivars Many cultivars exist with flowers in white or shades of pink as well as those in the Pewter Group, selected for their striking foliage colours and markings.

Cyclamen hederifolium

HARDINESS
Hardy.

HEIGHT AND SPREAD
Height and spread of flowers and foliage 10–15 cm (4–6 in).

FLOWERING TIME
Early autumn.

CYCLAMEN

THIS AUTUMN-FLOWERING CYCLAMEN IS A GREAT CHOICE FOR COOL, SHADY AREAS AND LOOKS GOOD WITH FERNS.

Description A tuberous perennial which blooms in early autumn. Handsome, heart-shaped, silver-marked, green leaves emerge shortly after the flowers finish. Leafless flower stalks are topped with pink or white nodding flowers that have upward-pointing petals.

Ideal position Sun or partial shade.

Ideal soil conditions Fertile, well-drained soil. Prefers dry conditions in summer.

Cultivation Set plants into the garden in spring or summer, or plant dormant tubers shallowly in summer. Make sure the smooth, unmarked side of the tuber is on the bottom. Mulch when the leaves wither.

Propagation Divide tubers in summer or grow from seed. Soak the seed overnight, then sow 6 mm (¼ in) deep in a pot. Enclose the pot in a plastic bag, then place it in a dark place until the seeds germinate.

Pest and disease prevention No serious pests or diseases.

Design tips Use hardy cyclamen in shady spots with ferns and hellebores *Helleborus* spp.

Cyclamen persicum

HARDINESS
Hardy.

HEIGHT AND SPREAD
10–20 cm (4–8 in) tall and wide.

FLOWERING TIME
Winter to early spring.

CYCLAMEN

THIS WINTER-FLOWERING CYCLAMEN IS IDEAL TO BRIGHTEN UP AN INDOOR SETTING WITH ITS EYE-CATCHING BLOOMS.

Description A tuberous perennial with thick, slender-stalked, rounded and heart-shaped, finely toothed, variegated leaves. Stems grow to 20 cm (8 in) and carry fragrant, single flowers in pink, rose, white, red and purple.

Ideal position Best grown as a houseplant.

Ideal soil conditions Evenly moist soil. Don't let plant sit in water.

Cultivation This cyclamen is a specialist plant requiring knowledge and experience. It needs a dormant period after flowering. Begin watering and fertilizing when new growth appears.

Propagation Best results gained from fresh seed. Soaking seed for up to 24 hours may help sometimes erratic germination. Plant into moist medium and keep in warm position. Keep potting mix moist.

Pest and disease prevention Root rot is a danger. Don't let it sit in water.

Design tips Primarily for indoors.

Cultivars 'Pearl Wave' has flowers with wavy-edged petals.

Delphinium Elatum Group

HARDINESS
Hardy.

HEIGHT AND SPREAD
1.35–1.8 m
(4½–6 ft) tall.
60–90 cm
(2–3 ft) wide.

FLOWERING TIME
Early to
midsummer.

DELPHINIUMS

MOST GARDEN DELPHINIUMS BELONG TO THIS GROUP. THERE IS A VAST ARRAY OF SHADES TO ADD COLOUR.

Description Stately border plants with dense flower clusters atop tall stems with deeply cut, palmately lobed leaves. Plants grow from stout crowns with thick, fleshy roots. The showy flowers of the various garden hybrids range in colour from white to all shades of true blue to lavender and into purple. Five petal-like sepals surround two to four small, true petals that are often called the "bee."

Ideal position Full sun and shelter from strong winds.

Ideal soil conditions Evenly moist but well-drained, fertile, humus-rich soil. A neutral to slightly acid soil is best.

Cultivation Delphiniums are heavy feeders and benefit from an annual balanced organic fertilizer in spring or a top-dressing of well-rotted manure. Set out new plants in spring. Mature plants produce many stems. Thin the clumps to three to five stems as they emerge. Cut off old flowering stems below the foliage. New shoots often emerge from the crown. When they develop, cut the old shoots to the ground. Divide overgrown plants and replant into soil enriched with organic matter.

Hybrid delphiniums continued

The ruffled flowers of delphiniums are a natural choice for a cottage garden.

Propagation Divide plants in spring. Take cuttings in spring from new shoots. Seeds may not produce identical plants to the parent.

Pest and disease prevention Exclude slugs with a barrier of wood ash or sand around the clumps. Dust parts affected by powdery mildew with sulphur.

Design tips Plant at the rear of borders where their showy spires will tower over other summer-blooming perennials such as phlox, lilies, lupins and bellflowers *Campanula* spp.

Hybrids A few popular selections are listed here. Plants from the 'Black Knight' and 'Galahad' group are Pacific Hybrids. These are widely available and have 3.5–5-cm (1½–2-in) single or semi-double flowers. 'Blue Nile' is a beautiful eye-catching blue with a white centre.

Other species *D. Belladonna* Group hybrids are hardy, compact plants. 'Bellamosum' has large deep blue flowers on 1.2-m (4-ft) stalks. 'Cliveden Beauty' has sky blue flowers with a white eye.

Dendranthema x *grandiflorum* syn. *Chrysanthemum*   ASTERACEAE

HARDINESS
Hardy to half-
hardy.

HEIGHT AND
SPREAD
45 cm–1.3 m
(1½–4 ft) tall.
60–75 cm
(24–30 in) wide.

FLOWERING TIME
Late summer to
mid-autumn.

OTHER COMMON
NAMES
Border
chrysanthemum.

GARDEN CHRYSANTHEMUM

CHRYSANTHEMUMS IN FLOWER ARE A
FAMILIAR SIGHT IN LATE SUMMER AND
ARE IDEAL FOR ADDING COLOUR TO
AN AUTUMN DISPLAY.

Description Garden chrysanthemums
have stout stems clothed in lobed
leaves. They grow from creeping
stems with tangled fibrous roots and
bloom in a wide variety of colours
from white to pale pink, rose,
burgundy, red, golden brown, gold,
yellow and cream. Flower shapes
range from button-like heads to
pompons (double ball-shaped
flowers), cushions (flat, fully double
flowers) and decoratives (large
double to semi-double heads).
There are even novelty hybrids

with spider-like heads (pictured on
page 190) and those with spoon-
shaped petals. Flower sizes range
from 2.5–15 cm (1–6 in).

Ideal position From full sun to light
shade in a sheltered site.

Ideal soil conditions Humus-rich,
well-drained soil.

Cultivation Many chrysanthemums
tend to sprawl in summer. Pinch the
stems once or twice in spring and
early summer to promote compact
growth. Stop pinching altogether in
summer. Stake larger varieties.
To encourage larger flowers, remove
axillary buds (those surrounding
the largest main bud).

Garden Chrysanthemum continued

Mixed colours of the spider form.

This process, called disbudding, allows the stem to direct its energy into producing one large flower. Chrysanthemums spread outward from the centre by creeping stems. Divide the fast-growing clumps every 1–2 years to keep them healthy and vigorous. In frost-prone areas lift plants in late autumn and store over winter.

Propagation Divide in spring. Tip cuttings taken in late spring or early summer root quickly.

Pest and disease prevention Aphids may attack young shoots. Spider mites may cause stippling and leaf curl. Spray with insecticidal soap or a botanical insecticide.

Design tips Use to brighten annual displays or mix with asters and anemones for autumn colour.

Cultivars The array of chrysanthemums available is astounding. Many of the large-flowered varieties are difficult to maintain in the average garden but the "Korean", "pompon" and "Rubellum" types do not need special attention. Very late-flowering varieties cannot tolerate frost and are best grown in greenhouses in pots.

Dianthus spp.

HARDINESS
Hardy.

HEIGHT AND SPREAD
45–60 cm
(1½–2 ft) tall.
30 cm (1 ft) wide.

FLOWERING TIME
Early to midsummer.

PINKS

SUMMER-FLOWERING PINKS ARE IDEAL FOR SUNNY BORDERS AND ROCK GARDENS.

Description This group consists of about 300 species of plants. They have narrow, blue-green grass-like leaves and fragrant white to pink or mauve flowers in open clusters on wiry stems. Flowers are single or double and some have markings of contrasting colours. *D.plumarius* (pictured above) is a distant parent of many of today's garden cultivars.

Ideal position An open, sunny site.

Ideal soil conditions Average, well-drained, sandy or loamy soil. Should be neutral or slightly acid for best growth. Alpine pinks need very sharply drained soil. Avoid sites that are wet in winter.

Cultivation Plants may be short-lived, so take cuttings to maintain stock. Divide clumps every 2–3 years to keep them vigorous. Remove flowers as they fade to promote continued flowering.

Propagation Layer or take stem cuttings from the foliage rosettes in summer. Strip leaves from the lower third of a 5–7.5 cm (2–3 in) cutting. Place in a medium of one part vermiculite and two parts sand or perlite to allow excellent drainage and good air circulation.

Pinks continued

Maiden pink *Dianthus deltoides*

Pest and disease prevention Usually trouble free. In wet summers slugs may be a problem. Plants may be prone to rot if they are sitting in wet soil.

Design tips Plant at the front of borders or use as an edging along paths.

Cultivars 'Doris' has double pink flowers, a long flowering season and is very reliable.

'Mrs Sinkins' has fragrant, double white flowers.

'Gran's Favourite' has fringed flowers with a pinkish-purple centre.

Other species D. alpinus, alpine pink. This clump-forming pink has

3.5-cm (1½-in), single pink flowers and is ideal for rockeries.

D. barbatus, sweet William. This slow-growing biennial or short-lived perennial forms tufts of deep green, lance-shaped leaves and dense, rounded clusters of 2.5-cm (1-in) bi-coloured pink, rose or white flowers. Sweet William self-seeds and grows to 45 cm (1½ ft), ideal for massed plantings and cottage gardens.

D. caryophyllus is a summer-flowering plant with perfumed purple, pink or white flowers. It is available from specialist nurseries.

D. deltoides, maiden pink (pictured above). A mat-forming pink with a mass of single rose-coloured flowers borne one to a

Cheddar pink *Dianthus gratianopolitanus*

stem. Good for rock gardens.

D. gratianopolitanus, cheddar pink (pictured above). Cheddar pink bears sweet-scented flowers to enjoy outdoors in the garden or indoors as cut flowers. This spring-blooming pink has 2.5-cm (1-in), fragrant white, rose or pink flowers borne singly or in pairs. It grows well in sunny rock gardens or cascading over walls. As an alternative, combine with other front-of-the-border plants such as sedum, thyme and lamb's ears *Stachys byzantina*. Interplant them with spiky foliage such as yuccas and grasses.

D. gratianopolitatus 'Flore Pleno' has double, fragrant flowers.

D. superbus, lilac pink. This stunning pink has deeply fringed pink, lavender or white flowers borne in open clusters on wiry stems.

Dicentra spectabilis

BLEEDING HEART

PLANT ELEGANT BLEEDING HEART WITH
SPRING BULBS, PRIMROSES AND BRUNNERA
FOR A STRIKING SPRING DISPLAY.

Description A popular, traditional
perennial with strings of heart-
shaped flowers held above deeply
divided blue-green foliage. Plants
grow from thick, fleshy roots. Bright
pink, heart-shaped flowers consist
of two reflexed lobes with a central
column that resembles a dangling
drop of blood.

Ideal position Partial shade.
Bleeding heart tolerates sun if the
soil stays moist.

Ideal soil conditions Evenly moist,
humus-rich soil.

Cultivation Bleeding heart will bloom
for 4–6 weeks in spring. Top-dress
with well-rotted manure in early
spring to maintain soil fertility.
If plants lose their vigour, you can
lift and divide clumps, but they may
not respond well to disturbance.
Replant them into soil that has been
enriched with organic matter.

Propagation Sow fresh seed outdoors
in summer or in spring indoors.
Take root cuttings in winter and
place in a cold frame.

Pest and disease prevention Slugs and
snails may attack spring foliage. Use
barriers or beer traps to deter them.

Western bleeding heart *Dicentra formosa*

HARDINESS
Hardy.

HEIGHT AND SPREAD
45 cm (1½ ft) tall.
45 cm (1½ ft) wide.

FLOWERING TIME
Early spring to early summer.

Design tips Combine with hostas or ground-cover plants that will fill the void left by the declining foliage.

Other species *D. eximia*, fringed bleeding heart, is often confused with *D. formosa*. *D. eximia* is from the mountains of eastern North America. 'Snowdrift' has pure white flowers and is available from specialist nurseries.

D. formosa, Western bleeding heart (pictured above), is, as its name suggests, from western areas of North America and is widely available. It is a spreading evergreen perennial with pink and red flowers in summer and autumn. It grows to 30–45 cm (1–1½ ft) tall and 45 cm (1½ ft) wide. Likes full sun to shade. 'Alba' has pure white flowers.

Dictamnus albus

HARDINESS
Hardy.

HEIGHT AND
SPREAD
60–120 cm
(2–4 ft) tall.
60 cm (2 ft) wide.

FLOWERING TIME
Early summer.

BURNING BUSH

BURNING BUSH IS EXQUISITE AND DELICATE
IN FOLIAGE AND FLOWER, SO SITE PLANTS
WHERE THEY ARE EASY TO ADMIRE.

Description Forms shrublike clumps
of stout stems with deep green,
pinnately lobed leaves and erect
flower spikes. Plants grow from
thick, woody crowns with fibrous
roots. The 2.5-cm (1-in), showy,
white flowers have five starry petals
and 10 long, curled stamens (male
reproductive structures). The seed
capsules are attractive in summer.

Ideal position Likes full sun to light
shade.

Ideal soil conditions Well-drained,
humus-rich soil.

Cultivation Burning bush is a long-
lived, trouble-free perennial that is
slow to establish and resents
disturbance once planted.

Propagation Sow seed outdoors in
autumn when ripe. Seedlings may
occasionally appear next season but
germination is usually much slower.
Transplant to permanent position
after 3 years.

Pest and disease prevention No
serious pests.

Design tips Combine with other
perennials that need good drainage,
such as oriental poppy *Papaver
orientale* and yarrow.

Cultivars Var. 'Purpureus' has dark-
veined, violet-purple flowers.

Digitalis spp.

HARDINESS
Hardy.

HEIGHT AND
SPREAD
75 cm (2½ ft) tall.
30 cm (1 ft) wide.

FLOWERING TIME
Plants flower
during late spring
and summer.

FOXGLOVE

FOXGLOVES ARE POPULAR, EASY-CARE
PERENNIALS AND BIENNIALS THAT ARE
PERFECT FOR MASS PLANTINGS.

Description The unusual foxglove species (above) has fuzzy, broad, lance-shaped leaves. Rosettes of foliage form at the base of the flowering stems and persist over winter. The 5–7.5-cm (2–3-in), tubular flowers are the colour of crushed strawberries and the flower spikes are the same height as more typical foxgloves. Foxgloves are poisonous if ingested and the foliage can irritate the skin.

Ideal position Likes full sun to partial shade.

Ideal soil conditions Well-drained, average garden soil.

Cultivation Divide overgrown clumps by removing new rosettes from the flower stalk and replant into soil that has been enriched with organic matter. Set out new plants in spring to flower the same season or in autumn to flower the following year. Remove spent flower stalks. Leave one stalk to self-seed.

Propagation Divide in autumn. Sow fresh seed outdoors in autumn or in late spring. Seedlings emerge the next spring and will flower in the second year.

Foxglove continued

Common foxglove *Digitalis purpurea*

Pest and disease prevention No serious pests or diseases.

Design tips Plant at the middle or rear of perennial gardens. In informal gardens, combine them with ferns and ornamental grasses. Use mass plantings along a wall or fence, or in combination with flowering shrubs.

Other species *D. ferruginea*, rusty foxglove, grows to 1–1.2 m (3 ½–4 ft) tall, with narrow spikes of 2.5-cm (1-in) rusty brown-and-white flowers.

D. grandiflora, yellow foxglove, has 5-cm (2-in) soft yellow flowers on 60–90 cm (2–3 ft) stalks. The lush foliage is also attractive.

D. lutea has small, creamy yellow flowers on narrow, 60–90 cm (2–3 ft) spikes.

D. purpurea, common foxglove (pictured above), is a biennial or short-lived perennial with 60–150 cm (2–5 ft) spikes of purple, rose, pink or white flowers. *Digitalis purpurea* f. *albiflora* has white flowers that are often lightly spotted brown inside. Excelsior Hybrids have dense spikes in a variety of colours.

Doronicum orientale

HARDINESS
Hardy.

HEIGHT AND SPREAD
30–60 cm
(1–2 ft) tall.
30 cm (1 ft) wide.

FLOWERING TIME
Spring and early summer.

LEOPARD'S BANE

BRIGHTLY COLOURED LEOPARD'S BANE IS AN EASY-CARE DAISY, PERFECT FOR SPRING FLOWER GARDENS.

Description Has deep green, triangular leaves in open clusters from a fibrous-rooted crown. A profusion of 2.5–5-cm (1–2-in) bright yellow, single daisies bloom on slender, leafless stems.

Ideal position Partial shade.

Ideal soil conditions Moist, humus-rich soil. Soil should not dry out while plant is actively growing.

Cultivation Leopard's bane emerges in spring when its yellow flowers are a cheering sight. It grows well among deciduous shrubs and trees.

Divide clumps every 2–3 years to keep them vigorous.

Propagation Divide in spring or autumn. Sow seed indoors in late winter or early spring.

Pest and disease prevention No serious pests or diseases.

Design tips Combine with clustered bellflower *Campanula glomerata*, spring bulbs and wildflowers.

Cultivars 'Magnificum' has showy 5-cm (2-in) flowers.

Echinacea purpurea

HARDINESS
Hardy.

HEIGHT AND
SPREAD
60–120 cm
(2–4 ft) tall.
30–60 cm
(1–2 ft) wide.

FLOWERING TIME
Mid- to late
summer.

PURPLE CONEFLOWER

PURPLE CONEFLOWERS ARE SHOWY, SUMMER
DAISIES THAT COMBINE WELL WITH MOST
PERENNIALS AND ORNAMENTAL GRASSES.

Description Purple coneflowers
have sparse, 15-cm (6-in) oval or
broadly lance-shaped leaves on
stout, hairy stems. Plants grow from
thick, deep taproots. Red-violet to
rose-pink flowers have broad,
drooping rays (petal-like structures)
surrounding raised, bristly cones.

Ideal position Full sun.

Ideal soil conditions Average to
humus-rich, moist, well-drained soil.

Cultivation Plants increase from
basal buds to form broad, long-lived
clumps. Division is seldom necessary

and is not recommended.

Propagation Sow seed indoors in
a warm place in spring. Take root
cuttings in late autumn.

Pest and disease prevention No
serious pests or diseases.

Design tips Plant in perennial
borders or meadow and prairie
gardens. Attracts butterflies.

Cultivars 'Alba' has creamy white
daisy flowers.
    'Kims Knee High' has clear pink
flowers with reflexed rays.
    'Magnus' has huge, flat, rose-
purple daisy flowers.

Epimedium x *versicolor*

HARDINESS
Hardy.

HEIGHT AND SPREAD
25–35 cm
(10–14 in) tall.
30 cm (1 ft) wide.

FLOWERING TIME
Early to mid-spring.

OTHER COMMON NAMES
Barrenwort.

EPIMEDIUM

EPIMEDIUM IS AN EXCELLENT WOODLAND GROUND-COVER PLANT THAT COMBINES WELL WITH HOSTAS AND FERNS.

Description Has semi-evergreen leaves divided into glossy, heart-shaped leaflets. The wiry, trailing stems have matted, fibrous roots. The unusual flowers have 8 yellow, petal-like sepals and 4 spurred petals that are tinged with red. They are held above the new leaves as they emerge.

Ideal position Partial to full shade. Avoid waterlogged soil, especially during winter.

Ideal soil conditions Moist, well-drained, humus-rich soil.

Cultivation Epimediums can thrive for years with little attention. They perform well under adverse conditions, even in the dry shade of mature trees. A spring mulch of leafmould is beneficial. Cut old foliage back in spring to allow the flowers to emerge freely.

Propagation Divide overgrown clumps in autumn.

Pest and disease prevention No serious pests or diseases.

Design tips Combine with bulbs, hellebores and ferns.

Cultivars 'Neosulphureum' has yellow flowers with short spurs.
    'Sulphureum' has very pretty, two-toned, yellow flowers.

Eremurus stenophyllus

HARDINESS
Hardy.

HEIGHT AND SPREAD
1–1.5 m
(3½–5 ft) tall.
60 cm (2 ft) wide.

FLOWERING TIME
Early summer.

FOXTAIL LILY

FOXTAIL LILY IS A ROBUST, STATELY PERENNIAL. ITS ELEGANT FLOWER SPIKES LOOK STUNNING PLANTED AGAINST A WALL.

Description These perennials have tall flower spikes and clumps of straplike foliage. Plants grow from a thickened crown with brittle, spreading roots. Starry, 2.5-cm (1-in), six-petalled flowers are crowded on tall, pointed spikes.

Ideal position Full sun to light shade. Avoid positions with soggy soil, which promotes root rot.

Ideal soil conditions Moist but well-drained, humus-rich soil.

Cultivation Plant crowns 10–15 cm (4–6 in) deep and space them 30 cm (12 in) apart. Mulch to protect from late frosts in very cold winters. Divide clumps if they become crowded.

Propagation Divide in autumn. Sow fresh seed outdoors in autumn.

Pest and disease prevention No serious pests or diseases.

Design tips Plant among perennials or against a wall or a hedge. Surround with bold poppies *Papaver* spp., daylilies *Hemerocallis* spp. and irises.

Other species *E. himalaicus* is from the Himalayas and has dense spikes of white flowers.

Erigeron glaucus

HARDINESS	Hardy.
HEIGHT AND SPREAD	25 cm (10 in) tall. 20 cm (8 in) wide.
FLOWERING TIME	Late spring and summer.

BEACH ASTER

THIS EASY-CARE PLANT PROVIDES GOOD GROUND COVER IN SEASIDE AREAS. IT'S ALSO GREAT IN ROCK GARDENS.

Description Low-growing, clump-forming plant. It forms a dense mat of grey-green foliage topped by pale lilac daisy flowers with yellow centres typical of the daisy family, in late spring and summer.

Ideal position Full sun.

Ideal soil conditions Sandy, well-drained soil.

Cultivation Fleabane is hardy and will thrive with little water. Space plants 20 25 cm (8–10 in) apart when planting. Cut back after flowering to encourage compact growth and discourage self-seeding.

Propagation Sow seed or divide mature plants in spring.

Pest and disease prevention No serious pests or diseases.

Design tips Plant in rock gardens or on banks.

Cultivars 'Albus' has white flowers.
  'Elstead Pink' has lovely dark pink flowers.
  'Roseus' has pink flowers.

Erigeron karvinskianus

HARDINESS
Hardy in mild
regions. Half-hardy
elsewhere.

HEIGHT AND
SPREAD
15–25 cm (6–10 in)
tall. Can spread 1 m
(3 ft) or more.

FLOWERING TIME
Summer.

FLEABANE

FLEABANE IS RELIABLE AND VIGOROUS. IT IS
IDEAL FOR GROWING IN AND OVER WALLS IN
SUNNY SITES.

Description Fleabane bears many
tiny, dainty, daisy-type flowers.
Masses of small, 2.5-cm (1-in),
daisy-type flowers with yellow
centres open white, then age
to shades of pink and purple.

Ideal position Full sun.

Ideal soil conditions Moderately
fertile, well-drained soil.

Cultivation Fleabane is fairly
drought-tolerant. Space plants
20–25 cm (8–10 in) apart when
planting. Cut back after flowering
to encourage compact growth. The
plant self-seeds readily.

Propagation Divide mature plants
in spring.

Pest and disease prevention No
serious pests or diseases.

Design tips Plant in rock gardens or
on banks. Looks particularly good
tumbling over stone walls.

Erigeron speciosus

HARDINESS
Hardy.

HEIGHT AND
SPREAD
45–75 cm
(1½–2½ ft) tall.
30–60 cm
(1–2 ft) wide.

FLOWERING TIME
Early to
midsummer.

DAISY FLEABANE

DAISY FLEABANE MAY BE DIFFICULT TO
SOURCE BUT IS LOVELY WITH LOW GRASSES.
THE FLOWERS ARE GOOD FOR CUTTING.

Description Has leafy clumps of
hairy, 15-cm (6-in), lance-shaped
leaves that spring from fibrous-
rooted crowns. The 3.5-cm (1½-in)
aster-like flowers of daisy fleabane
have white, pink, rose or purple rays
surrounding bright yellow centres.

Ideal position Full sun to light shade.

Ideal soil conditions Moist but well-
drained, average to humus-rich soil.

Cultivation Fleabanes are long-lived
perennials. Divide every 2–3 years.

Propagation Divide in autumn. Take
cuttings in spring before buds form.
Sow seed outdoors in autumn or
indoors in spring.

Pest and disease prevention No
serious pests or diseases.

Design tips Plant at the front of
borders with summer-flowering
perennials such as cranesbills
Geranium spp., cinquefoils
Potentilla spp. and phlox.

Hybrids Many cultivars are from
crosses with *E. speciosus*.
  'Azure Fairy' has semi-double,
lavender-blue flowers.
  'Foerster's Darling' has reddish
pink flowers.

Eryngium giganteum

HARDINESS
Hardy.

HEIGHT AND SPREAD
90–120 cm
(3–4 ft) tall.
30–75 cm
(1–2½ ft) wide.

FLOWERING TIME
Summer.

OTHER COMMON NAMES
Miss Willmott's Ghost

SEA HOLLY

THE ROUNDED FLOWER CLUSTERS AND SILVERY GREEN BRACTS OF SEA HOLLY ADD EXCITEMENT TO ANY PERENNIAL PLANTING.

Description Sea holly is an architectural plant with stiff flowering stems and mostly basal, pinnately divided leaves. Plants grow from thick taproots. Small, steel-blue, globose flower heads are surrounded by prickly bracts.

Ideal position Full sun. Extremely drought-tolerant once established.

Ideal soil conditions Average, well-drained soil.

Cultivation Set plants in permanent location while young. This sea holly may be short-lived.

Propagation Sow fresh seed outdoors in autumn. May also be propagated by root cuttings.

Pest and disease prevention No serious pests or diseases.

Design tips Plant in the middle of borders with goldenrod *Solidago* spp., asters, phlox and ornamental grasses.

Other species and hybrids *E. alpinum*, alpine sea holly, is similar but has larger, showier flowers and lobed leaves.

E. x *oliverianum*, has beautiful silvery leaves and silver-blue flowerheads. Longer lasting than its parent *E. giganteum*.

Eupatorium purpureum subsp. *maculatum*   ASTERACEAE

HARDINESS
Hardy.

HEIGHT AND SPREAD
1.2–1.8 m
(4–6 ft) tall.
90–120 cm
(3–4 ft) wide.

FLOWERING TIME
Late summer.

JOE PYE WEED

JOE PYE WEED IS A TALL, STATELY PERENNIAL THAT'S PERFECT FOR MOIST BORDERS AND MEADOW PLANTINGS.

Description The showy terminal flower clusters of Joe Pye weed are domed to rounded and consist of hundreds of small, fuzzy, rose-purple flowers.

Ideal position Full sun or light shade.

Ideal soil conditions Moist, humus-rich soil.

Cultivation Plants take 2–3 years to mature, so leave ample room when planting out young plants.

Propagation Divide plants in early spring or autumn.

Pest and disease prevention No serious pests or diseases.

Design tips Choose Joe Pye weeds for the middle or back of the border for a bold accent. Combine with tall perennials, such as asters, goldenrod *Solidago* spp., grasses, and especially perennials whose foliage will mask this plant's leaves, which have faded by the time the flowers are out.

Euphorbia amygdaloides

HARDINESS
Hardy.

HEIGHT AND SPREAD
90–105 cm
(3–3½ ft) tall.
90–105 cm
(3–3½ ft) wide.

FLOWERING TIME
Spring to summer.

WOOD SPURGE

WOOD SPURGE IS A DELIGHTFUL SPRING-FLOWERING PERENNIAL. USE IT WHEREVER YOU WANT FRESH SPRING COLOUR.

Description An erect perennial with dark green leaves. It grows from fleshy, fibrous roots. Grown for its flowers, which are surrounded by prominent, yellowish-green bracts. The sap can cause skin rashes.

Ideal position Full sun or part shade.

Ideal soil conditions Moist, well-drained soil.

Cultivation An easy-care plant. Divide when necessary.

Propagation Take cuttings, or divide in spring. Wear gloves. Sow seed in autumn or spring.

Pest and disease prevention No serious pests or diseases.

Design tips Plant at the front of the border. Combine with tall, spring-flowering perennials.

Cultivars 'Purpurea' (pictured above) has a more bushy habit with stems and foliage, which are often purplish, offset against bright green bracts.

'Variegata' has very pretty, yellow-edged leaves.

Varieties *E. amygdaloides* var. *robbiae* has dark green leaves held in distinctive rosettes on the non-flowering stems. It grows to 60 cm (2 ft) high.

Euphorbia myrsinites

HARDINESS
Frost-hardy.

HEIGHT AND SPREAD
15 cm (6 in) tall.
30–60 cm (1–2 ft) wide.

FLOWERING TIME
Spring.

SPURGE

PLANT THIS SPRAWLING SPURGE IN A SUNNY ROCK GARDEN, AT THE FRONT OF BORDERS, OR IN CONTAINERS.

Description A creeping plant, it has thick stems and blue-grey, wedge-shaped leaves. It grows from fleshy, fibrous roots and is a striking addition to the spring garden. Unusual flower heads have tiny, yellow flowers surrounded by showy, funnel-shaped, yellow bracts. The sap can cause skin rashes.

Ideal position Full sun to light shade.

Ideal soil conditions Average to humus-rich, well-drained soil. Plants will grow in poor, gravelly soils.

Cultivation Self-seeds freely. Divide the clumps when necessary, wearing gloves.

Propagation Take stem cuttings after flowering in spring. Divide mature plants in spring or autumn. Sow seed outdoors in autumn or spring, or indoors in early spring.

Pest and disease prevention No serious pests or diseases.

Design tips Combine with *Aubrieta* spp., phlox and bulbs.

Euphorbia polychroma

HARDINESS
Frost-hardy.

HEIGHT AND SPREAD
15–25 cm
(6–10 in) tall.
30–60 cm
(1–2 ft) wide.

FLOWERING TIME
Spring.

SPURGE

THIS CLUMP-FORMING SPURGE BLOOMS AT THE SAME TIME AS TULIPS, MAKING STRIKING COLOUR COMBINATIONS.

Description The plants are long-lived garden residents that need little care. The unusual flower heads consist of tiny, yellow flowers surrounded by showy, funnel-shaped, yellow bracts. The sap can cause skin rashes.

Ideal position Full sun or light shade.

Ideal soil conditions Average to rich, well-drained soil. Plants will grow in lighter soil in sun.

Cultivation Divide congested clumps if they overgrow their position.

Propagation Take stem cuttings in spring or sow seed in autumn or spring.

Pest and disease prevention No serious pests or diseases.

Design tips Plant at the front of the border or in a sunny rock garden. Combine with early-blooming perennials such as columbines *Aquilegia* spp., *Arabis* and *Aubrieta* spp., and fleabane *Erigeron* spp. For striking colour, use them with bulbs such as ornamental onions *Allium* spp., fritillaries *Fritillaria* spp. and daffodils.

Filipendula rubra

HARDINESS
Hardy.

HEIGHT AND
SPREAD
1.2–1.8 m
(4–6 ft) tall.
60–120 cm
(2–4 ft) wide.

FLOWERING TIME
Early summer.

QUEEN–OF–THE–PRAIRIE

MATURE CLUMPS OF THIS NORTH AMERICAN PLANT MAKE AN ARRESTING DISPLAY. COMBINE THEM WITH DAYLILIES AND PHLOX.

Description Queen-of-the-prairie is a towering perennial with huge flower heads on stout, leafy stalks. The showy, 30-cm (1-ft) leaves are deeply lobed and star-like. Plants grow from creeping stems. Small, five-petalled, pink flowers are crowded into large foamy heads.

Ideal position Full sun to light shade in reliably moist soil.

Ideal soil conditions Evenly moist, humus-rich soil.

Cultivation If leaves become tattered after bloom, cut plants to the ground; new leaves will emerge. Plants spread quickly in moist soil. Divide every 3–4 years to keep compact.

Propagation Lift and divide clumps in spring or autumn, or dig crowns from the edge.

Pest and disease prevention No serious pests or diseases.

Design tips Plant queen of-the-prairie at the rear of borders in dappled shade or beside ponds in open situations.

Cultivars 'Venusta' has deep rose-pink flowers and is widely available.

Gaillardia x grandiflora

HARDINESS
Frost-hardy.

HEIGHT AND SPREAD
60–90 cm
(2–3 ft) tall.
45 cm
(1½ ft) wide.

FLOWERING TIME
Throughout summer.

BLANKET FLOWER

GIVE BLANKET FLOWER A SUNNY, WELL-
DRAINED SPOT, AND IT WILL BEAR DAZZLING
ORANGE-AND-YELLOW BLOOMS ALL SUMMER.

Description The flowers are held
on loose stems with hairy, lobed
leaves. Plants grow from fibrous-
rooted crowns and may be short-
lived. Ragged yellow-and-orange,
daisy-like flowers have single or
double rows of toothed, petal-like
rays surrounding a yellow centre.

Ideal position Full sun.

Ideal soil conditions Average to poor,
well-drained soil. Rich, moist soil
causes overgrowth and flopping.

Cultivation Blanket flowers thrive in
well-drained soil in sun. Deadhead

regularly and cut down in autumn
to improve chances of overwintering.

Propagation Divide in early spring.
Sow seed indoors in spring. Seedlings
often bloom the first year.

Pest and disease prevention No
serious pests or diseases.

Design tips Use in mixed borders
and rock gardens.

Cultivars 'Dazzler' has yellow-tipped
petals surrounding an orange or
red centre.
　'Bremen' has copper-red, yellow-
tipped flowers.
　'Kobold' (pictured above) has
red-and-yellow flowers.

Gaura lindheimeri

HARDINESS
Hardy.

HEIGHT AND SPREAD
90–120 cm
(3–4 ft) tall.
90 cm (3 ft) wide.

FLOWERING TIME
Throughout summer.

WHITE GAURA

WHITE GAURA IS PERFECT FOR INFORMAL GARDENS. ITS FLOWER CLUSTERS LOOK LIKE A SWIRL OF DANCING BUTTERFLIES.

Description A shrubby perennial with airy flower clusters on wiry stems and small, hairy leaves. It grows from a thick, deep taproot. Unusual white flowers, tinged with pink, have four triangular petals and long, curled stamens (male reproductive structures) on spikes.

Ideal position Full sun. Extremely heat- and drought-tolerant.

Ideal soil conditions Moist, well-drained, average soil.

Cultivation White gaura is an easy-care perennial that thrives for years with little attention. Plants flower non-stop all summer. Remove old flower stalks to make way for the new ones.

Propagation Sow seed outdoors in spring or autumn. Take softwood cuttings in summer.

Pest and disease prevention No serious pests or diseases.

Design tips Combine them with low-mounding perennials such as verbenas *Verbena* spp., cranesbills *Geranium* spp. and sedums. In late summer they are beautiful with tawny ornamental grasses.

Gentiana asclepiadea

HARDINESS
Hardy.

HEIGHT AND SPREAD
60–90 cm
(2–3 ft) tall.
60 cm (2 ft) wide.

FLOWERING TIME
Late summer and autumn.

WILLOW GENTIAN

CHOOSE WILLOW GENTIAN TO PLANT IN BORDERS OR USE WITH FERNS AND WILDFLOWERS IN A WOODLAND GARDEN.

Description Willow gentian is a late-blooming perennial with leafy, arching stems that grow from a crown with thick, fleshy roots. The lance-shaped, opposite leaves have prominent veins. Deep blue flowers are carried in pairs along the arching stems. Each one is tubular, with five flaring, starry lobes.

Ideal position Sun to partial shade. Provide willow gentian with shade from hot afternoon sun to avoid leaf browning.

Ideal soil conditions Evenly moist, humus-rich soil.

Cultivation Gentians are long-lived perennials that thrive with little care. Plants seldom need division and dislike root disturbance.

Propagation Divide carefully in spring. Sow fresh seed outside in late summer or autumn.

Pest and disease prevention No serious pests or diseases.

Design tips Combine these elegant perennials with asters, goldenrods *Solidago* spp. and other autumn-flowering plants.

Geranium endressii and other spp.

HARDINESS
Hardy.

HEIGHT AND SPREAD
25–50 cm
(10–20 in) tall.
45 cm (18 in) wide.

FLOWERING TIME
Early to late summer.

CRANESBILLS, HARDY GERANIUMS

CRANESBILLS ARE PERFECT PLANTED AT THE FRONT OF BORDERS TO TIE PLANTINGS TOGETHER OR AS AN EDGING ALONG PATHS.

Description A mounding plant with deeply cut, five-lobed leaves arising from a slow-creeping, fibrous-rooted crown. Pink flowers appear from early to midsummer. Soft pink saucer-shaped, five-petalled flowers are carried in sparse clusters.

Ideal position Full sun to partial shade.

Ideal soil conditions Average to humus-rich soil that is not too dry.

Cultivation Plants spread reliably and can make good ground cover.

Propagation Divide between early autumn and spring. Take stem cuttings in summer or cut back after flowering and divide.

Pest and disease prevention No serious pests or diseases.

Design tips Combines well with many perennials in informal and cottage-garden schemes.

Other species *G. argenteum* is an alpine perennial with a silver sheen to the leaves that may be difficult to source. It has sparse, purple flowers.

G. cinereum, a grey-leaved cranesbill, is a low, spreading plant with small, deeply incised leaves and saucer-shaped, pink flowers veined with violet. They are best

Cranesbills continued

Cranesbill *Geranium clarkei*.

suited to the rock garden. 'Ballerina' (pictured opposite) is a cultivar with lilac-pink flowers with striking veins and purple eyes. 'Purple Pillow' has bold, purple flowers.

G. clarkei (above) is a floriferous species with delicate white, pink or lilac dark-veined flowers. The leaves are very deeply divided. 'Kashmir Purple' has purple-blue flowers. 'Kashmir White' has white flowers.

G. dalmaticum, Dalmatian cranesbill, is a low, rounded plant with small, curly, lobed leaves and 2.5-cm (1-in) shell-pink flowers. Plants spread rapidly by creeping stems. The variety 'Album' has white flowers.

G. himalayense is a mounding plant with deeply incised leaves and 5-cm (2-in) violet-blue flowers. 'Gravetye' is a compact grower with violet-centred, blue flowers. This group has the largest flowers of all cranesbills.

G. ibericum, from the Caucasus, is a robust plant with large seven- to nine-lobed leaves and 5-cm (2-in) purple-blue flowers from late spring to early summer.

G. macrorrhizum is fast spreading with fragrant, seven-lobed leaves and bright pink flowers. 'Album' has white flowers with pink sepals. 'Ingwersen's Variety' has light pink flowers and glossy leaves. Plants are covered with tiny, sticky hairs.

Cranesbill *Geranium* (Cinereum Group) *'Ballerina'*

G. maculatum, spotted cranesbill, is a woodland plant with five-lobed leaves and tall, sparsely flowering stalks of clear-pink or white flowers in late spring to early summer.

G. x *oxonianum* 'A.T. Johnson' has dozens of silvery pink flowers. 'Claridge Druce' has lilac-pink flowers. 'Wargrave Pink' has salmon-pink flowers.

G. pratense, meadow cranesbill, has deeply incised leaves and 3.5-cm (1½-in) purple flowers with red veins. 'Mrs. Kendall Clarke' has lilac-blue flowers in midsummer and may repeat flower.

G. sanguineum, bloody cranesbill, is a low, wide-spreading plant with deeply cut, starry leaves and flat, magenta flowers held just above the foliage. 'Shepherd's Warning' is low growing with deep rose-pink flowers. *G. sanguineum* var. *Striatum* is prostrate with pale pink, rose-veined flowers.

G. sylvaticum, wood cranesbill, blooms in late spring to early summer with lobed leaves and numerous lavender-blue flowers.

Gypsophila paniculata

HARDINESS
Hardy.

HEIGHT AND SPREAD
90–120 cm
(3–4 ft) tall.
60–90 cm
(2–3 ft) wide.

FLOWERING TIME
Summer.

BABY'S BREATH

BABY'S BREATH LOOKS GREAT WITH PERENNIALS THAT HAVE SPIKY LEAVES OR FLOWERS, SUCH AS FOXGLOVES AND YUCCAS.

Description Baby's breath is an old-fashioned perennial with sparse, smooth, blue-green foliage. The stems and basal leaves grow from a thick, deep taproot. Small, single or double white flowers are carried in large, domed, airy clusters.

Ideal position Full sun to light shade.

Ideal soil conditions Near-neutral to alkaline, moist, humus-rich soil.

Cultivation Set out in spring. Don't disturb the crowns once the plants are established. Good drainage is essential for longevity. Tall cultivars may need support.

Propagation Take cuttings in summer and plant in sandy compost. Difficult to raise from seed.

Pest and disease prevention No serious pests or diseases.

Design tips Use the airy sprays to hide the yellowing foliage of bulbs and perennials such as oriental poppy *Papaver orientale* that go dormant in summer.

Cultivars 'Bristol Fairy' has double flowers on compact plants.
  'Pink Fairy' has beautiful, double, pale pink flowers.

Helenium autumnale

HARDINESS
Hardy.

HEIGHT AND SPREAD
90–150 cm
(3–5 ft) tall.
60–90 cm
(2–3 ft) wide.

FLOWERING TIME
Late summer and autumn.

SNEEZEWEED

PLANT SNEEZEWEED WITH OTHER LATE-SUMMER PERENNIALS AT THE MIDDLE OR REAR OF THE BORDER OR EN MASSE.

Description A showy, late-season perennial with tall, leafy stems that spring from a fibrous-rooted crown. The hairy, lance-shaped leaves are edged with a few large teeth. The 5-cm (2-in), yellow, daisy-like flowers have broad, petal-like rays.

Ideal position Full sun or light shade.

Ideal soil conditions Evenly moist, humus-rich soil.

Cultivation Either stake or pinch the stem tips in early summer to promote compact growth. Divide clumps every 3–4 years.

Propagation Divide in spring. Take stem cuttings in early summer. Sow seed of the species indoors in late winter.

Pest and disease prevention No serious pests or diseases.

Design tips Sneezeweed offers wonderful late-season colour. Combine it with asters, goldenrod *Solidago* spp. and phlox *Phlox paniculata*.

Cultivars 'Butterpat' has bright yellow flowers.
'Moerheim Beauty' has stunning, deep orange flowers with brown centres.

Helianthus x *multiflorus*

HARDINESS
Hardy.

HEIGHT AND
SPREAD
2 m (6 ft) tall.
90 cm (3 ft) wide.

FLOWERING TIME
Late summer.

SUNFLOWER

SUNFLOWERS ADD BOLD SPLASHES OF COLOUR TO THE SUMMER-FLOWERING PERENNIAL GARDEN.

Description Stout stems clothed in wide, 20-cm (8-in), wedge-shaped leaves. Plants grow from stout, fibrous-rooted crowns. The 5–7.5-cm (2–3-in) daisy-like flowers have bright yellow, petal-like rays and yellow centres.

Ideal position Full sun.

Ideal soil conditions Moist, average to humus-rich soil.

Cultivation Sunflowers are easy to grow but need room to spread. Divide them every 3–4 years. The stems are usually self-supporting, but those of *Helianthus* x *multiflorus* will need staking.

Propagation Divide in autumn. Take stem cuttings in early summer or sow seed outdoors in autumn.

Pest and disease prevention No serious pests or diseases.

Design tips Combine with garden phlox *Phlox paniculata*, asters, goldenrod *Solidago* spp., sedums and ornamental grasses.

Other species *H.* x *laetiflorus* is a spreading plant with flowers 10–12 cm (4–5 in) across. 'Morning Sun' has large, semi-double flowers.

HARDINESS
Hardy.

HEIGHT AND
SPREAD
90–150 cm
(3–5 ft) tall.
60–120 cm
(2–4 ft) wide.

FLOWERING TIME
Midsummer.

HELIOPSIS

A BRIGHT, SUMMER DAISY, HELIOPSIS COMBINES WELL WITH SUMMER PERENNIALS AND ORNAMENTAL GRASSES.

Description Has 12.5-cm (5-in) triangular leaves covering a tall, bushy plant that grows from a fibrous-rooted crown. The golden yellow, 5–7.5-cm (2–3-in) flowers have broad, petal-like rays and yellow centres that brown with age.

Ideal position Full sun.

Ideal soil conditions Humus-rich, moist, well-drained soil.

Cultivation In rich soils, these plants spread quickly. Divide them every 2–3 years. May need staking.

Propagation Divide in spring. Take stem cuttings in late spring or early summer. Sow seed indoors in late winter or early spring.

Pest and disease prevention No serious pests or diseases.

Design tips Plant with garden phlox *Phlox paniculata*, gay feathers *Liatris* spp. and asters.

Cultivars 'Golden Plume' has double, dark-yellow flowers on 90–105-cm (3–3½-ft) plants.
'Summer Sun' has lovely, 10-cm (4-in) flowers on 90-cm (3-ft) stems.

Helleborus niger

HARDINESS
Hardy.

HEIGHT AND SPREAD
30–45 cm
(1–1½ ft) tall.
30–45 cm
(1–1½ ft) wide.

FLOWERING TIME
Winter and early spring.

CHRISTMAS ROSE

CHRISTMAS ROSE'S LOVELY FOLIAGE IS ATTRACTIVE ALL SEASON. USE THIS PERENNIAL IN SHADE GARDENS OR IN SPRING BORDERS.

Description Has deeply lobed, leathery leaves growing from a stout crown with fleshy roots. The flowers open pure white and may turn pink with age.

Ideal position Light to partial shade. Established plants can tolerate deep shade.

Ideal soil conditions Evenly moist, humus-rich soil.

Cultivation In spring, remove any damaged leaves from the plant. Plants take 2–3 years to become established and resent disturbance.

Divide only to propagate. Mulch in autumn.

Propagation Sow seed outdoors as soon as it is ripe, in early summer, and place in pots in a sheltered spot. Keep moist.

Pest and disease prevention Leaf spot can disfigure the leaves.

Design tips Combine with early-spring bulbs such as snowdrops.

Other species *H. argutifolius* is a taller plant with green flowers, ideal for woodland gardens.

H. orientalis, lenten rose, has produced many hybrids with flowers from white to deepest purple. Some are spotted.

Hemerocallis hybrids

HARDINESS
Hardy.

HEIGHT AND SPREAD
30–90 cm (1–3 ft) tall. 60–90 cm (2–3 ft) wide. There are miniature and standard sizes as well as extremely tall kinds.

FLOWERING TIME
Summer.

DAYLILY

STUNNING DAYLILY HYBRIDS ARE AMONG THE MOST POPULAR PERENNIALS—THEY ARE LONG-LIVED, EASY-CARE PLANTS.

Description Each flower only lasts a day but a profusion of new buds keeps the plants in bloom for up to a month. Daylily flowers vary in colour and form. The majority of the wild species are orange or yellow with wide petals and narrow, petal-like sepals. Modern hybrids come in many colours.

Ideal position Full sun to light shade. Most modern hybrids need at least 8 hours of direct sun to flower well. If grown in full shade they will produce very few or even no flowers at all.

Ideal soil conditions Evenly moist, average to humus-rich soil.

Cultivation Plant container-grown or bareroot plants in spring or autumn. Place the crowns just below the soil surface. Plants take a year to become established and then spread quickly to form dense clumps. Most hybrids and species can remain in place for many years without disturbance. Some have so many flower stalks that the flowers crowd together and lose their beauty—divide these every 3 years. Deadhead regularly to keep them looking their best. The foliage of most daylilies is retained all season in mild areas. In very cold regions the foliage may rot in hard frosts.

Daylily continued

Daylily cultivars are available in a huge range of colours.

Propagation Hybrids are propagated by division only in late summer or early autumn. Seed-grown plants are often inferior to the parent plant.

Pest and disease prevention Aphids and thrips may attack foliage and flower buds. Wash off aphids with a stream of water or spray them with insecticidal soap. Thrips make small white lines in the foliage and may deform flower buds if damage is severe. Spray with insecticidal soap or a botanical insecticide such as pyrethrin.

Design tips Perfect for planting en masse. Combine with summer-blooming perennials and grasses.

Cultivars Many cultivars are available in a full range of colours. Buy plants after you see them in flower to make sure they are the size and colour you want. A few old favourites are listed below.

'Catherine Woodbery' is shell-pink with a yellow throat.

'Corky' has bright, lemon-yellow flowers.

'Cherry Cheeks' has very pretty, rose-pink flowers.

'Ice Carnival' is nearly white.

'Buzz Bomb' has deep orange flowers with yellow throats.

Heuchera sanguinea hybrids

HARDINESS
Hardy.

HEIGHT AND SPREAD
30–75 cm
(1–2½ ft) tall.
30–60 cm
(1–2 ft) wide.

FLOWERING TIME
Late spring and summer.

CORAL BELLS

THE AIRY BLOOMS OF CORAL BELLS DANCE OVER ROUNDED LEAVES. THEY ARE IDEAL IN BORDERS AND IN LIGHT SHADE.

Description Forms neat clumps of scalloped leaves. The small, fringed, nodding flowers are carried in slender, branching clusters. The flower colours range from white through shades of pink and red.

Ideal position Full sun or partial shade.

Ideal soil conditions Moist but well-drained, humus-rich soil.

Cultivation Remove old flower stalks to promote re-flowering. As plants grow, they rise above the soil on woody crowns. Lift plants every 3–4 years and replant the

crowns in improved soil. Do not crowd the plants by packing too many in a small space or they will lose their vigour and bloom less.

Propagation Divide plants in autumn or plant seed in spring. Cultivars will need to be propagated by division as they do not come true from seed.

Pest and disease prevention No serious pests or diseases.

Design tips Plant coral bells at the front of the border, as an edging for beds, along paths or in a lightly shaded rock garden. They work well in containers. Combine with cranesbills *Geranium* spp., catmints

Coral bells continued

Heuchera flowers.

Nepeta spp., ornamental onions *Allium* spp. and columbines *Aquilegia* spp.

Hybrids Several garden hybrids have been bred that are attractive in foliage and in flower. The evergreen leaves may be deep green, red, purple, orange and many of the dark-leaved forms are mottled with silver. Plants grow from woody, fibrous-rooted crowns to produce mounds of rounded, lobed leaves. Mounds are about 30 cm (1 ft) tall and flower stems rise another 30 cm (1 ft) tall. Small, dainty, fringed flowers are carried in slender, branching clusters. Colours vary from white through shades of pink and red.

Flowers from late spring to summer— variable depending on the cultivar.

'Amber Waves' has yellow-orange leaves and small rose-pink flowers.

'Chocolate Ruffles' has leaves that are chocolate coloured above and red below.

'Palace Purple' has shiny, purple almost metallic leaves.

'Red Spangles' has purplish-green leaves and blood-red flowers.

Hibiscus moscheutos

HARDINESS
Frost hardy.

HEIGHT AND SPREAD
1.2 m (4 ft) tall.
90 cm (3 ft) wide.

FLOWERING TIME
Late summer.

ROSE MALLOW

ROSE MALLOW IS A NATIVE OF SOUTHERN USA WITH SHOWY FLOWERS IN WHITE, PINK, SALMON AND RED.

Description A shrub-like plant that grows from a thick, woody crown. The broad, oval leaves have three to five shallow lobes. The large, showy 15–20-cm (6–8-in) flowers have five pleated, white petals that surround a central, fuzzy column. The flowers have bright red centres.

Ideal position Full sun in a sheltered site.

Ideal soil conditions Evenly moist, humus-rich soil.

Cultivation Space young plants 60 cm (2 ft) apart. Clumps dislike disturbance. In cold regions grow as conservatory or greenhouse plants.

Propagation Take cuttings in summer. Remove the flower buds and cut the leaves back by one-half to reduce water loss. Seed mixtures such as 'Galaxy' are available. Soak seed before planting.

Pest and disease prevention No serious pests or diseases.

Design tips They make great accent plants and are lovely in borders with ornamental grasses and in containers.

Hosta hybrids

HARDINESS
Hardy.

HEIGHT AND
SPREAD
15–90 cm
(6–36 in) tall.
15–150 cm
(6–60 in) wide.

FLOWERING TIME
Mainly summer.

OTHER COMMON
NAMES
Plantain lily

HOSTA

HOSTAS MAKE EXCELLENT COMPANIONS FOR
SPRING BULBS BECAUSE THE LEAVES FILL THE
SPACE LEFT WHEN BULBS FINISH FLOWERING.

Description Hostas are indispensable
foliage plants for shady gardens.
Their thick, pleated or puckered
leaves grow from stout crowns with
thick, fleshy roots. Lavender, purple
or white flowers are carried on
slender spikes. Individual flowers
have three petals and three petal-
like sepals.

Ideal position Light shade. Will
survive in full shade. Filtered sun
encourages the best leaf colour in
the gold- and blue-leaved forms.
All hostas need protection from hot
sun. Variegated and yellow-leaved
cultivars are particularly susceptible
to leaf scorch.

Ideal soil conditions Evenly moist,
humus-rich soil.

Cultivation Hostas take several
years to reach mature form and
size, especially the large-leaved
cultivars. Allow ample room when
planting to accommodate their
ultimate size. New shoots are slow
to emerge in spring, so take care
not to damage them during spring
tidying. Plant small bulbs such as
snowdrops *Galanthus* spp. and
squills *Scilla* spp. around the
clumps to mark their location.

Propagation Divide in early spring.

Hostas come in a range of leaf and flower colours.

Pest and disease prevention Set beer traps to drown slugs and snails; use a barrier of wood ash or sand around each plant; or use a biological control such as nematodes.

Design tips Use the smaller cultivars to edge beds or as ground cover under shrubs and trees. Choose taller forms for creating drama in a mixed planting or alone as accent plants. Plant hostas with ferns, sedges *Carex* spp. and shade perennials.

Cultivars Hundreds of cultivars of this popular foliage plant are available; only a few are listed below.

'August Moon' has large, golden-yellow leaves.

'Francee' is medium-sized with white-edged, deep green leaves.

'Golden Tiara' is small to medium with gold-edged leaves.

'Honeybells' has fragrant, white flowers tinged with violet and large, glossy, green leaves.

'Royal Standard' has medium-sized, glossy, green leaves and fragrant, white flowers.

'Sum and Substance' has huge, golden yellow leaves.

H. sieboldiara var. *elegans* has elegant blue-grey leaves and white flowers.

Iberis sempervirens   CRUCIFERAE/BRASSICACEAE

HARDINESS
Hardy.

HEIGHT AND
SPREAD
15–30 cm
(6–12 in) tall.
30–45 cm
(1–1½ ft) wide.

FLOWERING TIME
Late spring and
early summer.

PERENNIAL CANDYTUFT

GIVE CANDYTUFT WELL-DRAINED SOIL AND
IT WILL REWARD YOU WITH MOUNDS OF
STUNNING, WHITE FLOWERS.

Description A sub-shrub with
persistent stems tightly clothed in
3.5-cm (1½-in), narrow, deep green
leaves. Plants grow from fibrous-
rooted crowns. The tight, rounded
clusters consist of many 6-mm (¼-in),
four-petalled flowers.

Ideal position Full sun.

Ideal soil conditions Average to
humus-rich, well-drained soil.

Cultivation Space plants 30–45 cm
(1–1½ ft) apart in informal plantings
or 15 cm (6 in) apart for edging.

Cut back after flowering to promote
compact growth.

Propagation Take semi-ripe cuttings
in early summer.

Pest and disease prevention No
serious pests or diseases.

Design tips Use to edge plantings,
paths or walls. Plant in rock gardens.

Cultivars 'Snowflake' has delightfully
large, white flower clusters on
20–25-cm (8–10-in) stems.

Impatiens New Guinea hybrids

HARDINESS
Tender.

HEIGHT AND SPREAD
30 cm (12 in) tall.
35–40 cm
(14–16 in) wide.

FLOWERING TIME
Late spring to early autumn.

NEW GUINEA BUSY LIZZIE

NEW GUINEA BUSY LIZZIES, LIKE THEIR
ANNUAL RELATIVES, MAKE EXCELLENT
CONTAINER PLANTS.

Description Upright, mounded plants.
Their pointed, green leaves can be
brilliantly variegated in red, cream
or bronze. The 5-cm (2-in) wide, flat
flowers come in a variety of colours,
including orange, red, purple, pink
and lavender. They are perennial in
very mild, frost-free areas but are
usually grown as annuals.

Ideal position Sun to partial shade.

Ideal soil conditions Average to
moist, well-drained soil with added
organic matter.

Cultivation Provide a sheltered
position and ample moisture. Tip-
prune young plants to form neat,
well-rounded, shrubby growth.

Propagation Buy young plants and
set them out 30–45 cm (1–1½ ft)
apart in late spring. Take cuttings in
late summer and pot up rooted
cuttings in autumn; keep in a sunny
window until the following spring.

Pest and disease prevention No
serious pests or diseases.

Design tips Enjoy the showy leaves
and jewel-like flowers in beds,
borders and containers.

Impatiens walleriana

HARDINESS
Tender.

HEIGHT AND
SPREAD
15–60 cm
(6–24 in) tall.
15–60 cm
(6–24 in) wide.

FLOWERING TIME
Early summer until
mid-autumn.

BUSY LIZZIE

BUSY LIZZIES ARE POPULAR FOR POTS, WINDOW
BOXES AND HANGING BASKETS AND ADD
COLOUR TO SHADY AREAS.

Description Busy Lizzies are tender
perennials also grown as tender
annuals. Plants form neat, shrubby
mounds of well-branched, succulent
stems. The lance-shaped, green or
bronze-brown leaves have slightly
scalloped edges. The plants are
covered with flat, spurred flowers
over a long period.

Ideal position Partial to full shade.

Ideal soil conditions Average to
moist, well-drained soil with added
organic matter.

Cultivation Keep well watered and
tip-prune young plants to produce
well-rounded, bushy plants.

Propagation Cuttings strike easily
in warmer months. Sow seed indoors
in a warm place in spring. Maintain
a steady temperature and keep moist
until seedlings appear. Set plants out
in early summer.

Pest and disease prevention No
serious pests or diseases.

Design tips Impatiens are the stars
of shady gardens. Mix them with
other annuals and perennials in
beds and borders.

Incarvillea delavayi

HARDINESS
Hardy.

HEIGHT AND
SPREAD
45–60 cm
(1½–2 ft) tall.
45 cm
(1½ ft) wide.

FLOWERING TIME
Late spring and
early summer.

INCARVILLEA

COMBINE THESE EXOTIC-LOOKING PLANTS
WITH CANDYTUFT AND SEDUM IN BORDERS.

Description Showy plants with 30-cm
(1-ft), pinnately divided leaves. They
are slow to emerge in spring. The
5–7.5-cm (2–3-in), tubular, rose-pink
flowers have flat, five-petalled faces.
They are borne in clusters 30–45 cm
(1–1½ ft) above the foliage. The
seed pods are attractive.

Ideal position Full sun in an open
position.

Ideal soil conditions Average to
humus-rich, well-drained soil.

Cultivation Easy to grow. Mulch
plants to protect them in areas with
very hard frosts.

Propagation Sow seed in late winter
or spring in a warm place. Keep the
soil moist and cover with clear
plastic wrap to encourage humidity.
Seedlings will soon develop. Divide
large plants in spring or autumn.

Pest and disease prevention Slugs
and snails may attack these plants.

Design tips Plant with spring- and
summer-flowering perennials for a
stunning flower display.

Iris spp.

HARDINESS
Hardy.

HEIGHT AND
SPREAD
30–90 cm
(1–3 ft) tall.
30–60 cm
(1–2 ft) wide.

FLOWERING TIME
Early to mid-
summer; some
cultivars may
flower again.

IRIS

THE STRAPLIKE FOLIAGE AND GRACEFUL
FLOWERS OF IRISES COMBINE WELL WITH
ROUNDED PERENNIALS SUCH AS PEONIES.

Description Plants form tight fans of narrow, swordlike leaves from slow-creeping rhizomes. Flowers range in colour from pure white, cream and yellow to all shades of blue, violet and purple. Some cultivars come close to true red. The flowers have three segments, called "falls," which ring the outside of the flowers. They are usually reflexed downward and bear a central white or yellow blaze. The centre has three slender segments called "standards." They are often upright but can also be flat or reflexed.

Ideal position Full sun to partial shade.

Ideal soil conditions Evenly moist, humus-rich soil.

Cultivation Irises are easy-care perennials. They thrive for many years without division. If flowering begins to wane or plants outgrow their position, divide and re-plant into soil that has been enriched with organic matter.

Propagation Divide plants in autumn or spring. Seed collected from cultivars will be variable and often inferior to the parent plant. Contact with the sap may irritate skin.

Pest and disease prevention *Iris sibirica* is usually trouble free.

Siberian iris *Iris sibirica*

Bearded irises can suffer from rot if the soil is too wet; excess moisture in the soil may also cause leaf spot.

Design tips Plant in formal or informal gardens with perennials, ornamental grasses and ferns. Combine with rounded perennials such as peonies and cranesbills *Geranium* spp. beside ponds. Ferns, hostas, primroses and astilbes are good companions.

Cultivars 'Butter and Sugar' has creamy white and yellow flowers on 60-cm (2 ft) stems.

'Ego' has rich blue, ruffled flowers on 75-cm (2½-ft) stems.

'Flight of Butterflies' has bright-blue, heavily veined flowers on 90-cm (36-in) stems

'Orville Fay' is medium blue with 90-cm (3-ft) stems.

'Perry's Blue' has pale-blue flowers with traditional form.

Other species Bearded Hybrids (pictured opposite) are even more popular than Siberian irises. They have showy, fragrant flowers with wide, bearded falls and wide, upright stands. Plants range in size from about 30 cm (12 in) to over 70 cm (28 in) tall. They like moderately fertile soil with good drainage and a sunny spot. Hundreds of cultivars are available. Some of the best include 'Brown Lasso', with ruffled, butterscotch flowers, 'Jane Phillips', with sky-blue flowers and 'Superstition', with indigo, almost black flowers.

Iris continued

Japanese iris *Iris ensata*

I. cristata, crested iris, is a 6-cm (3-in) spring woodland iris with sky-blue flowers. Prefers semi-shade.

I. ensata, Japanese iris (pictured above), is a very pretty iris with lovely blue or purple flowers. Many stunning cultivars are available with flattened flowers up to 20 cm (8 in) across. Prefers moist soil and full sun.

I. pseudacorus, yellow flag, is a stout 90–120-cm (3–4-ft) iris with bright yellow flowers. Grows well in full sun to partial shade. Thrives in moist soil or shallow water.

I. tectorum, crested iris, is a short, stout 30–45-cm (1–1½-ft) iris with delicate, flattened, spotted lilac-blue flowers. Prefers a sheltered warm spot and moist soil.

I. versicolor, blue flag iris, is a tall 45–90-cm (1½–3-ft) iris with purple-blue flowers. Likes moist soil or shallow water.

Kniphofia uvaria and hybrids

HARDINESS
Hardy.

HEIGHT AND
SPREAD
90–150 cm
(3–5 ft) tall.
60–120 cm
(2–4 ft) wide.

FLOWERING TIME
Summer.

OTHER COMMON
NAMES
Torch lily.

RED-HOT POKER

THE BOLD, VERTICAL FORM OF RED-HOT
POKER ADDS DRAMATIC ACCENTS TO
PERENNIAL BORDERS AND ROCK GARDENS.

Description Red-hot poker is a
commanding perennial from South
Africa with tufts of narrow, evergreen
leaves from a fleshy, rooted crown.
Long, slender spikes consist of tightly
packed, tubular flowers. The lowest
on the spike are yellow-white and
the upper ones are red.

Ideal position Full sun. Established
plants may be quite drought-tolerant.

Ideal soil conditions Deep, humus-
rich, well-drained soil.

Cultivation Set out young plants
60–75 cm (2–2½ ft) apart. Leave
established plants undisturbed.
Plants increase to form broad,
floriferous clumps. Mulch young
plants over winter.

Propagation Divide clumps in spring.
Sow seed in late winter in a warm
place at a depth of 6 mm (¼ in).
Keep in a light place and don't allow
the surface of the compost to dry
out. Grow on in cooler conditions
and plant out after all risk of frost.

Pest and disease prevention Provide
excellent drainage for *Kniphofia*
hybrids to avoid crown rot.

Red-hot poker continued

Kniphofia hybrid

Design tips The bold, vertical form of red-hot pokers adds excitement to perennial borders and rock gardens. Combine with ornamental grasses, wormwoods *Artemisia* spp., dahlias and other summer perennials.

Hybrids 'Ice Queen' grows to 1.05 m (3½ ft) tall with a spread to 1.05 m (3½ ft) . It has lovely, green, budded flowers, which open to pale yellow.

'Little Maid' is a dwarf form that grows to 60 cm (2 ft) with pale green buds opening to cream-coloured flowers.

'Percy's Pride' is a taller-growing cultivar, to 90 cm (3 ft), with pale yellow flowers.

'Royal Standard', a striking bi-colour, grows to 1.2 m (4 ft) with spikes of fat red buds that open and age to lemon-yellow.

Lavandula angustifolia

HARDINESS
Hardy.

HEIGHT AND SPREAD
60 cm (2 ft) tall.
60–90 cm
(2–3 ft) wide.

FLOWERING TIME
Early to late summer.

ENGLISH LAVENDER

ENGLISH LAVENDER IS A COMPACT, VERY FRAGRANT PLANT WITH FLOWERS THAT ATTRACT BEES.

Description Grey-green leaves clothe soft, hairy stems topped with spikes of purple-blue flowers. The 12-mm (½-in) fragrant flowers are carried in tight, narrow clusters.

Ideal position Full sun. Extremely drought-tolerant.

Ideal soil conditions Average, well-drained soil.

Cultivation Cut back flower stems in autumn and, in mild areas, trim back the foliage but do not cut into old wood. In colder areas, trim back in spring.

Propagation Take tip cuttings in summer.

Pest and disease prevention No serious pests or diseases.

Design tips Plant lavender in ornamental, wildlife-friendly and herb gardens. Also use as an edging plant. In borders, combine with other plants that need excellent drainage, such as yarrows.

Cultivars 'Hidcote' grows 60 cm (2 ft) tall with dark purple flowers.
'Rosea' has pale pink flowers.
'Munstead' has lavender-blue flowers on 45-cm (1½ ft) plants.
'Twickel Purple' has purple flowers on 60-cm (2-ft) plants.

Leucanthemum x superbum

HARDINESS
Hardy.

HEIGHT AND SPREAD
30–90 cm
(1–3 ft) tall.
60 cm (2 ft) wide.

FLOWERING TIME
Throughout summer.

SHASTA DAISY

SHASTA DAISY IS A ROBUST, SHOWY PLANT. COMBINE WITH OTHER SUMMER-BLOOMING PERENNIALS SUCH AS DAYLILIES AND IRISES.

Description Has dense clusters of shiny, 25-cm (10-in), deep green, toothed leaves and short, creeping, fibrous-rooted stems. Bright white, 7.5-cm (3-in) daisies with large, bright yellow centres are carried on stout, leafy stems. Double-flowered cultivars are available.

Ideal position Full sun but tolerates light shade.

Ideal soil conditions Average to rich, well-drained soil. Dislikes very dry or waterlogged soil.

Cultivation Shasta daisies are easy-care perennials. Deadhead plants to promote continued flowering. Plants grow quickly, often outgrowing allotted space. Divide and replant clumps in organically enriched soil every 2–3 years to keep them vigorous and free-flowering.

Propagation Divide in early spring or late summer.

Pest and disease prevention No serious pests or diseases.

Design tips Plant shasta daisies with blanket flowers *Gaillardia* spp. and coreopsis.

Liatris spicata

HARDINESS
Hardy.

HEIGHT AND
SPREAD
60–120 cm
(2–4 ft) tall.
30–60 cm
(1–2 ft) wide.

FLOWERING TIME
Late summer.

OTHER COMMON
NAMES
Blazing star.

GAY FEATHER

SPIKY GAY FEATHER IS A STRIKING PERENNIAL WITH FLOWERHEADS THAT, UNUSUALLY, OPEN FROM TOP TO BOTTOM.

Description The erect stems arise from basal tufts of grass-like, medium green foliage. Plants grow from a fat corm. Rose-purple flowers are carried on slender flower spikes in small heads that are crowded together into dense spikes. Large clumps may need staking.

Ideal position Full sun. Plants tend to flop in partial shade.

Ideal soil conditions Average to humus-rich, moist soil.

Cultivation Clumps increase slowly and seldom need division.

Propagation Divide plants in spring. Sow seed outdoors in autumn.

Pest and disease prevention No serious pests or diseases.

Design tips Lovely in perennial gardens and meadow plantings. Combine with purple coneflowers *Echinacea purpurea*, coreopsis and with ornamental grasses.

Cultivars 'Kobold' is a popular cultivar with rose pink flowers on 45–75-cm (1½–2½-ft) stems. It flowers earlier in summer and may repeat flower if deadheaded.

Ligularia dentata

HARDINESS
Hardy.

HEIGHT AND
SPREAD
1.2–1.5 m
(4–5 ft) tall.
90 cm (3 ft) wide.

FLOWERING TIME
Late summer.

LIGULARIA

LIGULARIA IS A DRAMATIC ACCENT PLANT
FOR MOIST SOIL. IT COMBINES WELL WITH
SPIKY PLANTS.

Description Ligularia has impressive
30–60-cm (1–2-ft), round or kidney-
shaped leaves on long stalks. Plants
grow from stout crowns with fleshy
roots. The 12.5-cm (5-in) bright
orange-yellow flowers, carried in
open clusters, are like spidery daisies.

Ideal position Light to partial shade.

Ideal soil conditions Consistently
moist, humus-rich soil. Plants do
not tolerate dry soil.

Cultivation The leaves lose water
rapidly. In heat, they can wilt but
they recover as temperatures cool.

The plants form big clumps but
don't need frequent division.

Propagation Lift clumps in early
spring or autumn and cut crowns
apart. Replant into enriched soil.

Pest and disease prevention Slugs
may be a problem.

Design tips Ligularias are bold plants.
Use beside ponds or with ferns,
astilbes, hostas, irises and grasses.

Cultivars 'Desdemona' has purple
spring leaves, which fade to green,
with purple undersides.

Lobelia cardinalis

HARDINESS
Frost-hardy.

HEIGHT AND SPREAD
60–90 cm
(2–3 ft) tall.
30–60 cm
(1–2 ft) wide.

FLOWERING TIME
Mid- to late summer.

CARDINAL FLOWER

THE BRILLIANT, SCARLET BLOOMS OF CARDINAL FLOWER MAKE AN EYE-CATCHING ADDITION TO ANY BORDER WITH MOIST SOIL.

Description Has fiery-coloured flower spikes on leafy stems and grows from a fibrous-rooted crown. The lance-shaped leaves may be green or red-bronze. Brilliant scarlet tubular flowers have three lower and two upper petals.

Ideal position Full sun to partial shade.

Ideal soil conditions Evenly moist, humus-rich soil.

Cultivation Cardinal flowers are shallow-rooted. Where winters are cold, mulch plants to protect the crowns. Replant in spring if frost has lifted the crowns. May be short-lived, but self-sows prolifically. Contact with the sap may irritate skin.

Propagation Divide in late autumn or spring. Sow the fine seed, uncovered, indoors in late winter.

Pest and disease prevention Virus diseases spread by aphids may be a problem.

Design tips Cardinal flowers look attractive around pools or in informal plantings. Combine them with irises, hostas and ferns.

Cultivars 'Bee's Flame' has stunning, bright crimson flowers and dark red leaves.

Lupinus hybrids

PAPILIONACEAE

LUPIN

SPIKY LUPIN FLOWERS, IN MANY COLOURS,
OFFER CHEERFUL VERTICAL ACCENTS IN
EARLY-SUMMER BORDERS.

Description Has dramatic flower
spikes on stout stems with large,
palmately divided leaves. Plants
grow from thick roots. The 18-mm
(¾-in) pealike flowers come in a
range of colours and are crowded
into bold, towering spikes.

Ideal position Full sun to light shade.

Ideal soil conditions Well-drained,
neutral to acid soil. Dislike dry
conditions in spring but will not
tolerate winter wet.

Cultivation Lupins flower best in
a sunny spot and can be cut back
after the first flush to provide
a few more late-summer blooms.
They are often short-lived.

Propagation Sow seed inside in a
warm place in late winter. Before
sowing, soak seeds overnight or
"chip" them by nicking the hard
coat. Seeds are available that will
flower in their first year from sowing.

Pest and disease prevention No
serious pests or diseases.

Design tips Plant lupins with other
cottage-garden perennials such as
columbines *Aquilegia* spp. and
cranesbills *Geranium* spp.

Lychnis coronaria

HARDINESS
Hardy.

HEIGHT AND SPREAD
60–90 cm
(2–3 ft) tall.
30–45 cm
(1–1½ ft) wide.

FLOWERING TIME
Summer.

ROSE CAMPION

THE SOFT, SILVERY LEAVES AND SHOCKING-PINK FLOWERS OF ROSE CAMPION ADD EXCITEMENT TO BEDS AND BORDERS.

Description The deep pink, five-petalled flowers are carried in branched clusters atop long, grey, woolly stems. Leaves are covered in "wool".

Ideal position Full sun.

Ideal soil conditions Well-drained soil. Avoid sites that are wet in winter.

Cultivation Divide clumps every 2–3 years in spring to keep the plants vigorous. Plants may be short-lived, but self-sown seedlings are numerous.

Propagation Sow seed outdoors as soon as ripe or remove small crowns from the edge of the clump in spring.

Pest and disease prevention No serious pests or diseases.

Design tips Plant rose campion in formal and informal beds and borders or in rock gardens. Use the strong-coloured flowers to spice up a subdued scheme of blues and pale yellows. Combine with catmints *Nepeta* spp., cranesbills *Geranium* spp. and blue-leaved grasses. Plant in colour combinations with yarrows and marguerites *Argyranthemum frutescens*.

Macleaya cordata

PAPAVERACEAE

HARDINESS
Hardy.

HEIGHT AND SPREAD
1.5–2.5 m
(5–8 ft) tall.
1.2 m (4 ft) or
more wide.

FLOWERING TIME
Summer.

PLUME POPPY

PLUME POPPY LOOKS DRAMATIC IN CLUMPS AT
THE BACK OF BORDERS WITH TALL PERENNIALS.

Description The imposing plume poppy is shrub-like in stature with 25-cm (10-in) lobed leaves clothing erect stems. Plants grow from stout, creeping roots and quickly become invasive. The 30-cm (1-ft) plumes consist of small, cream flowers that give way to showy, flat, rose-coloured seedpods.

Ideal position Full sun to partial shade. Stems are not as sturdy on shade-grown plants.

Ideal soil conditions Moist, well-drained, average to humus-rich soil.

Cultivation Established clumps of plume poppy can double in size each season. Control is inevitably necessary to avert a total takeover. Chop off the creeping roots with a spade as soon as you see new stems emerging.

Propagation Remove new offsets in summer or take stem cuttings.

Pest and disease prevention No serious pests or diseases.

Design tips Place plume poppies at the rear of borders where there is ample room for them to grow. A mature clump is a lovely sight.

Mertensia virginica syn. *M. pulmonarioides*   BORAGINACEAE

HARDINESS
Hardy.

HEIGHT AND
SPREAD
30–60 cm
(1–2 ft) tall.
30–60 cm
(1–2 ft) wide.

FLOWERING TIME
Spring.

VIRGINIA BLUEBELL

PLANT THIS NORTH AMERICAN PERENNIAL IN
A WOODLAND GARDEN WITH SPRING BULBS.

Description Virginia bluebells bear
lovely, graceful, spring flowers on
arching stems clothed with thin,
blue-green leaves. Plants grow from
thick roots and go dormant after
flowering. Nodding, sky-blue bells
open from pink buds. The flowers
are attractive to bees.

Ideal position Partial shade.

Ideal soil conditions Consistently
moist, well-drained, humus-rich soil.

Cultivation Virginia bluebells emerge
early in spring and go dormant soon
after flowering so can leave gaps in
plantings. Place them where you
will not dig them up by accident.

Propagation Divide large clumps
after flowering in spring. Leave at
least one bud per division. Sow
seed when fresh.

Pest and disease prevention No
serious pests or diseases.

Design tips Interplant clumps of
Virginia bluebells with foliage plants
such as ferns and hostas to fill gaps
left by still-dormant plants.

Miscanthus sinensis

HARDINESS
Hardy.

HEIGHT AND
SPREAD
90–150 cm
(3–5 ft) tall.
90 cm (3 ft)
wide or more.

FLOWERING TIME
Late summer and
early autumn.

SILVER GRASS

SILVER GRASS IS ONE OF THE BEST LARGE
ORNAMENTAL GRASSES. ITS FLOWERHEADS
ARE ATTRACTIVE IN AUTUMN.

Description Large clumps of long,
pointed, sharp-edged leaves. Flower
plumes above the foliage are in hues
from silver to reddish purple.

Ideal position Full sun.

Ideal soil conditions Light, moist,
humus-rich soil. Protect from
excessive winter wet.

Cultivation Set container-grown
plants 60–120 cm (2–4 ft) apart
in spring. Divide in spring when
clumps begin to die in the centre.

Propagation By seed or division.

Pest and disease prevention No
serious pests or diseases.

Design tips Combine with asters
and goldenrod *Solidago* spp. to
create a stunning autumn show.

Cultivars 'Cabaret' grows to 1.8 m
(6 ft); its leaves have white stripes
in the centre. The flowers bloom
pink in autumn, then become
cream coloured.

'Morning Light', one of the best
cultivars, grows to 1.2 m (4 ft) with
narrow, white-edged leaves and
reddish bronze autumn flowers that
later turn a cream colour.

Monarda didyma

HARDINESS
Hardy.

HEIGHT AND SPREAD
60–90 cm
(2–3 ft) tall.
60 cm (2 ft) wide.

FLOWERING TIME
Summer to early autumn.

OTHER COMMON NAMES
Bergamot.

BEE BALM

BEE BALM'S LOVELY FLOWERS ADD COLOUR TO THE SUMMER GARDEN AND ATTRACT BEES. THE LEAVES ARE AROMATIC.

Description Sturdy flower stems grow from fast-creeping runners. Tight heads of tubular, red flowers are surrounded by a whorl of coloured leafy bracts.

Ideal position Full sun to partial shade.

Ideal soil conditions Evenly moist, well-drained, humus-rich soil. Protect from excessive winter wet.

Cultivation Plants can spread quickly. Divide every 2–3 years.

Propagation Divide in spring. Sow seed in spring.

Pest and disease prevention Powdery mildew causes white blotches on the foliage and may cover the entire plant. Thin the stems to allow good air circulation. Cut affected plants to the ground.

Design tips Plant in mixed and wildlife-friendly borders.

Cultivars 'Blue Stocking' has very pretty violet flowers.
'Cambridge Scarlet' (pictured above) has brilliant scarlet flowers.
'Mahogany' has ruby-red flowers.
'Marshall's Delight' is a mildew-resistant pink.
'Prairie Night' is dark lilac.
'Snow Queen' is creamy white.

Nepeta spp.

HARDINESS
Hardy.

HEIGHT AND SPREAD
45–90 cm
(1½–3 ft) tall.
60–90 cm
(2–3 ft) wide.

FLOWERING TIME
Early to late summer.

CATMINT

CATMINT'S SPIKES OF DAINTY, VIOLET-BLUE FLOWERS ARE PERFECT FOR EDGING PATHS, AND FOR BEDS OR BORDERS.

Description The wiry stems are clothed in soft, hairy, grey-green, oval leaves and grow from fibrous-rooted crowns. Violet-blue, terminal flower clusters are carried in whorls on slender spikes.

Ideal position Full sun.

Ideal soil conditions Average to humus-rich, well-drained soil. Plants also tolerate poor, dry soil.

Cultivation Clumps get quite leggy after flowering. Trim flower stalks to encourage fresh growth and repeat flowering.

Propagation Divide in spring or autumn. Take cuttings in summer.

Pest and disease prevention No serious pests or diseases. Cats find the plants irresistible and may destroy them.

Design tips In borders, combine with bellflowers *Campanula* spp., cranesbills *Geranium* spp., coreopsis and ornamental grasses.

Cultivars 'Six Hills Giant' has deep purple-blue flowers.

Other species *N. racemosa* grows to 30–45 cm (1–1½ ft) tall. Lavender-blue flowers cover the plants for a long period. 'Snowflake' has white flowers.

Oenothera speciosa

HARDINESS
Hardy.

HEIGHT AND SPREAD
30–60 cm (1–2 ft) tall. 60 cm (2 ft) or more wide.

FLOWERING TIME
Late spring and early summer.

WHITE EVENING PRIMROSE

THIS EVENING PRIMROSE LOOKS WONDERFUL EN MASSE IN LOW-MAINTENANCE AREAS SUCH AS DRY, SUNNY SLOPES.

Description Evening primroses spread by underground runners. They flower during the day, unlike the many night-blooming species of the *Oenothera* genus. White, cup-shaped flowers, 5 cm (2 in) across, fade to soft pink and turn toward the sun. Varieties are available that are night-scented.

Ideal position Full sun to very light shade.

Ideal soil conditions Well-drained, average soil.

Cultivation Set plants about 60 cm (2 ft) apart in spring or autumn. Plant where the spread won't become a problem as plants will self-seed readily.

Propagation Propagate by division in early spring or autumn after flowering.

Pest and disease prevention No serious pests or diseases.

Design tips Grow in drifts and in cottage-garden schemes.

Cultivars 'Rosea' grows to 37.5 cm (15 in) and has clear pink, 7.5-cm (3-in) flowers.

Paeonia lactiflora hybrids

HARDINESS
Hardy.

HEIGHT AND SPREAD
45–90 cm
(1½–3 ft) tall.
90 cm (3 ft) wide.

FLOWERING TIME
Early summer.

PEONY

COMBINE THE LOVELY GARDEN PEONY WITH EARLY LILIES IN BEDS AND BORDERS OR USE THEM IN MASS PLANTINGS.

Description Shrub-like with sturdy stalks clothed in shiny green leaves. Plants grow from thick, fleshy roots and may be very long-lived. Flowers range in colour from white, cream and yellow to pink, rose, burgundy and scarlet and may be single, semi-double or double.

Ideal position Full sun to light shade.

Ideal soil conditions Moist, humus-rich soil. Good drainage is important. Will not tolerate being waterlogged.

Cultivation Plant container-grown peonies in autumn. Do not plant too deeply, especially in heavy soils. Plant bare-root plants in spring; they may establish better than container-grown plants. Feed in autumn. Taller selections and those with double flowers may need staking. Plants may grow undisturbed for years but if roots become too crowded, flowering will wane. Lift plants in autumn, divide the roots, leaving four or five eyes (buds) per division, and re-plant about 5 cm (2 in) below the surface into soil that has been enriched with organic matter.

Propagation Divide in autumn.

Pest and disease prevention Spray or dust foliage with an organically

Peonies with single and semi-double flowers may be more resistant to wind damage.

acceptable fungicide such as sulphur or bordeaux mix to discourage the fungal disease botrytis.

Design tips Early-summer perennials such as irises, foxgloves *Digitalis* spp., columbines *Aquilegia* spp. and early lilies are excellent companions.

Cultivars There are many cultivars available in a range of different colours and forms.

'Duchess de Nemours' is an early white double.

'Bowl of Beauty' is a large, pink to red-tinted form with a dense central cluster of white to cream stamens.

'Gay Paree' has cerise-and-white flowers.

'Kansas' has magenta-purple petals and is a sturdy plant.

'Sara Bernhardt' is a fragrant, rose-pink double-flowered form.

'Sea Shell' is a tall, pink single-flowered form.

'Whitleyi Major' has fragrant, pure white flowers.

Papaver orientale

HARDINESS
Hardy.

HEIGHT AND
SPREAD
60–90 cm
(2–3 ft) tall.
60–90 cm
(2–3 ft) wide.

FLOWERING TIME
Early summer.

ORIENTAL POPPY

ORIENTAL POPPIES ARE PRIZED FOR THEIR
COLOURFUL, CRÊPE-PAPER-LIKE FLOWERS.
PLANT THEM WITH BORDER PERENNIALS.

Description Plants produce rosettes
of coarse, hairy, lobed foliage from
a thick taproot. The 7.5–10-cm
(3–4-in) flowers have crinkled,
scarlet-red petals, often with black
blotches at their base.

Ideal position Full sun. Established
plants are tough and long-lived.

Ideal soil conditions Average, well-
drained, humus-rich soil.

Cultivation Plants may need support
as clumps can flop, especially after
rain. Self-seeds freely.

Propagation Take root cuttings
in winter.

Pest and disease prevention No
serious pests or diseases.

Design tips Combine with
ornamental grasses and bushy
plants such as catmints *Nepeta* spp.
or asters.

Cultivars 'Beauty of Livermere' has
deep crimson flowers with a large
black blotch.
   'Karine' has shell-pink single
flowers.
   'Patty's Plum' has ruffled, purple
petals.
   'Perry's White' has large, white
flowers with overlapping petals.

Penstemon barbatus

SCROPHULARIACEAE

HARDINESS
Varies from hardy
to frost-hardy.

HEIGHT AND
SPREAD
45–90 cm
(1½–3 ft) tall.
30–60 cm
(1–2 ft) wide.

FLOWERING TIME
Cultivars flower
from summer into
autumn.

PENSTEMON

COMBINE PENSTEMON'S FOXGLOVE-LIKE
SPIRES WITH ROUNDED PLANTS SUCH AS
CRANESBILLS, YARROWS AND HEUCHERAS.

Description This North and Central
American plant has erect flower
spikes clothed in shiny, broadly
lance-shaped leaves. Flowering
stems and basal foliage rosettes
grow from fibrous-rooted crowns.
It has 2.5–3.5-cm (1–1½-in), irregular,
tubular pink flowers. Seed mixes
of this species with a wider range
of colours are available.

Ideal position Full sun to light shade.

Ideal soil conditions Average to
humus-rich, well-drained soil. Good
drainage and shelter are essential
for success.

Cultivation In their native habitat,
plants form dense clumps with
maturity. Hardiness varies with
cultivars and in areas with cold
winters, a dry winter mulch is
advised. Cultivars may be short-lived.
Deadhead regularly.

Propagation Sow seed indoors in
winter after pre-chilling the seeds.
Seedlings may flower the first year.

Pest and disease prevention No
serious pests or diseases.

Design tips Plant penstemons in
mixed borders, and smaller forms in
rock gardens. Cultivars are suitable
for containers.

Penstemon continued

Penstemon digitalis 'Husker Red' with dark-red foliage.

Cultivars 'Cambridge Mixed' are compact plants in shades of pink, blue and purple.

'Elfin Pink' has bright pink flowers on 30-cm (1-ft) stems.

'Jingle Bells' has bright scarlet flowers on 1.2-m (4-ft) stems.

Other species *P. digitalis*, foxglove penstemon, has 75–150-cm (2½–5-ft) tall stems with clusters of 2.5-cm (1-in), white flowers and shiny, deep green leaves. Plants thrive in moist soil. 'Husker Red' (pictured above) has deep ruby-red leaves.

P. hirsutus, hairy penstemon, is a fuzzy form with purple flowers. Var. 'Pygmaeus' is a dwarf selection only 12 cm (5 in) high.

P. pinifolius is a shrubby plant with small, scarlet flowers and stiff, needle-like leaves.

P. smallii, Small's penstemon, has dense clusters of rose-purple flowers. Plants prefer well-drained, dry soil and are often short-lived.

Hybrids Many hybrids of mixed origin are available.

'Alice Hindley' has delicate mauve flowers.

'Apple Blossom' has pale-pink flowers.

'Firebird' *P. Schoenholzeri* has scarlet flowers.

'Mother of Pearl' has pale purple flowers with veined throats.

Perovskia atriplicifolia

HARDINESS
Hardy.

HEIGHT AND SPREAD
90–120 cm
(3–4 ft) tall.
30–60 cm
(1–2 ft) wide.

FLOWERING TIME
Late summer to early autumn.

RUSSIAN SAGE

THE AIRY, GREY FLOWER BUDS AND SOFT BLUE FLOWERS MIX WELL WITH YELLOW, PINK, DEEP-BLUE AND PURPLE FLOWERS.

Description A shrubby, branching perennial with erect stems clothed in grey-green, deeply lobed leaves. Plants grow from fibrous-rooted crowns. Small, irregularly shaped, blue flowers are carried in profusion on slender sprays.

Ideal position Full sun.

Ideal soil conditions Average to poor, well-drained soil. Good drainage is essential for success.

Cultivation The stems of Russian sage can become very bushy and woody. Prune back hard to a low framework in spring.

Propagation Take stem cuttings in early summer.

Pest and disease prevention No serious pests or diseases.

Design tips Plant towards the middle or back of borders. Combine with yarrow, gay feather *Liatris* spp., balloon flower *Platycodon grandiflorus*, sedum, phlox and ornamental grasses.

Cultivars 'Blue Spire' has violet-blue flowers on strong, upright stems up to 1.2 m (4 ft) tall.

HARDINESS
Hardy.

HEIGHT AND
SPREAD
25–38 cm
(10–15 in) tall.
30–60 cm
(1–2 ft) wide.

FLOWERING TIME
Late spring.

BLUE PHLOX

BLUE PHLOX LOOKS GREAT IN WOODLAND
GARDENS WITH SPRING BULBS, WILDFLOWERS
AND FERNS.

Description Blue phlox is a sweet-scented, woodland species with creeping stems clothed in evergreen, oval leaves. Plants have fibrous, white roots. Lavender-blue to sky-blue flowers are borne in open clusters, on upright stems.

Ideal position Partial shade.

Ideal soil conditions Evenly moist, humus-rich soil.

Cultivation Divide only if spreading over other plants.

Propagation Take cuttings in summer from non-flowering stems. Sow seed in autumn or spring.

Pest and disease prevention Powdery mildew may attack. Spray with sulphur to contain the disease.

Design tips Grows well around flowering shrubs as ground cover.

Hybrids *P.* 'Chattahoochee' has clusters of lavender-blue flowers with red eyes.

Other species *P. stolonifera*, creeping phlox, forms low mats of rounded foliage and upright spikes of blue or pink flowers similar to *P. divaricata*.

Phlox paniculata

HARDINESS
Hardy.

HEIGHT AND
SPREAD
90–120 cm
(3–4 ft) tall.
60 cm (2 ft) wide.

FLOWERING TIME
Mid- to late
summer.

PHLOX

PHLOX ARE BEAUTIFUL AND VERSATILE
GARDEN PERENNIALS. COMBINE WITH DAISIES,
BEE BALM AND PENSTEMONS.

Description Has domed clusters of
fragrant, richly coloured flowers atop
stiff, leafy stems. Plants grow from
fibrous-rooted crowns. Flowers range
from magenta to pink and white.

Ideal position Full sun to light shade.

Ideal soil conditions Moist but well-
drained, humus-rich soil.

Cultivation Divide clumps every
3–4 years to keep them vigorous.

Propagation Divide in spring. Take
stem cuttings late spring or early
summer and root cuttings in autumn.

Pest and disease prevention
Powdery mildew is the bane of
phlox growers. It causes white
patches on the leaves or, in bad
cases, turns entire leaves white.
To avoid problems, thin the stems
before plants bloom to increase air
circulation. Select resistant cultivars,
especially hybrids with *P. maculata*.

Design tips Perfect in mixed borders
and on the edges of lightly shaded
woodland gardens.

Cultivars Many selections are
available. They vary in their
flowering time, mildew resistance
and flower size.
    'Bright Eyes' is pink with
crimson eyes and is mildew-resistant.

Phlox continued

Phlox paniculata 'Mount Fuji' may repeat flower in late summer if deadheaded.

'Blue Paradise' has mid-blue flowers with a dark eye.

'David' has large heads of white flowers and is mildew-resistant.

'Mount Fuji' (pictured above) is a compact, late-summer white.

'Prospero' has lilac flowers with white-edged petals.

Other species *P. carolina* subsp. *angusta*, has glossy, oval leaves and elongated clusters of lavender, pink or white flowers in early summer. 'Bill Baker' has medium pink flowers. 'Miss Lingard' has white flowers with yellow eyes.

P. maculata, early phlox, is similar to *P. carolina* but the foliage is lance-shaped. 'Alpha' has rose-pink flowers with a darker eye. 'Omega' has white flowers with lilac-pink eyes.

Physostegia virginiana

HARDINESS
Hardy.

HEIGHT AND SPREAD
60–120 cm
(2–4 ft)tall.
60 cm (2 ft) wide.

FLOWERING TIME
Late summer.

OBEDIENT PLANT

PLANT CULTIVARS IN MIXED BORDERS WITH ASTER, GOLDENROD, PHLOX AND ORNAMENTAL GRASSES.

Description This perennial is named for the tendency of its flowers to remain in any position when shifted in their four-ranked clusters. Plants grow from creeping stems. The tubular, two-lipped flowers are rose-pink to lilac-pink.

Ideal position Full sun to light shade.

Ideal soil conditions Moist to wet, humus-rich soil.

Cultivation Tends to flop if the soil is too rich. Stake as necessary. Divide every 2–4 years to contain.

Propagation Divide in spring. Sow seed in autumn.

Pest and disease prevention No serious pests or diseases.

Design tips Use in formal beds, borders and cottage gardens. It is lovely in any informal planting.

Cultivars 'Rosea' has large, bright pink flowers on 1-m (3-ft) stems.
'Summer Snow' has white flowers on 1-m (3-ft) stems.
'Vivid' has pretty, vibrant, purple-pink flowers.

Platycodon grandiflorus

HARDINESS
Hardy.

HEIGHT AND SPREAD
60 cm (2 ft) tall.
30–60 cm
(1–2 ft) wide.

FLOWERING TIME
Summer.

BALLOON FLOWER

THE RICH BLUE BLOOMS OF BALLOON FLOWER
OPEN FROM CURIOUS, INFLATED BUDS. ENJOY
WITH OTHER SUMMER-BLOOMING PERENNIALS.

Description Balloon flowers are
showy, summer-blooming plants
with saucer-shaped flowers on
succulent stems clothed in toothed,
triangular leaves. Plants grow from
thick, fleshy roots. The rich blue
flowers have five-pointed petals.

Ideal position Full sun to light shade.

Ideal soil conditions Well-drained,
average to humus-rich soil that does
not dry out.

Cultivation New shoots are slow to
emerge. Take care not to damage
them. Remove spent flowers to
encourage bloom. Established
clumps dislike disturbance.

Propagation Divide clumps if
necessary, but regrowth may be poor.
Take basal cuttings with a piece of
crown attached. Sow seed outdoors
in autumn.

Pest and disease prevention No
serious pests or diseases.

Design tips Plant with summer
perennials such as yellow yarrows
Achillea spp., sages *Salvia* spp. and
bergamot *Monarda* spp.

Cultivars 'Apoyama Group' have blue-
violet flowers on 15-cm (6-in) plants.
'Shell Pink' has pale pink flowers
on 60-cm (2-ft) plants.

Polemonium caeruleum

HARDINESS
Hardy.

HEIGHT AND SPREAD
45–75 cm
(1½–2½ ft) tall.
30–45 cm
(1–1½ ft) wide.

FLOWERING TIME
Throughout summer.

JACOB'S LADDER

JACOB'S LADDER IS IMPRESSIVE WHEN USED IN NATURALISTIC AND COTTAGE GARDENS WITH ASTILBE, IRISES AND FERNS.

Description Jacob's ladder has tall, leafy stems crowned with loose clusters of nodding flowers. The showy leaves are pinnately divided with many leaflets. Plants grow from fibrous-rooted crowns, with saucer-shaped soft blue flowers.

Ideal position Full sun to partial shade.

Ideal soil conditions Evenly moist, humus-rich soil.

Cultivation Deadhead regularly to encourage further flowers. Plants seldom need division.

Propagation Sow seed outdoors in autumn. Self-sown seedlings may appear.

Pest and disease prevention No serious pests or diseases.

Design tips Plant in borders with *Aruncus dioicus*, phlox and ornamental grasses. Massed plantings are effective in wild gardens.

Varieties *P. caeruleum* var. *album* has white flowers.

Other species *P. reptans*, creeping Jacob's ladder, is a woodland plant with light blue flowers on 20–40-cm (8–16-in) stems. A good summer ground-cover plant.

Polygonatum odoratum　　　　　　　CONVALLARIACEAE

HARDINESS
Hardy.

HEIGHT AND
SPREAD
45–75 cm
(1½–2½ ft) tall.
60 cm (2 ft) wide.

FLOWERING TIME
Spring.

ANGLED SOLOMON'S SEAL

ANGLED SOLOMON'S SEAL PROVIDES GRACE
AND BEAUTY TO A SHADY GARDEN. COMBINE
IT WITH HOSTAS AND IRISES.

Description Has graceful, arching
stems with broad, oval, angled, green
leaves, arranged like stairs, up the
stem. Tubular, pale green, fragrant
flowers are carried in clusters at the
nodes. Showy blue-black fruit is
produced in late summer.

Ideal position Partial to full shade.

Ideal soil conditions Moist, humus-
rich soil.

Cultivation Spreads from thick,
creeping rhizomes to form wide
clumps. Divide to control its spread.

Propagation Divide clumps in
spring or sow fresh seed outdoors
in autumn.

Pest and disease prevention Sawfly
may attack the plants. In serious
infestations, spray may be necessary.

Design tips Combine with hostas,
lungworts *Pulmonaria* spp., irises,
wildflowers and ferns. Use massed
plantings under shrubs.

Cultivars *P. odoratum* var.
pluriforum 'Variegatum' (pictured
above) is prized for its broad, oval
leaves with creamy white margins.
P. odoratum 'Flore Pleno' has
double white flowers.

Primula Polyanthus Group

HARDINESS
Hardy.

HEIGHT AND SPREAD
20–30 cm
(8–12 in) tall.
30 cm (1 ft) wide.

FLOWERING TIME
Late winter and
early spring.

POLYANTHUS

PLANT BRIGHT-COLOURED POLYANTHUS WITH
SPRING BULBS SUCH AS DAFFODILS, EARLY
TULIPS AND BLUEBELLS.

Description Polyanthus primroses
are hybrids with large, showy
flowers in a rainbow of colours.
The broad, crinkled leaves rise
directly from stout crowns with
thick, fibrous roots. Flat, five-petalled
flowers vary in colour from white,
cream and yellow to pink, rose, red
and purple. Many bi-coloured forms
are available.

Ideal position Sun to light shade.

Ideal soil conditions Evenly moist,
well-drained, humus-rich soil.

Cultivation Easy-to-grow perennials
often sold as bedding plants. Divide
overgrown clumps after flowering
and re-plant into soil that is enriched
with organic matter.

Propagation Divide in autumn. Sow
seed outside in winter in trays and
cover with fine grit. Seeds may need
pre-chilling if sown indoors.

Pest and disease prevention No
serious pests or diseases.

Design tips Combine with early-
blooming perennials such as
hellebores *Helleborus* spp., lungworts
Pulmonaria spp. and forget-me-nots
Myosotis spp. Wildflowers and ferns
are excellent companions.

Polyanthus continued

Drumstick primula *Primula denticulata*

Hybrids Many hybrids and seed-grown strains are available.

The Gold-laced Group are particularly eye-catching with golden-eyed, dark red or purple flowers with a thin gold edge.

Other species *P. auricula*. Auriculas have thick, spoon-shaped, evergreen leaves and showy clusters of white, pink, yellow, green, purple and bi-coloured flowers. Most auriculas are thought to belong to *P. x pubescens*, not *P. auricula*.

P. denticulata, drumstick primula (pictured above), bears round heads of small, pink, lavender or white flowers on tall stalks. Leafy clumps develop as flowers fade.

P. elatior, oxlip, has broad, puckered leaves and open clusters of nodding, soft yellow flowers.

P. japonica has yellow-green foliage and pink, rose or white flowers in tiered clusters on tall stems.

P. sieboldii has fuzzy, heart-shaped, toothed leaves and open clusters of pink, rose or white flowers with notched petals.

P. veris, cowslip primrose, has fragrant, nodding, yellow flowers and broad evergreen leaves.

P. vulgaris has wrinkled, evergreen leaves and dainty, pale yellow flowers.

Pulmonaria saccharata

HARDINESS
Hardy.

HEIGHT AND
SPREAD
25–30 cm
(10–12 in) tall.
30–60 cm
(1–2 ft) wide.

FLOWERING TIME
Spring.

LUNGWORT

LUNGWORT IS A LOVELY SPRING-FLOWERING
FOLIAGE PLANT. IT ADDS A DRAMATIC TOUCH
TO SHADY GARDENS.

Description Has wide, hairy leaves
variously spotted and blotched with
silver. Plants grow from crowns
with thick, fibrous roots. The
nodding, five-petalled flowers vary
in colour from pink to blue.

Ideal position Partial to full shade.

Ideal soil conditions Moist, humus-
rich soil.

Cultivation Keep soil moist and
remove dead leaves after flowering.

Propagation Divide in spring, after
flowering, or in autumn.

Pest and disease prevention No
serious pests or diseases.

Design tips Plant lungwort with
spring bulbs, primroses, foamflowers
Tiarella spp., wildflowers and ferns.

Cultivars The Argentea Group has
plants with beautiful silvery-grey
leaves.
  'Dora Bielefeld' has spotted
leaves and large pink flowers.

Other species *P. angustifolia* has
plain narrow leaves and gentian-
blue flowers.
  P. longifolia has long, heavily
spotted leaves and flowers that turn
from pink to blue.

Pulsatilla vulgaris

HARDINESS
Hardy.

HEIGHT AND SPREAD
10–20 cm
(4–8 in) tall.
15–20 cm
(6–8 in) wide.

FLOWERING TIME
Mid- to late spring.

PASQUE FLOWER

THE PASQUE FLOWER IS NATIVE TO MOUNTAIN MEADOWS AND PERFECT FOR PLANTING IN ROCK GARDENS.

Description Pasque flowers are spring-blooming perennials with cupped flowers over rosettes of deeply incised, lobed leaves clothed in soft hairs. Plants grow from deep, fibrous roots. The purple flowers have five starry petals surrounding a central ring of fuzzy, orange-yellow stamens (male reproductive structures). Clusters of fuzzy seeds follow the flowers.

Ideal position Full sun in a very well-drained site.

Ideal soil conditions Average to humus-rich, very well-drained soil. Does not tolerate winter wet.

Cultivation Pasque flower begins blooming in mid-spring. When the flowers fade, the flower stems grow in length and bear pretty seedheads. It seldom needs division and dislikes disturbance.

Propagation Sow seed as soon as it is ripe.

Pest and disease prevention No serious pests or diseases.

Design tips Great companions for pasque flowers are bulbs such as grape hyacinths, primulas, candytuft *Iberis sempervirens* and alpine forms of *Aquilegia* spp.

Pasque flower *Pulsatilla vulgaris* var. 'Rubra'

Cultivars Var. 'Rubra' (pictured above) has purple- or rust-red flowers.

'Alba' has white flowers with bright, yellow centres.

Other species *P. bungeana*, available only from specialist nurseries, has bell-shaped, violet-blue, upward-facing flowers and grows to only 5 cm (2 in) tall.

P. halleri is an unusual species with very hairy, fine, silky foliage. The flowers are white, lavender or purple. *P. hallerie* subsp. *slavica* has hairy, woolly foliage that is less divided than that of *P. halleri* and charming, deep violet flowers. It may be difficult to source.

P. montana has very fine, divided leaves. The bell-shaped flowers are deep blue to purple. The flower stems are 15 cm (6 in) tall but can grow to 45 cm (18 in) when in seed.

Ranunculus aconitifolius

HARDINESS
Hardy.

HEIGHT AND
SPREAD
60 cm (24 in) tall.
45 cm (18 in) wide.

FLOWERING TIME
Late spring and
early summer

WHITE BUTTERCUP

THIS WOODLAND PLANT HAS PRETTY, SINGLE
WHITE FLOWERS WITH A GOLDEN EYE. THE
DOUBLE FORM HAS BUTTON-LIKE FLOWERS.

Description A clump-forming plant
with fibrous, fleshy roots, it produces
sprays of pink-tinged flower buds
that open into white saucer-shaped
flowers in late spring. The mainly
basal leaves are divided into
3 to 5 lobes and a dark, glossy
green in colour.

Ideal position Dappled to full shade.

Ideal soil conditions Moist, humus-
rich to heavy soil.

Cultivation An easy, spreading plant
that prefers a little sun but will
tolerate shade and heavy, clay soils

as long as the ground is reliably
moist. If clumps become too large,
dig them up and divide in autumn.

Propagation By seed sown outdoors
when ripe or by division in autumn.

Pest and disease prevention No
serious pests or diseases.

Design tips The freely branched
stems and loose sprays of charming
flowers make this an ideal plant for
informal, cottage-garden planting
schemes. Combine it with hostas
and moisture-loving *Iris sibirica* in
a damp, shady spot.

Cultivars 'Flore Pleno', the double
form, has button-like flowers with
numerous white petals.

Rodgersia pinnata

HARDINESS
Hardy.

HEIGHT AND SPREAD
90–120 cm
(3–4 ft) tall.
90 cm (3 ft) wide.

FLOWERING TIME
Summer.

RODGERSIA

RODGERSIA IS A BOLD PERENNIAL IDEALLY SUITED TO BOG GARDENS, BUT HAPPY IN ANY SITE GIVEN ENOUGH MOISTURE.

Description Rodgersia has large, pinnately compound leaves that are bronze-tinged when young. It grows from a stout, branching root. The small, pink flowers are carried in plume-like clusters.

Ideal position Sun to partial shade. Mulch to retain moisture.

Ideal soil conditions Fertile, moist, humus-rich soil.

Cultivation Rodgersias form clumps from crowns that are long-lived. Give each plant at least 90 cm (3 ft).

Propagation Divide in early spring. Sow seed outdoors in autumn.

Pest and disease prevention No serious pests or diseases.

Design tips Plant near water or in open situations with irises, astilbes, ferns, ligularias and other moisture lovers.

Other species *R. aesculifolia* has long, palmately divided leaves and creamy white or pink flowers. Can reach 1.5 m (5 ft).

    R. sambucifolia is similar to *R. pinnata* but with white flowers.

Rudbeckia fulgida

HARDINESS
Hardy.

HEIGHT AND SPREAD
45–90 cm
(1½–3 ft) tall.
60 cm (2 ft) wide.

FLOWERING TIME
Late summer and early autumn.

OTHER COMMON NAMES
Black-eyed Susan.

CONEFLOWER

CONEFLOWERS ARE VERSATILE PERENNIALS PERFECT FOR MIXED BORDERS, WILD GARDENS AND EVEN CONTAINERS.

Description Coneflowers are showy summer daisies with oval to broadly lance-shaped, rough, hairy foliage on stiff stems. Plants grow from fibrous-rooted crowns. The daisy-like flowers have yellow-orange rays (petal-like structures) and conical, dark brown centres.

Ideal position Full sun to light shade.

Ideal soil conditions Fertile, moist but well-drained soil that does not dry out.

Cultivation Coneflowers are tough, long-lived perennials. They spread outward to form large clumps. The edges of the clumps are the most vigorous. Divide every 3–4 years in spring and re-plant into soil enriched with organic matter.

Propagation Divide in spring. Sow seed outdoors in autumn or indoors in a warm place in late winter.

Pest and disease prevention No serious pests or diseases.

Design tips For a wonderful late-summer flower display, plant coneflowers with echinaceas, sedums, phlox, bergamot *Monarda* spp.,

One of the many popular *Rudbeckia* cultivars

chrysanthemums and ornamental grasses.

Varieties *R. fulgida* var. *sullivantii* 'Goldsturm' is a popular compact cultivar of this variety with deep yellow flowers. The variety *speciosa* has narrow leaves and smaller flowers.

Other species There are many species, each with distinctive cultivars. Some are listed below.

R. hirta has the distinctive green-centred cultivar, 'Green Eyes', as well as golden-orange 'Goldilocks'. 'Becky Mixed' is a bushy dwarf cultivar available in a variety of colours ranging from deep orange to light lemon-yellow. *R. hirta*

cultivars are usually grown as half-hardy annuals as they won't survive below 0˚C (32˚F).

R. laciniata is a tall-growing, hardy plant with single flowers and is the parent of a number of double forms, including 'Goldquelle'.

Ruta graveolens

HARDINESS
Hardy.

HEIGHT AND SPREAD
30–60 cm
(1–2 ft) tall.
60 cm (2 ft) wide.

FLOWERING TIME
Summer.

RUE

RUE IS A TRADITIONAL PLANT FOR HERB GARDENS BUT IS A WONDERFUL FOIL FOR BOLD, COLOURFUL FLOWERS.

Description Rue has small, yellow flowers that are carried in open clusters above lacy, aromatic, blue-grey foliage. Brushing against the leaves may cause skin irritation in sunlight.

Ideal position Full sun and in the middle of a border.

Ideal soil conditions Average to poor, well-drained soil.

Cultivation Rue forms broad, dense clumps that seldom need division.

Propagation Take stem cuttings in late spring or early summer.

Pest and disease prevention No serious pests or diseases.

Design tips Choose rue for herb gardens or for the middle or back of mixed beds and borders so people won't brush by it. Combine with hyssop *Hyssopus officinalis*, yarrow, ornamental onions and ornamental grasses. For contrast, plant with bold flowers such as balloon flower *Platycodon grandiflorus*.

Salvia elegans

HARDINESS
Half-hardy.

HEIGHT AND
SPREAD
90 cm (3 ft) tall.
60 cm (2 ft) wide.

FLOWERING TIME
Midsummer to
early autumn.

PINEAPPLE SAGE

USE PINEAPPLE SAGE IN HERB AND COTTAGE
GARDENS. THE FOLIAGE EXUDES
A WONDERFUL PINEAPPLE SCENT.

Description This perennial has
beautiful, trumpet-shaped, bright red
flowers and attractive light green
foliage which releases its scent when
crushed or rubbed between the fingers.

Ideal position Full sun.

Ideal soil conditions Well-drained,
alkaline soil.

Cultivation Pineapple sage needs a
warm site and plants are best lifted
and potted up in containers
in autumn for overwintering inside.
Keep watering to a minimum
in winter.

Propagation Take stem or root
cuttings during summer.

Pest and disease prevention No
serious pests or diseases.

Design tips Use pineapple sage
for structure and foliage interest in
formal beds and borders. It's a good
filler for the rear of the border or
where its clear, red blooms can be
incorporated into a late-summer
colour scheme.

Salvia officinalis

HARDINESS
Hardy.

HEIGHT AND
SPREAD
30–60 cm
(1–2 ft) tall.
60 cm (2 ft) wide.

FLOWERING TIME
Summer.

COMMON SAGE

COMMON SAGE IS AN EVERGREEN AROMATIC
HERB THAT BLENDS EQUALLY WELL INTO
FLOWER GARDENS AND HERB GARDENS.

Description The broad, lance-shaped, opposite leaves are sea-green to purple-green with a crinkled surface. The pink or purple flowers are less showy than those of other sages but are an added bonus to the leaves. Plants grow from fibrous-rooted crowns.

Ideal position Full sun.

Ideal soil conditions Well-drained, alkaline soil.

Cultivation Sage grows to form a small shrub. Prune lightly in spring to encourage growth and again after flowering.

Propagation Take stem cuttings in late spring to early summer.

Pest and disease prevention No serious pests or diseases.

Design tips Use sage in herb and cottage gardens or for winter structure and foliage interest in beds and borders.

Cultivars The pretty 'Purpurascens' (pictured above) has leaves tinged with purple.
'Tricolor' has grey-green leaves tinged with yellow and pink to red.

Salvia pratensis

HARDINESS	Hardy.
HEIGHT AND SPREAD	60–90 cm (2–3 ft) tall. 60–90 cm (2–3 ft) wide.
FLOWERING TIME	Summer
OTHER COMMON NAMES	Meadow clary.

MEADOW SAGE

MEADOW SAGE IS AN IDEAL PERENNIAL FOR NATURALISTIC PLANTINGS BECAUSE IT DOES NOT REQUIRE SUPPORT OR STAKING.

Description An easy-care herbaceous perennial. The plant forms an attractive mound of basal, grey-green leaves and flowers on stout stems. The hooded flowers vary from pale to dark violet-purple and are carried on spikes up to 90 cm (3 ft) tall. They are attractive to bees.

Ideal position Full sun.

Ideal soil conditions Well-drained, moist, reasonably fertile soil.

Cultivation Plant in particularly well-drained soil. Cultivars can be cut back in late spring to produce stronger flowering in late summer.

Propagation By seed or by division or softwood cuttings in spring.

Pest and disease prevention No serious pests or diseases.

Design tips Well suited to the middle of the border where both the foliage and the taller flower spikes can be fully appreciated.

Cultivars Cultivars are available in white, pink and shades of blue.

Salvia x *superba*

HARDINESS
Hardy.

HEIGHT AND SPREAD
60–90 cm
(2–3 ft) tall.
60 cm (2 ft) wide.

FLOWERING TIME
Early to mid-summer.

SAGE

THE SPIKY BLOOMS OF THIS SAGE COMBINE WONDERFULLY WITH ROUNDED PERENNIALS SUCH AS CRANESBILLS.

Description A bushy, well-branched plant with aromatic, triangular leaves. It grows from a fibrous-rooted crown. Violet-blue flowers are carried on narrow spikes.

Ideal position Full sun.

Ideal soil conditions Any reasonable, well-drained soil.

Cultivation After flowering wanes, cut back flowering stems to promote fresh growth. May repeat flower. Plants seldom need division.

Propagation Divide in spring or autumn. Take cuttings in spring.

Pest and disease prevention No serious pests or diseases.

Design tips Plant in borders with summer perennials such as yarrow, lamb's-ears *Stachys byzantina*, daylilies, coreopsis and ornamental grasses.

Cultivars These are now listed under a similar sage, *S.* x *sylvestris*.
　'Blue Queen' has violet-blue flowers.
　'May Night' has violet-blue flowers on bushy plants.

Sanguinaria canadensis

HARDINESS
Hardy.

HEIGHT AND
SPREAD
15–20 cm
(6–8 in) tall.
30 cm (12 in) wide.

FLOWERING TIME
Mid- to late spring.

BLOODROOT

BLOODROOT, FROM CANADA AND NORTH
AMERICA, IS PERFECT IN WOODLAND
GARDENS WITH SPRING BULBS AND FERNS.

Description A single, deeply cut,
seven-lobed leaf emerges wrapped
around the single flower bud. Plants
grow from a thick, creeping rhizome.
The snow-white flowers have 8 to
11 narrow petals surrounding a
cluster of yellow-orange stamens
(male reproductive structures).
Flowers last a few days.

Ideal position Light to full shade.
Spring sun is important but summer
shade is necessary. Plants do not
tolerate summer drought.

Ideal soil conditions Moist, humus-
rich soil.

Cultivation The foliage remains
attractive all summer if moisture is
available. Plants form dense clumps
that may resent division.

Propagation Divide, if necessary,
in late summer. Sow fresh seed
outdoors in autumn.

Pest and disease prevention No
serious pests or diseases.

Design tips Plant bloodroot under
deciduous shrubs. Use as a ground-
cover plant.

Cultivars A stunning, fully double
form with magnificent, long-lasting
flowers is available.

Sanguisorba canadensis

HARDINESS
Hardy.

HEIGHT AND SPREAD
1.2–1.5 m
(4–5 ft) tall.
1.2 m (4 ft) wide.

FLOWERING TIME
Late summer.

CANADIAN BURNET

THE TALL, ELEGANT, BOTTLEBRUSHES OF CANADIAN BURNET LOOK STUNNING AT THE REAR OF A MIXED BORDER.

Description Plants grow from thick, fleshy roots. Flowers appear in late summer atop stout stems clothed in pinnately divided leaves with oblong leaflets. The fuzzy, white flowers lack petals and are tightly packed into dense spikes.

Ideal position Full sun to partial shade.

Ideal soil conditions Average to moist, humus-rich soil.

Cultivation Will grow in any reasonably fertile soil but prefers a moist situation.

Propagation Divide in spring. Sow seed outdoors in autumn.

Pest and disease prevention No serious pests or diseases.

Design tips Plant at the rear of the border with phlox, monkshood *Aconitum* spp., asters, sedum and ornamental grasses.

Other species *S. obtusa* grows to 90–120 cm (3–4 ft) with drooping, rose-pink flower clusters and grey-green leaves with rounded leaflets.

Santolina chamaecyparissus

HARDINESS
Hardy.

HEIGHT AND SPREAD
30–60 cm
(1–2 ft) tall.
60 cm (2 ft) wide.

FLOWERING TIME
Summer.

COTTON LAVENDER

PRETTY COTTON LAVENDER IS PERFECT FOR EDGING PATHS AND BEDS AND IDEAL IN A MEDITERRANEAN SCHEME.

Description Cotton lavender is a compact, semi-woody plant with small, white, woolly, pinnately divided leaves topped with yellow flowers in summer. Plants grow from fibrous-rooted crowns. The button-like yellow flowers are held above the foliage on thin stalks.

Ideal position Full sun. Plants tolerate drought, poor soil and salt.

Ideal soil conditions Average, very well-drained soil.

Cultivation Cut back in early spring to promote strong, healthy growth

and trim flower stalks in autumn. In cold areas, leave intact and trim in spring.

Propagation Take stem cuttings in summer from non-flowering shoots.

Pest and disease prevention No serious pests or diseases.

Design tips Combine with other perennials that need good drainage, such as pinks *Dianthus* spp., and sedums.

Other species *S. rosmarinifolia*, is similar but has bright green foliage and paler yellow flowers.

Saponaria x lempergii

HARDINESS
Half-hardy.

HEIGHT AND
SPREAD
10–15 cm
(4–6 in) tall.
30–35 cm
(12–14 in) wide.

FLOWERING TIME
Summer.

SOAPWORT

THE MOUNDS OF PRETTY FLOWERS ON
SOAPWORT LOOK LOVELY AT THE FRONT
OF BORDERS AND IN ROCK GARDENS.

Description Soapwort has mounds
of flowers on sprawling stems with
oval leaves. Plants grow from
fibrous-rooted crowns. The 2.5-cm
(1-in), pale pink flowers have five
squared petals.

Ideal position Full sun.

Ideal soil conditions Average, well-
drained soil.

Cultivation Divide to control the
spread. Cut back after flowering.

Propagation Divide in autumn. Take
cuttings in early summer.

Pest and disease prevention No
serious pests or diseases.

Design tips Plant soapwort along
paths, along the edges of beds, at the
front of borders or in rock gardens.

Other species *S. ocymoides*, Tumbling
Ted, is a sprawling, hardy plant with
clusters of 6-mm (¼-in), bright pink
flowers. 'Rubra Compacta' forms
tight mounds with deep pink to
crimson flowers.

S. officinalis, Bouncing Bet, is a
hardy, spreading plant with stems to
90 cm (3 ft) and rounded clusters of
pale pink flowers.

Saxifraga stolonifera

HARDINESS
Frost-hardy.

HEIGHT AND
SPREAD
15 cm (6 in) tall.
30 cm (1 ft) wide.

FLOWERING TIME
Late summer.

MOTHER OF THOUSANDS

IN A SHADY GARDEN, THE SILVERY FOLIAGE
MAKES GOOD GROUND COVER AMONG
BULBS, WILDFLOWERS AND FERNS.

Description An attractive ground-cover plant with round leaves that resemble bedding geraniums. The evergreen leaves are attractively veined with silver. The tiny, white flowers have five petals, two of which are longer than the others.

Ideal position Partial to full shade.

Ideal soil conditions Moist, humus-rich soil.

Cultivation Plants spread quickly to form dense, weed-proof mats. Easily pulled if they spread out of bounds.

Propagation Remove and replant rooted offsets in autumn. Sow seed outdoors in autumn.

Pest and disease prevention No serious pests or diseases.

Landscape use Use as ground cover under flowering shrubs and small trees. The plants also perform admirably in pots.

Cultivars 'Tricolor' has pink and cream variegation but is less hardy.

Other species *S.* x *urbium*, London pride, has toothed, spoon-shaped, evergreen leaves and clusters of small, white, pink-spotted flowers.

Scabiosa caucasica

HARDINESS
Hardy.

HEIGHT AND SPREAD
45–60 cm
(1½–2 ft) tall.
30–60 cm
(1–2 ft) wide.

FLOWERING TIME
Summer.

SCABIOUS

TO INCREASE THE VISUAL IMPACT OF THIS
DELICATE FLOWER, PLANT IT IN GROUPS
WHERE THE FLOWERS SEEM TO DANCE.

Description Scabious, with its
pincushion flowers, is perfect for
cottage gardens. The stems are
loosely clothed in lance-shaped to
three-lobed leaves. The unusual, soft
blue flowers are packed into flat,
5–7.5-cm (2–3-in) heads that rise
above the leaves on slender stems.
The flowers increase in size as they
near the margins of the heads.

Ideal position Full sun.

Ideal soil conditions Moderately fertile,
well-drained, neutral to alkaline soil.

Cultivation Plants form good-sized
clumps. Divide every 3–4 years if
plants become overcrowded.
Deadheading will prolong flowering.

Propagation Divide in spring or
autumn. Sow seed in spring.

Pest and disease prevention No
serious pests or diseases.

Design tips The airy flowers look
beautiful above low, mounded plants
such as phlox, pinks *Dianthus* spp.
and yarrows. They combine well with
bergamot *Monarda* spp., daylilies
and columbines *Aquilegia* spp. and
attract bees.

Pincushion flower *Scabiosa caucasica* 'Clive Greaves'

Cultivars 'Alba' has white flowers.

'Clive Greaves' (pictured above) has large, lavender-blue heads.

'Miss Wilmot' has pure white flowers with creamy white centres.

Other species *S. atropurpurea* is a tall, branching, often short-lived plant with wiry stems, which carry deep purple, blue or lavender blooms. Flower season can be extended if flowers are regularly deadheaded. This species has some wonderful, double cultivars that are almost black, such as 'Chile Black'.

S. columbaria 'Misty Butterflies' has flowers with a blend of pink to lavender-blue and held over grey-green foliage.

S. graminfolia (pictured opposite) has grass-like foliage topped with pink to lilac flowers on slender stalks.

S. lucida forms tufted clumps of silvery green foliage with pale lilac summer flowers held erect on thin, wiry stems.

Sedum spectabile

HARDINESS
Hardy.

HEIGHT AND SPREAD
30–60 cm
(1–2 ft) tall.
60 cm (2 ft) wide.

FLOWERING TIME
Mid- to late summer.

OTHER COMMON NAMES
Stonecrop,
Ice plant.

SEDUM

VERSATILE LATE-FLOWERING SEDUMS LOOK
STUNNING WHEN USED IN LARGE SWEEPS
OR CLUMPS.

Description Late-summer perennials
with clusters of pink flowers atop
thick, fleshy stems clothed in broad,
grey-green leaves. Plants grow from
fibrous-rooted crowns. Small, bright
pink flowers are borne in 10–15-cm
(4–6-in) domed clusters. The flowers
attract bees and butterflies and the
brown seed heads hold their shape
all winter.

Ideal position Full sun. Extremely
drought- and heat-tolerant.

Ideal soil conditions Average to light,
well-drained soil.

Cultivation Clumps get quite full
with age and may fall open. Divide
overgrown plants.

Propagation Divide in spring. Take
cuttings of non-flowering shoots in
summer. Sow seed in spring.

Pest and disease prevention No
serious pests or diseases.

Design tips Plant in sunny borders,
wildlife gardens and rock gardens.
Combine with yarrow, purple
coneflower *Echinacea purpurea*
and ornamental grasses.

Cultivars 'Brilliant' has striking
brilliant pink flowers.
'Stardust' has white flowers.

Sedum spurium 'Dragon's Blood'

Hybrids Several hybrid cultivars are available. 'Autumn Joy' syn. 'Herbstfreude' is similar to *S. spectabile* but more robust and with darker flowers.

'Ruby Glow' has sprawling stems with purple-tinged leaves and ruby-red flowers.

Other species *S. aizoon* is an upright plant with oval, toothed leaves and flat, 7.5–10-cm (3–4-in) clusters of yellow flowers.

S. album is a creeping plant with evergreen leaves and 2.5–5-cm (1–2-in) clusters of white flowers.

S. kamtschaticum, also evergreen or semi-evergreen, is a creeping plant with yellow flowers. A variegated form is available with mid-green leaves that have cream borders. It works well in rock gardens.

S. spurium, Caucasian stonecrop, has rounded, evergreen leaves that form mats, and open clusters of pink flowers. 'Dragon's Blood' (pictured above) has red-tinged foliage and rose-red flowers. 'Tricolor' has leaves variegated with pink, white and green.

S. telephium is a deciduous plant. Cultivars have very dark purple leaves and pink flowers.

Silene fimbriata

CAMPION

PUT CAMPION IN A ROCKERY OR THE FRONT OF A BORDER WHERE ITS LOOSE FLOWER STEMS WON'T BE OVERSHADOWED.

Description Good carpeting plant with hairy, upright, leafy stems carrying interesting flowers with light green, inflated calyces holding white, fringed petals.

Ideal position Sun to partial shade.

Ideal soil conditions Average to very well-drained soil.

Cultivation Cut back flowering stems at the end of the season to promote growth and next year's flowers.

Propagation Stem cuttings in spring. Sow seed in spring or early autumn.

Pest and disease prevention No serious pests or diseases.

Design tips This campion makes a wonderful ground-cover plant. It is perfect for rock gardens and sloping beds and borders.

Other species *S. acaulis*, moss campion, is a useful, hardy plant for the rock garden. It forms green cushions with pink flowers during summer. Flowering may be sparse if summers are hot.

S. uniflora flowers through summer. The double-flowering 'Robin Whitebreast' is a hardy garden plant.

Smilacina syn. *Maianthemum racemosa*   CONVALLARIACEAE

HARDINESS
Hardy.

HEIGHT AND SPREAD
60–90 cm
(2–3 ft) tall.
60 cm (2 ft) or
more wide.

FLOWERING TIME
Late spring.

FALSE SPIKENARD

FALSE SPIKENARD THRIVES IN SHADE. YOU'LL ENJOY THE FLOWERS IN SPRING, FOLIAGE IN SUMMER AND BERRIES IN AUTUMN.

Description Erect, arching stems bear broad, glossy, green leaves arranged like ascending stairs. Plants grow from a thick, creeping rhizome. Small, starry, creamy white flowers are borne in terminal, plume-like clusters. Red berries ripen in late summer.

Ideal position Light to full shade.

Ideal soil conditions Evenly moist, humus-rich, neutral to acid soil.

Cultivation Divide tangled rhizomes if plants overgrow their position.

Propagation Divide in spring. Sow seed in autumn.

Pest and disease prevention No serious pests or diseases.

Design tips Plant in woodland gardens with hostas, bleeding hearts *Dicentra* spp., columbines *Aquilegia* spp., wildflowers and ferns. Very useful for a shady border.

Other species *S. stellata* has narrow, blue-green foliage and small clusters of 6-mm (¼-in) white flowers. The attractive berries are striped with red or pink.

Solidago canadensis   ASTERACEAE

HARDINESS
Hardy.

HEIGHT AND
SPREAD
60–150 cm
(2–5 ft) tall.
90–150 cm
(3–5 ft) wide.

FLOWERING TIME
Late summer into
autumn.

CANADIAN GOLDENROD

PLANT THE ROBUST CANADIAN GOLDENROD AT THE BACK OF BORDERS AND IN WILD GARDENS.

Description A common wildflower of wasteland with plumed flower clusters and toothed, lance-shaped leaves. Grows from creeping rhizomes and can become invasive. The small, bright yellow flowers are grouped into large, plumed heads.

Ideal position Full sun to light shade.

Ideal soil conditions Average to poor, well-drained soil.

Cultivation Spreads rapidly and needs frequent division.

Propagation Divide in spring or after flowering has ended. Take cuttings in early summer.

Pest and disease prevention May be prone to mildew. Dividing regularly will help.

Design tips Combine with phlox, asters, sunflowers *Helianthus* spp. and gay feathers *Liatris* spp.

Hybrids 'Goldenmosa' is compact at 60–75 cm (2–2½ ft) tall. 'Goldkind' (Golden Baby) has dense, conical sprays and is 60 cm (24 in) tall.

Stachys byzantina

HARDINESS
Hardy.

HEIGHT AND SPREAD
15–37.5 cm
(6–15 in) tall.
30–60 cm
(1–2 ft) wide.

FLOWERING TIME
Summer.

LAMB'S EARS

THE PRETTY, MAT-FORMING FOLIAGE OF LAMB'S EARS MAKES IT AN EXCELLENT EDGING PLANT FOR GROWING ALONG PATHS.

Description Lamb's ears are eye-catching plants with basal rosettes of elongated, densely white, woolly leaves. The leaves have the same soft feeling as lamb's wool, hence the name. These sun-loving plants grow from slow-creeping stems. Small, two-lipped rose-purple flowers are carried on woolly flower stalks. Many people consider the flowers unattractive and remove them from the plant.

Ideal position Full sun.

Ideal soil conditions Very well-drained, average to poor soil. Drought-tolerant.

Cultivation Lamb's ears form dense, broad clumps of tightly packed foliage. Divide overgrown clumps to control their spread.

Propagation Divide plants in spring.

Pest and disease prevention Dislikes wet, heavy soil which can cause powdery mildew. Provide very good drainage.

Design tips Choose lamb's ears for the front of sunny beds and borders. Combine these plantings with irises, coral bells *Heuchera* spp., ornamental onions *Allium* spp., yuccas and sedums.

Lamb's ears continued

Lamb's ears *Stachys byzantina* 'Cotton Boll'

Cultivars 'Big Ears' grows larger than most lamb's ears and has purple flowers borne on tall spikes.

'Cotton Boll' (pictured above) has larger, less-woolly leaves and flowerheads that look like cotton-wool balls.

'Primrose Heron' has soft, primrose-yellow foliage in spring.

'Silver Carpet' is a neat, compact cultivar with leaves that are more intensely silvery than other cultivars.

Other species *S. coccinea* is a long-flowering, evergreen perennial with red flowers. It grows to 60 cm (2 ft) tall and can flower from spring through to autumn, but is half-hardy.

S. macrantha has erect stems that grow to 60 cm (2 ft) tall and spreads slowly. It bears purple-pink flowers from late spring to late summer. It is hardy.

Stokesia laevis

HARDINESS
Hardy.

HEIGHT AND SPREAD
30–60 cm
(1–2 ft) tall.
60 cm (2 ft) wide.

FLOWERING TIME
Summer.

STOKES'S ASTER

STOKES'S ASTER IS ATTRACTIVE IN FOLIAGE AND FLOWER AND IT LOOKS WONDERFUL IN FORMAL OR INFORMAL GARDENS.

Description The broad, lance-shaped leaves are deep green with a white mid-vein. The evergreen leaves form a rosette growing from a crown with thick, fibrous roots. The 5–7.5-cm (2–3-in) daisy-like flowers have ragged blue to purple rays and fuzzy white centres.

Ideal position Full sun and a sheltered spot.

Ideal soil conditions Average to humus-rich, well-drained soil. Good drainage is essential over winter.

Cultivation Plants grow particularly well when left undisturbed. Divide in spring as necessary.

Propagation Divide in early spring. Sow seed outdoors in autumn.

Pest and disease prevention Excessive winter wet can cause rotting.

Design tips Combine with verbenas *Verbena* spp., phlox, goldenrod *Solidago* spp. and ornamental grasses.

Cultivars 'Alba' has white flowers.
'Blue Star' has very pretty lavender-blue flowers.

Symphytum ibericum

HARDINESS
Hardy.

HEIGHT AND
SPREAD
Foliage to 30 cm
(1 ft) tall.
60 cm (2 ft) wide.
Flowers to 45 cm
(1½ ft) tall.

FLOWERING TIME
Spring to summer.

YELLOW COMFREY

YELLOW COMFREY IS AN EXCELLENT, EASY-
CARE GROUND-COVER PLANT FOR SHADY
SPOTS IN YOUR GARDEN.

Description It produces dense,
spreading clumps that tend to crowd
out most weeds. Clusters of white to
creamy yellow, tubular flowers, 18 mm
(¾ in) long, rise above the foliage.

Ideal position Sun or partial shade.

Ideal soil conditions Ideally, fertile
well-drained soil. Tolerates most soils
once established.

Cultivation Set plants 45–60 cm
(1½–2 ft) apart in spring or autumn.
Once established, plants need
virtually no care.

Propagation Propagate by division
in spring or autumn.

Pest and disease prevention No
serious pests or diseases.

Design tips Yellow comfrey is
an excellent, easy-care, weed-
suppressing ground-cover plant.

Cultivars 'All Gold' has pretty,
golden-yellow leaves in spring.
Flowers vary in colour from pink
to pale mauve.

Other species *S. x uplandicum* is a
particularly good source of nutrients.
Pick out leaves into a bucket filled
with water and cover. After 3–4
weeks the liquid can be strained
and used as a plant feed.

Thalictrum aquilegiifolium

HARDINESS
Hardy.

HEIGHT AND SPREAD
60–120 cm
(2–4 ft) tall.
30–60 cm
(1–2 ft) wide.

FLOWERING TIME
Late spring and early summer.

MEADOW RUE

MEADOW RUE PERFORMS WELL BESIDE PONDS OR ALONG STREAMS WITH IRISES, HOSTAS, DAYLILIES AND FERNS.

Description Has billowy plumes crowning erect stalks clothed in intricately divided leaves that resemble those of columbines. Plants grow from fibrous-rooted crowns. The 1-cm (½-in) lavender or white flowers consist of many fuzzy stamens (male reproductive structures) in dense clusters.

Ideal position Full sun or partial shade.

Ideal soil conditions Fertile, humus-rich, well-drained soil.

Cultivation Clumps spread slowly and seldom need division.

Propagation Divide in spring or autumn. Sow seed outdoors in autumn.

Pest and disease prevention No serious pests or diseases.

Design tips A strong-growing plant for a mixed border in dappled shade.

Cultivars Var. 'Album' has white flowers.
'Thundercloud' has lilac-purple flowers.

Other species *T. flavum* subsp. *glaucum* has powdery blue-grey foliage and flattened heads of soft, sulphur-yellow flowers.

Thermopsis villosa

HARDINESS
Hardy.

HEIGHT AND SPREAD
90 cm (3 ft) tall.
60cm (2 ft) wide.

FLOWERING TIME
Late spring or early summer.

CAROLINA LUPIN

THIS AMERICAN LUPIN IS LOVELY AT THE EDGE OF AN OPEN WOODLAND OR IN LIGHTLY SHADED WILD GARDENS.

Description Produces upright flower spikes atop stout stems clothed in three-lobed, grey-green leaves. Plants grow from stout, fibrous-rooted crowns. Lemon-yellow, pea-shaped flowers are tightly packed into 20–30-cm (8–12-in) clusters.

Ideal position Full sun to light shade.

Ideal soil conditions Average to rich, well-drained soil.

Cultivation Clumps grow slowly to shrub-like proportions but seldom need division. If foliage declines after bloom, cut it down to the ground.

Propagation Take cuttings in early summer from sideshoots. Sow seed outdoors in autumn. Sow seed indoors in early spring after soaking it in hot water for 12–24 hours.

Pest and disease prevention No serious pests or diseases.

Design tips Plant toward the rear of the garden with peonies, blue star *Amsonia tabernae-montana*, cranesbills *Geranium* spp. and other rounded or mounding plants.

Tiarella cordifolia

HARDINESS
Hardy.

HEIGHT AND
SPREAD
15–25 cm
(6–10 in) tall.
30–60 cm (1–2 ft)
wide or more.

FLOWERING TIME
Spring.

FOAMFLOWER

AS THE CONSUMMATE GROUND COVER,
FOAMFLOWER'S FOLIAGE MATS DISCOURAGE
WEEDS UNDER SHRUBS AND TREES.

Description Woodland plants with
fuzzy flowers and rosettes of
triangular, three-lobed hairy leaves.
Plants grow from fibrous-rooted
crowns and creeping stems. The
small, starry white flowers are borne
in spike-like clusters. They are often
tinged with pink.

Ideal position Partial to full shade.

Ideal soil conditions Evenly moist,
humus-rich, slightly acid soil.

Cultivation Spreads by creeping
stems to form broad mats. Divide
plants to control spread.

Propagation Remove runners in late
summer and treat them as cuttings
if they lack roots of their own. Sow
seed in spring.

Pest and disease prevention No
serious pests or diseases.

Landscape use In woodland gardens
combine them with bulbs, ferns,
flowers such as bleeding heart
Dicentra spp. and bloodroot
Sanguinaria canadensis, as well
as hostas and irises.

Other species *T. wherryi* is a clump-
forming species with many pink-
tinged flower spikes rising above
deeply lobed leaves in late spring.
Best in light shade.

Tradescantia Andersoniana Group

HARDINESS
Hardy.

HEIGHT AND
SPREAD
30–60 cm
(1–2 ft) tall.
45 cm (1½ ft) wide.

FLOWERING TIME
Summer.

SPIDERWORT

EACH SPIDERWORT FLOWER LASTS ONLY A
DAY, BUT ONE PLANT PRODUCES SO MANY
YOU'LL ENJOY THEM FOR MONTHS.

Description Has satiny flowers borne
in clusters at the tips of the stems.
The 2.5–3.5-cm (1–1½-in) flowers
have three rounded blue, purple
or white petals. Plants grow from
thick, spidery roots. Related to the
popular houseplants.

Ideal position Full sun to partial shade.

Ideal soil conditions Moist, humus-
rich soil.

Cultivation After flowering, plants
tend to look shabby. Cut them to
the ground to encourage new
growth. Plants in dry situations tend
to go dormant in summer.

Propagation Divide in autumn. Self-
sown seedlings often appear.

Pest and disease prevention No
serious pests or diseases.

Design tips Plant in informal
gardens with bellflowers
Campanula spp., columbines
Aquilegia spp., hostas and ferns.
In formal gardens combine them
with other spring-blooming
perennials.

Cultivars 'Blue Stone' has rich
medium blue flowers.

'J.C. Weguelin' is sky-blue and
'Purple Dane' has intense purple
flowers. 'Osprey' is white.

Tricyrtis hirta

HARDINESS
Hardy.

HEIGHT AND SPREAD
60–90 cm
(2–3 ft) tall.
30–60 cm
(1–2 ft) wide.

FLOWERING TIME
Early autumn.

TOAD LILY

THE JAPANESE TOAD LILY IS BEST PLANTED WHERE IT CAN BE FULLY APPRECIATED AT CLOSE RANGE.

Description The tall, arching stems are clothed in alternate, broadly lance-shaped leaves that have prominent veins. The purple-spotted white flowers face upwards with three petals and three petal-like sepals around a central column. The flowers are carried in the leaf axils on the upper one-third of the stem.

Ideal position Partial to full shade in a sheltered spot.

Ideal soil conditions Evenly moist, humus-rich soil. Do not let soil dry out in summer.

Cultivation Plants spread by creeping stems to form handsome clumps that seldom need division. In areas with cold winters, provide a thick mulch: plants are covered by snow in their native habitat.

Propagation Divide clumps in spring. Sow seed outdoors in autumn for best results.

Pest and disease prevention No serious pests or diseases.

Design tips Large groups of toad lilies are effective when planted with astilbes, hostas, ferns and other moisture-lovers.

Tropaeolum speciosum

HARDINESS
Half-hardy.

HEIGHT AND SPREAD
2.7 m (9 ft) tall.
Up to 1.8 m
(6 ft) wide.

FLOWERING TIME
Summer to autumn.

OTHER COMMON NAMES
Flame flower,
Flame nasturtium.

FLAME CREEPER

A VERY PRETTY PERENNIAL CLIMBER, FLAME CREEPER IS PERFECT FOR GROWING THROUGH A HEDGE AND ADDING COLOUR.

Description Flame creeper is a perennial climber. Its delicate shoots are covered with apple-green foliage. The flowers are bright scarlet and followed by blue-black fruits.

Ideal position Plant where the roots are in shade but the stems can reach the sun.

Ideal soil conditions Fertile, moist, well-drained soil.

Cultivation Give support to the climbing stems, either by growing through shrubs, hedges or up a wall. The secret to a healthy flame creeper is good drainage, feeding when in growth and just enough moisture.

Propagation Start seed or tubers early indoors and transplant after all danger of frost is past. Be careful when moving them, their roots are very delicate. Take cuttings in late summer.

Pest and disease prevention No serious pests or diseases.

Design tips The bright foliage and colourful flowers stand out well against dark-leaved shrubs.

Uvularia grandiflora

HARDINESS
Hardy.

HEIGHT AND SPREAD
30–75 cm
(1–2½ ft) tall.
30–60 cm
(1–2 ft) wide.

FLOWERING TIME
Mid- to late spring.

LARGE MERRYBELLS

THE GRACEFUL, NODDING FLOWERS OF
LARGE MERRYBELLS LOOK WONDERFUL
WITH OTHER LATE-SPRING BULBS.

Description Plants grow from
rhizomes with brittle white roots.
The nodding, bell-shaped, lemon-
yellow flowers have three petals
and three petal-like sepals that twist
in the middle and are on slender
stalks clothed in grey-green leaves.

Ideal position Partial to full shade.

Ideal soil conditions Moist, fertile,
humus-rich soil.

Cultivation Large merrybells spreads
to form tight, attractive clumps. When
flowers fade, the foliage expands to
provide good ground cover.

Propagation Divide plants before
flowering in early spring.

Pest and disease prevention No
serious pests or diseases.

Design tips Plant large merrybells in
woodland gardens with other bulbs
and flowers such as late daffodils and
bloodroot *Sanguinaria canadensis*.

Other species *U. sessilifolia* is a
slender, delicate plant with straw-
coloured flowers and narrow leaves.

Verbascum chaixii

HARDINESS
Hardy.

HEIGHT AND SPREAD
90 cm (3 ft) tall.
45 cm (18 in) wide.

FLOWERING TIME
Summer.

NETTLE–LEAVED MULLEIN

COMBINE NETTLE-LEAVED MULLEIN WITH FINE-LEAVED PLANTS, SUCH AS CATMINT, AS WELL AS GERANIUMS.

Description Nettle-leaved mullein has thick flower spikes and stout stems with broadly oval, pointed leaves. The small, five-petalled white to yellow flowers are tightly packed into dense clusters.

Ideal position Full sun.

Ideal soil conditions Average to dry, well-drained soil.

Cultivation Long-lived plants spread slowly to form clumps and seldom need division.

Propagation Sow seed outdoors in autumn. Take root cuttings in late winter or early spring.

Pest and disease prevention No serious pests or diseases.

Design tips Plant in borders with fine-textured perennials, such as coreopsis *Coreopsis verticillata* and cranesbills *Geranium* spp.

Cultivars 'Album' (above) has white flowers with purple eyes. 'Cotswold Queen' has lovely yellow flowers with purple stamens and purple blotches at the base of the petals, and 'Cherry Helen' has rusty to cherry-red flowers.

Verbena bonariensis

HARDINESS
Frost-hardy.

HEIGHT AND SPREAD
2 m (6 ft) tall.
45 cm (18 in) wide.

FLOWERING TIME
Midsummer to early autumn

VERBENA

A POPULAR PERENNIAL, THIS AIRY, BRANCHING PLANT ADDS DOTS OF BRIGHT PURPLE COLOUR TO SUMMER DISPLAYS.

Description Tall, upright plant with long, wiry stems that rise up from a basal clump of dark green leaves and branch towards the top. From midsummer until mid-autumn, small, flattish heads of bright purple-blue flowers bloom at the tips of the branches.

Ideal position Full sun and a sheltered position.

Ideal soil conditions Average, very well-drained soil.

Cultivation Fairly easy to grow as long as you give plants a sunny, sheltered site out of strong winds, and where the soil will not become too wet over winter. In cold regions, mulch the top with dry leaves or straw to protect the crown of the plant. May not survive very cold winters.

Propagation By seed sown indoors in early spring or from stem-tip cuttings in summer.

Pest and disease prevention No serious pests or diseases.

Design tips This verbena, although tall, can be planted at the front of beds and borders: its airy stems allow you to look through to other plants behind. A wonderful companion for tall, tawny-coloured grasses.

Veronica spicata

HARDINESS
Hardy.

HEIGHT AND SPREAD
30–60 cm
(1–2 ft) tall.
45–60 cm
(1½–2 ft) wide.

FLOWERING TIME
Summer.

SPEEDWELL

THIS SPIKY SPEEDWELL IS A GOOD COMPANION FOR ORNAMENTAL GRASSES AND SUMMER-BLOOMING PERENNIALS.

Description Has pointed flower clusters atop leafy stems. The leaves are oval to oblong and clothed in soft hair. Plants grow from fibrous-rooted crowns. The small, two-lipped clear blue flowers are tightly packed into erect spikes.

Ideal position Full sun.

Ideal soil conditions Average, well-drained soil.

Cultivation Plants grow slowly to form neat, attractive clumps. Cut plants back if they get leggy and to encourage fresh growth and continued flowering. Dislikes winter wet.

Propagation Divide in spring or autumn. Take stem cuttings in late spring or early summer and remove any flower buds.

Pest and disease prevention No serious pests or diseases.

Design tips These spiky perennials combine well with other summer perennials that need good drainage, such as yarrows *Achillea* spp,. catmints *Nepeta* spp., and ornamental grasses. Their spiky forms add interest to plantings.

Viola and cvs.

HARDINESS
Hardy.

HEIGHT AND
SPREAD
5–15 cm
(2–6 in) tall.
20–30 cm
(8–12 in) wide.

FLOWERING TIME
Spring.

VIOLA, PANSY

IN INFORMAL GARDENS, PLANT VIOLAS WITH
BULBS, WILDFLOWERS, HOSTAS AND EARLY-
BLOOMING PERENNIALS.

Description Violas are robust plants
with delicate early-season flowers.
Some of them are scented. They
produce rosettes of heart-shaped
leaves from creeping, fibrous-rooted
rhizomes. The flowers range from
deep purple to blue, yellow, mauve
and bi-colours, and all of them have
five petals. Two point upwards and
three point outwards and down.
The two outward-facing petals
have fuzzy beards.

Ideal position Sun to partial shade.

Ideal soil conditions Well-drained,
fairly fertile soil.

Cultivation Violas are easy to grow.
They will spread and make themselves
at home in any garden.

Propagation Divide plants after
flowering or take cuttings in summer
for planting out in autumn. Sow seed
in late summer and barely cover.

Pest and disease prevention No
serious pests or diseases.

Design tips Violas make attractive
ground cover in light shade. All
violas work well in containers.

Viola continued

Viola 'Jackanapes'

Species *V. odorata* (pictured on page 305) is a semi-evergreen with scented flowers, usually deep purple or white. Self-seeds readily.

V. cornuta, the horned violet, is a spreading evergreen that bears an abundance of spurred lilac to violet flowers that are lightly scented. The petals are more separated than those of *V. odorata*. *V. cornuta* Alba Group has white flowers.

V. sororia, woolly blue-violet, is a stemless perennial with sharply pointed, hairy leaves. 'Freckles' has pale blue flowers flecked with purple.

Hybrids *V. odorata* has been cross-bred with other species to give rise to hundreds of cultivars and hybrids of mixed parentage.

'Beshlie' has pale yellow, fragrant flowers with long stems.

'Huntercombe Purple' has purple flowers wth small cream-coloured eyes.

'Jackanapes' (pictured above) has destinctive two-toned (brown and yellow) flowers.

'Little David' has slightly frilly cream flowers with purple borders.

'Maggie Mott' has pretty blue-purple flowers.

'Magic' has deep purple flowers with purple and cream centres.

'Nellie Britton' has lavender-pink flowers.

Yucca filamentosa

HARDINESS
Frost-hardy.

HEIGHT AND SPREAD
2 m (6 ft) tall
60–90 cm
(2–3 ft) wide.

FLOWERING TIME
Mid- to late summer.

YUCCA

THE SPIKY CLUMPS OF YUCCA ADD A
DRAMATIC ACCENT TO ANY PLANTING.
THE SHOWY FLOWERS ARE A BONUS!

Description It grows from a woody
crown with fleshy roots. Produces
tall, elongated clusters of nodding,
bell-like creamy white flowers and
rosettes of sword-shaped blue-green
leaves to 75 cm (30 in) long. The
flowers have three petals and three
petal-like sepals that form a bell.

Ideal position Full sun.

Ideal soil conditions Average, well-
drained soil.

Cultivation Plants thrive for years
with little care. After flowering, the
main crown dies but auxiliary crowns

keep growing. In areas with very
cold winters, mulch the crowns.

Propagation Remove suckers from
the clump in spring.

Pest and disease prevention No
serious pests or diseases.

Design tips Plant in dry borders or
rock gardens as accent plants or in
seaside gardens. Contrast the stiff
foliage with soft or delicate plants
such as lamb's ears *Stachys
byzantina*, sedums and verbenas
Verbena spp.

Cultivars 'Bright Edge' (pictured
above) has tall, striking, yellow-
variegated leaves.

INDEX

Page references in *italics* indicate
photos and illustrations.

A

Acanthaceae 114–15, *114–15*
Acanthus mollis 45, 114–15, *114*
A. spinosus 115, *115*
Achillea spp. 17, 37, 40, 66, 89, 118,
    262, 304
A. filipendulina 24, 116–18, *116*
A. millefolium 16–17, 117–18, *117–18*
Aconitum carmichaelii 40, 119, *119*
Actaea alba 27, 120, *120*
A. racemosa see Cimicifuga racemosa
Agapanthus africanus 40, 121–3, *121*
A. campanulatus *122*, 123
A. inapertus 123
A. praecox subsp. orientalis 'Albus'
    123, *123*
Agavaceae 307, *307*
Ajuga reptans *17*, *21*, *22*, 23, 27, 40,
    124, *124*
Alcea rosea 40, 125, *125*
Alchemilla mollis 24, 40, 63, 126, *126*
Alkanet 132, *132*
Allium cristophii 127, *127*, 291
Alstroemeria 129, *129*
A. aurea 40, 48, 54, 128–9, *128–9*
Amsonia spp. 37, *38*
A. tabernaemontana 130, *130*, 296
Anaphalis triplinervis 131, *131*
Anchusa azurea 132, *132*
Anemone 134, *134*
Anemone blanda 133, *133*

A. coronaria 134, *134*
A. nemorosa 135, *135*
A. x hybrida *12*, 17, *34*, 40, 64, *64*,
    110, 136, *136*, 151, 164, *164*
Angelica archangelica 137, *137*
Antennaria dioica 138, *138*
Anthemis tinctoria 81, 139, *139*
Apiaceae 137, *137*, 156, *156*, 206, *206*
Apocynaceae 130, *130*
Aquilegia spp. 12, *12*, 36, 40, *97*,
    141–2, *141–2*, 210, 226, 244,
    253, 268, 284, 289, 298
A. coerulea 142
A. canadensis 27, 140, *140*
A. chrysantha 142
A. flabellata 142
Arabis spp. 13, 27, 40, 143, *143*, 210
A. caucasica 22
Araceae 145, *145*, 166, *166*
Arenaria montana 144, *144*
Argyranthemum frutescens 245
Arisaema triphyllum 37, 145, *145*
Aristolochiaceae 150, *150*
Armeria maritima 40, 58, 66, 68,
    89, 146, *146*
Artemisia absinthium 43, 68, 147,
    147, 238
A. lactiflora 148, *148*
Aruncus dioicus 40, 52, 149, *149*, 263
Asarum canadense 140
A. europaeum 45, 150, *150*
Asphodelaceae 202, *202*, 237–8, *237–8*
Aster 153, *153*
Aster spp. 37, 50, 59, 101, 178, 190,
    206–7, 214, 219–21, 248, 254,
    261, 280, 290
A. novae-angliae 40, 151, *151*
A. novae-belgii 152, *152*
A. x frikartii 40, 153, *153*
Asteraceae 116–18, *116–18*, 131, *131*,
    138–9, *138–9*, 147–8, *147–8*,
    151–3, *151–3*, 164, *164*, 172–4,
    172–4, 180–1, *180–1*, 189–90,
    189–90, 199–200, *199–200*,
    203–5, *203–5*, 207, *207*, 212,

H

I

J–K

L

Tropaeolaceae 300, *300*
Tropaeolum speciosum 300, *300*
Turtleheads 52, 178, *178*

U–V

Uvularia grandiflora 27, 301, *301*
U. sessilifolia 301
Uvulariaceae 299, *299*, 301, *301*
Valerian, red 50, 97, 157, 175, *175*
Valerianaceae 175, *175*
Verbascum spp. 45, 64, 156
V. chaixii 302, *302*
Verbena bonariensis 303
Verbenaceae 303, *303*
Veronica spicata 59, 304, *304*
Viburnum spp. 119
Viola odorata 22, 41, 305–6, *305–6*
V. sonoria 306
Violaceae 305–6, *305–6*
Violet 120

W

Watering 90–1, *90–1*, 105
Weeds 98–9, *98–9*
White baneberry 120, *120*
White guara 66, 213, *213*
White mugwort 148, *148*
Willow gentian 214, *214*
Windflower 133, *133*
Wood spurge 208, *208*
Wormwood 68, 147, *147*, 238

Y

Yarrow 16–17, *19, 24*, 37, 50, 66, 89,
   91, 97, 108, 115–18, *116–18*,
   132, 170, 172, 180, 196, 239,
   245, 255, 257, 262, 274, 278,
   284, 286, 304
Yellow chamomile *81*, 139, *139*
Yucca filamentosa 45, 61, 307, *307*

Acknowledgments

KEY l=left; r=right; c=centre; t=top; b=bottom.

AA=Allan Armitage; AL=Andrew Lawson; Aus=Auscape; BCL=Bruce Coleman Ltd; CM=Cheryl Maddocks; CN= Clive Nichols; DF=Derek Fell; DW=David Wallace; GB=Gillian Beckett; GPL=Garden Picture Library; HSC=Harry Smith Collection; iS=istockphoto.com; JC=John Callanan; JP=Jerry Pavia; JY=James Young; LC=Leigh Clapp; PH=Photos Horticultural; SH=Shutterstock; SM=Stirling Macoboy; SOM=S. & O. Mathews; TE=Thomas Eltzroth; TPL=photolibrary.com; TR=Tony Rodd; WO=Weldon Owen; WR=Weldon Russell

1t, c LC; b Aus/Rob Walls 2c WO/JY 5c TE 6t TE; c SOM; b AL 7t SOM; c WO/JY 10c WO 12br TE 13t WO/JY 14tr, bl WO/JY 15t PH 17t WO/JY 18b PH 19t WO/JY 20br PH 21t SOM; cr PH 22t WO/JY 23cl DF; bl WO/JY 25c WO 26bl PH 27tr WO/JY 29t CN 30br CN 32c CN 34bl PH 35b CN 36bl CN 37tl SH 38br PH 39t CN 42tr WO; br PH 43t PH 44tr WO/JY; bl PH 45tr WO/JY; br PH 46bl WO/JY; t PH 47t WO 48b WO/JY 49t iS 50b SOM 51t CN; br WO/JY 52t JP; b AL 53t WO/JY 54t WO/JY 55tr SH 56b DF 57t EWA Photo Library; b SOM 58t, b WO/JY 59t WO/JY 60t WO/JY 61 Aus/Jerry Harpur 62bl AL 63t WO/JY 64b TE 65t TR; b PH 66t TE 67 GPL/Roger Hyam 68t TE 68–69b WO/JY 69t WO/JY 70c BCL/Eric Crichton 72t; c WR; b SH 73t WR 74t, b CN 76bl PH; br DW 78cl CN; bl, br DF 79t WO/JY; bl, br DF 80tl, tr WR/CM 81t GPL 83c CN 84tl, tc, tr DW; b AL 85tr CN 86c CN 88bl PH 89tl DW; br WO/JY 91tl SOM 93tr CN 96br PH 97tr DW; cl PH 98b PH 99tr APL/Corbis/Wolfgang Kaehler 100bl PH 101 PH 102c WO; b PH 105t PH; b Premaphotos Wildlife/K.G. Preston-Mafham 106b CN 108cl PH; br GPL/Brigitte Thomas 109tr, tc, tl DW 110bl, bc, br DW 111tr WO/JY 112c CN 114t JC 115t GP.com/Graham Rice 116t TE 117t Corbis 118t WO/JY 119t TR 120t PH 121t GP.com/Judy White 122t GPL/Mark Bolton 123t GPL/Brian Carter 124t WO/JY 125t TE 126t JC 127t WO/JY 128t GPL/J. Sira 129t GP.com/Judy White 130t PH 131t PH 132t TE 133t GPL/John Glover 134t GPL/John Glover 135t GPL/John Glover 136t JC 137t GPL/Brian Carter 138t GB 139t GPL/Gary Rogers 140t DF 141t JC 142t GPL/Neil Holmes 143t PH 144t TE 145t Nancy J. Ondra 146t TE 147t TE 148t TE 149t PH 150t PH 151t HSC 152t TE 153t WO 154t WO/JY 155t JC 156t JC 157t WR 158t JC 159t WO/JY 160t AL 161t GP.com/Judy White 162t SM 163t PH 164t DF 165t JP 166t HSC 167t PH 168t HSC 169t TR 170t JC 171t TE 172t JP 173t HSC 174t PH 175t JC 176t WR 177t WO/JY 178t Anita Sabrese 179t TE 180t WO/JY 181t APL/Corbis/Hal Horowitz 182t GPL/Mayer/Le Scanff 183t GP.com/Judy White 184t GPL/Mark Bolton 185t GB 186t WO/JY 187t JC 188t GPL/Rajeev Jhanji 189t WR 190t WO/JY 191t JC 192t GPL/John Glover 193t GPL/David Askham 194t WO/JY 195t GP.com/Judy White 196t TE 197t PH 198t WO 199t WO/JY 200t WO 201t TE 202t TE 203t WO/JY 204t WO 205t JC 206t APL/Corbis/Tania Midgley 207t HSC 208t GPL 209t WO/JY 210t GB 211t PH 212t WO/JY 213t JC 214t PH 215t JC 216t TPL 217t WO/JY 218t TE 219t

WO/JY 220t TPL 221t TE 222t WO/JY 223t WO/JY 224t WO 225t iS 226t WO
227t TE 228t WO/JY 229t WO/JY 230t TE 231t GPL 232t GPL/Lamontagne 233t
PH 234t WO 235t WO/JY 236t WO/JY 237t WO/JY 238t Aus/Jaime Plaza van
Roon 239t TR 240t JC 241t TE 242t PH 243t TE 244t CN 245t APL/ Corbis/Eric
Crichton 246t GPL/Brian Carter 247t TE 248t GB 249t WO/JY 250t TE 251t WO
252t DF 253t GPL/Marijke Heuff 254t JC 255t PH 256t WO/JY 257t PH 258t DF
259t TE 260t TE 261t TE 262t TE 263t WO 264t AA 265t TE 266t WO/JY 267t
WO/JY 268t WO/JY 269t WO/JY 270t TPL 271t Michael Dirr 272t PH 273t
WO/JY 274t GDR 275t WR 276t WO/JY 277t JY 278t PH 279t WO/JY 280t
John J. Smith 281t TR 282t TE 283t TR 284t GPL 285t WO/JY 286t PH 287t
WO/JY 288t SH 289t AA 290t TR 291t TE 292t WO/JY 293t TE 294t GB 295t SH
296t HSC 297t PH 298t TE 299t TR 300t PH 301t WO/JY 302t TE 303t iS 304t JC
305t TE 306t PH 307t WO/JY.

Illustrations by Tony Britt-Lewis, Edwina Riddell, Barbara Rodanska,
Jan Smith, Kathie Smith.